The grass withers, the flowers fade, but the Word of our God shall stand forever.
Isaiah 40:8

THE GREATEST BOOK EVER WRITTEN

By Dr. Rochunga Pudaite
With James C. Hefley, Ph.D

Hannibal Books
Hannibal, Missouri—"America's Home Town"
Printed in the United States of America
Cover design by Cyndi Allison
(Use coupon in back to order extra copies of this and other
helpful books from the publisher.)

What others say about "The Greatest Book Ever Written"

Dr. Richard Halverson, Chaplain of the United States Senate: "For many years, I've known Rochunga Pudaite as a man of exceptional devotion to Jesus Christ with an unwavering commitment to the Scriptures. This book reflects the heart and mind of its author. It will be of great benefit to both the seeker and the disciple."

Dr. Jerry Vines, President of the Southern Baptist Convention: "You will gain a new appreciation for the uniqueness and the divine nature of the Bible."

Elaine M. Townsend, widow of the founder and long-time general director of the Wycliffe Bible Translators: "This book will renew your love for the Scriptures."

Dr. Harold Lindsell, Editor Emeritus of Christianity Today: "My heart was touched and my spirit lifted as I read stories, old and new, of what God has done by His Spirit though the reading of the Word of God."

Dr. Barry Moore, world-wide Canadian evangelist: "This book is excellent. It will be an inspiration to the layman in strengthening his faith in the Bible as the Living Word of God."

Adrian Rogers, pastor and former president of the Southern Baptist Convention: "....a masterpiece of spiritual inspiration and a treasury of spiritual knowledge. "

Dr. Stuart Briscoe, author, pastor, and conference speaker: "....A great book about the greatest Book."

Dr. Jimmy Draper, pastor, and former president of the Southern Baptist Convention: "...A treasure of stories and inspirational material that will be a blessing to any reader. "

Dr. Gene M. Williams, President, Luther Rice Seminary, author, and conference speaker: "...Presents history, apologetics, and sociology as evidences of the good accomplishments in this world through the influence of the Bible."

Wallace Henley, pastor, novelist, and former White House aide: "Perhaps no one has put the Bible in more homes than Rochunga Pudaite. And no one is better qualified than he to report its broad impact!"

David Baker, pastor and noted evangelist. "...This book is really 'good stuff.' Add it to your 'must read' list today."

*Dedicated to my beloved
Mawii,
without whose help
this work could not have been
done*

Table of Contents

1 "The Book That Liberated My People"
. . . . *one*

2 "The Book of Truth and Miracles"
. . . . *eleven*

3 "The Book of Almost 2,000 Languages"
. . . . *twenty-seven*

4 "The Book That Triumphs Over Its Enemies"
. . . . *forty-one*

5 "The Book That Is Incomparable to all Other Scriptures"
. . . . *sixty-one*

6 "The Book That Meets Our Deepest Needs"
. . . . *eighty-one*

7 "The Book That Carries a Mandate for Caring"
. . . . *ninety-nine*

8 "The Book That Builds Civilized Culture"
. . . . *one hundred thirteen*

9 "The Book That Made America Great"
. . . . *one hundred twenty-nine*

10 "The Book That Builds the Church"
. . . . *one hundred forty-nine*

11 "The Book Which the Whole World Must Read"
. . . . *one hundred sixty-five*

A Personal Word From the Author
. . . . *one hundred and eighty-one*

Sources and Bibliography
. . . . *one hundred and eighty-two*

Index
. . . . *one hundred and eighty-eight*

Chapter 1

"The Book That Liberated My People"

The Book before me on my desk is the Bible. Although this translation is in English, the Bible is Everyman's Book. It is the Book for the Armenians of the Soviet Union, for the Aucas of Ecuador, and for the Hmars, my people in India.

More than any other book, it is the Book responsible for lifting my people out of poverty and superstition to become one of the most advanced, peace-loving ethnic groups in all of Asia.

Before I write about the greatness of the Bible in other areas, I must tell you what its message did for my people.

The Hmars are of Mongolian descent and migrated from central China across the lower Himalayas into northeast India where other tribal peoples lived. They settled in the hilly states of Manipur, Mizoram, Assam, and Tripura. Here they waged tribal warfare in which they took enemy heads in battle and hung them over the doors of their bamboo huts as trophies of victory.

After the Hmars came to India, a wise man in the tribe predicted the coming of white-skinned people who would load guns from the bottom. "These bottom-loaders," the Hmar seer said, "will be followed by other white-skinned persons telling us of a new religion not requiring sacrifice of animals or chickens."

It happened just as the wise man foretold. The British, who had already taken over most of India, moved into the jungled Himalayan foothills. The foreign colonials loaded their guns from the bottom and called my Hmar people "barbaric tribesmen." When they began making incursions into Hmar territory, Hmar warriors swooped down on a British tea plantation and took more than 100 heads. British General Lord Roberts set off with two columns of crack troops in hot pursuit. They killed a few Hmars, but the majority fled into the deep forest and across the Barak River where the British dared not follow.

That's where the Hmars were when a great spiritual revival swept over Wales shortly after the turn of the 20th century.

Watkin Roberts, a chemist, had read Lord Roberts' account of the pursuit of the Hmar headhunters and was stirred by the Welsh Revival to take the Bible to the Hmars. In 1910 Roberts entered Manipur state from the south shortly after an American Baptist missionary, William Pettigrew, began work among the Naga people in the north.

At that time there were known to be only 132 Christians among over a million people in Manipur. There were no Christians among the Hmars where Roberts wanted to go. The British agent, however, said it was too dangerous to enter Hmar territory and urged Roberts to work with the more peaceful Lushai Tribe. Roberts set to work to translate the Bible into the Lushai language.

That year, my father, Chawnga, and another teenage Hmar, walked six days to the Lushai village of Aijal where they hoped to sell some chickens for a profit. Along the way they met three strange white men who said they were missionaries. My father and his friend called the eldest Mr. Old White Man, the second Mr. Other White Man, and the Third Mr. Young White Man. Mr. Youngman, who was only 22, told my father and his friend in the Lushai language that his name was Watkin Roberts and that he had come from a far off land called Wales the year before the flowering of the bamboo [1908].

Mr. Youngman showed the two young Hmars a book, which he said was the Word of the true and only God. "You do not need to sacrifice chickens or animals any more," he said. "God tells us in His book that He sent His Son to be the sacrifice for our sins."

The friendly foreigner talked to the two young Hmars a long time about believing in God's Son and taking His ways as their own. My father and his friend could not accept this for they knew the Hmars would regard them as outcasts if they did not sacrifice and take heads according to the teachings of the old ones.

In the months following, my father and other Hmars kept hearing amazing stories about this Mr. Youngman who had a book that he claimed was the Word of the one true God. In one instance, Mr. Youngman was said to have traveled day and night to save the slaves of a dying Lushai chief, who were to be buried with their master. The slaves were already buried to their waist when he arrived. Mr. Youngman ordered his native helpers to dig them out, and no one dared lay a hand on the Welchman.

One day, in the providence of God, missionary Roberts received a gift of five pounds, worth about 25 dollars in American currency, from a Christian woman in Hemstead, England. "I'm sending this money," she said, "for you to use in winning at least one Indian soul." Roberts used the money to print a few hundred copies of the Gospel of John in Lushai.

Roberts got a list of all the Lushai and Hmar village chiefs known to the British. He sent a copy of the Gospel in Lushai to all the chiefs through the British messenger-mail service. The chief in my father's village of Senvon received one of the Lushai Gospels. He asked a Lushai tribesman to read the book to him. The chief then asked, "What did the one called Jesus mean when he said, 'You must be born again to enter the kingdom of Heaven.'" Unable to answer the question, the Lushai noted, "At the end of the book is the name and address of the white man who sent it. Send a messenger and ask him to come and explain the words to you."

The chief dispatched a message to Roberts, asking, "Come and tell us the meaning of the book you sent." Roberts asked the British agent for the area for permission to go. The official bluntly said, "No. When I go in there, I take along over a hundred soldiers for protection. I can't spare a single soldier to escort you."

"But I have an invitation from the chief of Senvon village to explain the Gospel," Roberts persisted.

The agent laughed. "That's an invitation to have your head lopped off. They'll never let you out alive. They'll kill some pigs and cows and make a celebration out of you."

Roberts was determined to go. Taking a Lushai interpreter who could speak Hmar fluently, he arrived in Senvon village on January 29, 1910.

Instead of killing the missionary, the chief and the villagers gave him gifts and listened respectfully to his message. For four days the Welsh missionary was unable to help the people understand how God had sought to make peace with man. On the fifth day he was preparing to leave, when the Lushai interpreter took him aside and told him a story.

"When two tribes are at war," the interpreter said, "the side that wishes to make peace goes to a mountaintop nearest to the enemy camp at sunrise and beats a big war drum three times. If the other side replies before sundown by beating their war drum, that means, 'come to the boundary and let's talk it over.' The chief who wants to make peace kills an animal and lets the blood of the animal flow along the boundary line. Then he and his enemy place their hands on the slain animal while their spokesmen negotiate. When they reach an understanding, the chiefs embrace and share in a peace dinner."

That evening missionary Roberts told the Hmar chief and others gathered around that God so loved the world that He sent His Son to die on the cross—the "boundary line" between God and man—to make peace with man. The Bible, Roberts said, "is a record of God's treaty with man and His invitation for man to come to the boundary and accept God's sacrifice for peace."

Roberts then invited the chief and the other Hmar listeners to make peace with the great God of the Bible by accepting His Son's death as the sacrifice for their sins. The chief and others solemnly announced that they wished to do so. One of those who accepted God's peace treaty was my father, Chawnga.

My father became one of the first Hmar preachers. He traveled by foot and canoe all over Hmar country telling people to come to the "boundary" and accept God's sacrifice for their sins. He dearly loved Mr. Youngman, who was only a few years older than himself. "Mr. Youngman," my father would say, "is not like the other British. He does not demand that tribals carry his baggage. He never insists that we follow European ways. He treats us with dignity and tells us to build our own churches after the way the Bible teaches."

The British agent was unhappy with what was happening among the Hmars. In his view, missionary Roberts and the Hmar preachers were destroying the old traditions and stirring up trouble in the tribal villages. The agent forced Roberts to leave, even though the missionary had only completed part of the Lushai Bible translation. He had my father brutally whipped when he refused to stop preaching.

The British officials could not keep my father and other Hmar believers from following the call of God. One of them was my mother's younger brother, Lienrum. He set out on foot for a distant village called Suongsang. He arrived shortly before sunset and was confronted by the chief who ordered him to leave. He slipped around and found a house where he could spend the night.

Shortly after dark the chief discovered he was still in the village. Thrusting a handful of rice into his hand, the chief said, "This is to show you we are a hospitable people. Eat it and be gone into the forest. Do not return."

Lienrum walked a little way and climbed into a tree where he was enveloped by mosquitos. Amidst the buzzing God gave him a song about the insignificance of our suffering in comparison to the glory of being in the presence of Jesus where we will go after death. One verse after another came to him as he sang. Each time when he started singing the noise of the mosquitos seemed to become part of the music. "By morning," he reported later, "I didn't even know they were biting anymore."

When the sun arose he walked back into the village and began singing with great joy the song God had given him.

The chief came out of his hut. "What are you doing? How can you be so happy when we put you out among the mosquitos last night?"

"Listen to my song about where I am going," Leinrum said. The chief gave rapt attention as Lienrum sang. A broad smile spread across his face. "You must sing this to all of us."

In no time a great crowd gathered and Leinrum sang every stanza of his song. It was the only sermon he could preach. After awhile the people sang with him.

They questioned him between verses: "Is it really so?" "Is the life beyond death really that wonderful?" "Where did you learn all of this?" "It's in a book called the Bible. Mr. Youngman brought part of it to Senvon village and showed us these things. When I believed, darkness didn't matter anymore. To the God we worship, night and day are the same."

While the chief and villagers listened agape, Lienrum continued. "Last night you sent me to the forest. You thought I would be unhappy. But all the mosquitos sang with me and played music as I sang."

"So I bring this message to you, revered chief. We are all sinners who have broken God's laws. But Jesus Christ, God's only Son, died on a cross to pay the price of our sin. That cross is the boundary of sin between God and man where God makes peace with those who believe. God speaks in the Bible to invite you to come to the boundary and accept His sacrifice for peace."

The chief begged Lienrum to stay longer. "I will go home and bring my family to live in your village," he said.

"Good, good," the chief agreed. "I'll send some men to bring your belongings so you will return quickly."

Lienrum and his family moved into the village. By the end of that year God had blessed them with a large church.

My father, Lienrum, and the other preachers continued to defy the British agent. They kept preaching and evangelizing. Churches sprang up in almost every Hmar village. Thousands of Hmars accepted God's peace treaty with great joy and began to live by Bible principles. They stopped quarrelling, fighting, drinking, and living in fear of evil spirits. The men even stopped beating wives. They worked harder and began taking steps to see that their children received an education.

My father was preaching when I went forward to say, "I will accept Jesus as my Savior."

A few months later, just after my tenth birthday, my father reminded me that my name Rochunga meant "God's Treasure." He told me for the first time that I had been dedicated as a baby by the church elders to translate the Bible for our people. "Many of our people do speak Lushai," he said. "But we must have the Bible in our own language, if they are to understand from our hearts. You must go to school and learn English to help you write the Bible in Hmar. We will have copies printed for everyone and teach them all to read."

The nearest mission school was far over the mountains. I would have to walk 96 dangerous miles through a jungle infested by tigers and other wild animals. I was fearful of the long, gruelling trip, though my father said he would walk with me and that God would protect us.

One Sunday morning my father preached from John 13:1 in the Lushai translation: " ... Having loved His own which were in the world, He loved them unto the horizon." As we walked toward home, I reminded my father, "You said God's love is unto the horizon, but you did not tell me how far the horizon is. If God loves me only as far as I can see, how can I trust Him? How far is the horizon?"

My father did not answer that question directly, but a few days later he took me to the top of nearby Sumtuk Mountain. There we climbed a tree from which we could see down the great Cachar Valley of Assam for over 100 miles.

"Down there," my father pointed, "is where your grandfather and others raided the British tea plantation and took over a hundred heads. Now look to the long mountain range beyond. Do you see the peak where the heaven kisses the earth?"

"Yes, my father," I replied, puzzled. "But why do you ask?"

"Because, my son, if you were to journey many weeks and come to the top of that mountain and looked, you would see another just like that one. Then if you journeyed on again for many days and weeks to the second mountain and looked again, you would see yet another. The horizon is never ending, my son. There is no place in the world where the love of God has not touched or cannot reach."

After five nights and six days, we reached the mission school unharmed. My father arranged for me to board with a young medical worker at a cost of three rupees (then about 45 cents) per month, plus whatever work I might be assigned. I milked the cows each morning, took them to their grazing fields and got them in the evening, and helped in the garden and with household chores as well. I went from this school to Jordhat Christian High School and from there to college. With help from World Vision and Dr. Billy Graham I came to America and studied at Wheaton College before enrolling for graduate work at Northern Illinois University. Along the way God gave me a beautiful Hmar girl named Mawii as my wife.

God enabled me to translate the New Testament into Hmar while I was a student at Wheaton. The British and Foreign Bible Society printed 10,000 copies for shipment to Hmarland by year's end, 1960. No one was prouder than my father Chawnga.

When the Bibles arrived the Hmar churches had a day of dedication and celebration in every village. The first printing sold out in six months and a second printing of 10,000 was ordered. Every Hmar family wanted a copy of God's Word in their own language.

Mawii and I were led by God, in 1959, to start Partnership Mission through which American Christians provided funds for building schools and a strong mission base among the Hmars. My father and other Christian tribal leaders trained hundreds of young Hmar men and women to take the Bible to neighboring tribal groups.

In 1971 God gave me another vision. One day I was praying when my concentration kept being broken by the telephone company jingle, "Let your fingers do the walking." Finally, in frustration, I stopped praying.

When I rose from prayer in my office in Wheaton, my eyes caught two telephone directories on my desk. Suddenly the idea was clear. These books listed the names and addresses of everyone in Calcutta and New Delhi, India. These were educated people, wealthy enough to afford telephones, the very leaders who could help evangelize India. We could organize Christians in America and elsewhere to mail New Testaments to reach the previously unreachable.

So Mawii and I joined with Bible loving American co-workers in organizing Bibles For The World. We provide hundreds of thousands of Bibles each year for Christians to mail to persons whose addresses are listed in the telephone directories of over 40 countries, including Bangladesh, Afghanistan, Tanzania, Zimbabwe, and even the Soviet Union. By 1990 there will be over a billion telephone addresses to which God's Word can be mailed. Our goal is to send God's Word to every telephone subscriber in the world!

What of the Hmars in the almost eight decades since Mr. Youngman brought the Bible to my people and my father (who is still living at age 97) received Christ?

Thanks to our God and the enlightenment of His Word, over 95 percent of the present 125.000 Hmar population are Bible-believing Christians. They now have the complete Bible in Hmar and worship in over 500 churches. Their children attend some 80 church-sponsored elementary schools, seven junior highs, and four high schools—one with an enrollment of about a thousand. There is even a good hospital, staffed by Hmar doctors and nurses.

Over 500 Hmars serve as missionaries to neighboring tribes where they have started several hundred churches. Hmar missionary evangelists have also taken food to villages of other tribes caught up in famine and war.

Does it surprise you that 85 percent of the Hmars can read and write, a phenomenal percentage in India? Or that per family income is much higher than the average in the nation. One of our latest projects is coffee. Government agricultural experts say the Hmars have the best land for growing coffee in all of India. The Hmars now have over a half million coffee trees and expect to have five million in just a few years. Like Maxwell House, we say Hmar coffee is good to the last drop.

Dozens of Hmars have distinguished themselves as national diplomats and civil administrators. One Hmar holds the rank of ambassador in the Indian Embassy in Yugoslavia. Another is the Indian charge d'affaires in Saudi Arabia. Another is the highest ranking civil servant of India. Another is the administrator of a large state.

Every year the government gives tests to select the outstanding young men for government service. Less than 100 are selected in the whole country. For several years one or two Hmars have been in each group of winners. And there is only about one Hmar for every 7,000 people in India. Pardon me if this sounds like boasting, but I am proud of what the Bible has done for our people.

When I was a boy the Hmars had no post offices, telephones, or auto roads of any kind. The Hmars were not even listed on the census roll as an ethnic group. By the time I was in college, they were beginning to become known. I was invited to present information to Prime Minister

Nehru on tribal needs. After an hour-long meeting, Nehru promised me that the Hmars would be on the next census and they would receive post offices. Today there are good hard-surface roads to some villages, as well as telephones and even television. However, my home village of Senvon is still reached only by a trail. But the road and the telephone line are just a few miles away.

The influence of the Bible has served as a check on the spread of Communism and terrorism in the tribal areas. Communist political candidates have suffered serious defeats in my home state of Manipur. At the behest of then Prime Minister Indira Gandhi, I was appointed to lead a peace mission to Mizo tribesmen, who had been trained for terrorism in Communist China and had been killing people and blowing up government buildings. They wanted political independence from India.

The rebel leaders trusted me because I was a Hmar and a Christian. On this critical day in 1975, Independence Day in India, I was resting in a house in the state of Mizoram. Suddenly a young Mizo burst into the room and pushed a revolver into my chest. "I am here to eliminate you," he announced.

I looked him straight in the eye and said, "I follow the Bible. I am an agent of peace who is trying to get the killing to stop."

The intruder just stared at me, stony faced and silent. "Before you carry out your job," I said, "will you kneel with me and let me pray for you? Then you can do whatever you must."

I closed my eyes and asked that the Mizo intruder be kept from harm and not killed, and that grievances be settled so peace would come. "Lord, open the eyes of our tribal people so they may see the beauty of their fellowman," I prayed. "Show them Your love from Your Word. Help them to live in peace."

When I finished he started walking away. "Wait," I requested. "Will you be my messenger and tell your people that I come in peace and goodwill? Tell your people not to explode any bombs today. That will be the signal that a confidence exists between us."

He slipped away without saying a word. I waited, listening, hoping, praying. The long day passed. After dark the governor called. "Come and join me in a celebration. This marks the beginning of good will. This is the first day since 1966 that a bomb has not gone off in the capital of this state."

Thanks largely to the influence of the Bible, the rebellion has ceased. The shootings have stopped and the people are at peace.

I now spend most of my time in the U.S.A. and in traveling. But at least once a year I return for an extended visit to my homeland. On my last trip there the future of the Hmars and surrounding tribes looked brighter than ever. Every year there are more churches, schools, missionary evangelists, and ministries to the needy. I tell every scholar and government official who will listen, "None of this would have happened without the Bible. I myself would likely still be an ignorant tribesman, if the Bible had not come to our people."

I often say that my people, the Hmars, have been transformed from headhunters to hearthunters. It is so. Their experience testifies that the Bible is indeed the greatest Book ever written. Above all other books, it is the one Book that reveals the mind of God, the heart of man, the way of salvation, and the blessedness of believers. It is the Book without peer as a literary miracle. It is unmatched by any other book, religious or otherwise, in wisdom and knowledge of the most important issues in life. It is the one Book that tells us where we come from, why we are here, and where we are going.

It is the Book that sets people free from spiritual and economic bondage. It is the Book that has stood and survived through the ages against legions of bitter enemies. It is the Book with the greatest appeal for all humanity, the Book that changes history, the Book that made America great, the Book that builds the church, and the Book which should be read and obeyed by every person in the world.

Beyond all other books, the Bible is the greatest Book ever written. If you do not believe this now, I challenge you to read the following chapters and then decide.

Chapter 2

"The Book of Truth and Miracles"

I was thinking about the greatness of the Bible when I first flew over the Bible lands in the fall of 1954. The KLM Super Constellation was carrying me from India to Scotland, where I was to begin training for translating the Bible into the Hmar language. Our beloved Mr. Youngman, Watkin Roberts, the Welsh missionary who brought the Bible to the Hmars, was making my trip possible, with assistance from Bob Pierce, the founder of World Vision, and Billy Graham. I had been reading from the book of Isaiah, chapter 43, "Fear not: for I have redeemed thee; I have called thee by thy name; thou art mine." We had crossed Pakistan and were over Iran when the pilot announced that we were approaching the Persian Gulf and would soon be flying over Iraq, Syria, Lebanon, and then the Mediterranean Sea and Greece.

The Bible lands from 20,000 feet!

Peering far off to the right, I saw two wiggly brown lines—the Tigris and the Euphrates rivers—coming together in the brown desert at the head of the blue gulf. Buried somewhere down there under the desert sand was the ancestral home of Abraham, and perhaps even the Garden of Eden. I tried to visualize a robed man—Abraham—riding on a camel at the head of a caravan, leaving his homeland of Ur of the Chaldees, following God's call "unto a land that I will show thee." (Genesis 12:1).

Time seemed to stand still as the lands of the Bible slowly passed under me. Down there was where the inspired authors of the books of the Bible had penned the greatest Book ever written—the Book expressing "the most sublime philosophy" (Sir Isaac Newton), "our only safe guide" (Daniel Webster), the Book "of all others to read at all ages and in all conditions of human life" (John Quincy Adams), the Book which "contains all things desirable to man" (Abraham Lincoln), the Book "which gives me comfort and boundless joy" (Mahatma Gandhi), and the Book which had transformed my people from headhunters to heart hunters. Down there Adam, Noah, Abraham, Moses, David, Solomon, the great Hebrew prophets, Jesus of Nazareth and His apostles, and Paul had walked! Down there the Book of books had been written!

Years later, after I translated the New Testament into Hmar, I made my first land pilgrimage across the world of the Bible. I walked where Abraham, Moses, Jesus, and Paul walked. I stood at the foot of a barren, rugged mountain, and gazed up to the peak where it is believed Moses received the Ten Commandments. I climbed beautiful Mount Nebo from which the great Lawgiver viewed the Promised Land. I mixed with pilgrims from many nations at Bethlehem, traversed the dusty streets of Nazareth, and set sail on the Sea of Galilee.

Later I reverently paused in the traditional Garden of Gethsemane and felt the bark of the hoary olive trees under which Jesus may have prayed. I marched along the Way of the Cross, surveyed skull-faced Golgotha, and stood in awe at an empty tomb from which some think Jesus arose. Scene upon scene from the Bible brought remembrances from the reading of Scripture as I walked the sacred paths. In my imagination I could hear the prophets and apostles and our Lord Himself speaking the words that are preserved for all humanity and all time in this Book of books.

Never has there been a book like the Bible. Never has there been such a treasury of sacred, holy literature in one volume.

God did not drop the Bible from Heaven by parachute, a portion at a time, to be picked up by a holy man and shared with others. On the other hand, no book was ever planned and written like the Bible.

Books in ancient times were not produced as they are today. Printing was unknown. Every letter, symbol, and picture had to be handwritten, just as it was done among my people, the Hmars, before the coming of Christianity and printing technology.

"Books" in Mesopotamia during Abraham's time were on baked clay tablets. The Romans treated the skin of lambs and calves to make a paper called vellum which they lengthened and stretched into a scroll.

The Egyptians made papyrus paper from a reed-like plant which grew wild at the mouth of the Nile and along the Mediterranean shore. They pasted papyrus sheets together to make a long strip and attached the ends to wooden rollers. The reader simply unrolled the roll.

"Bible" is from the Greek word byblos, meaning book. Byblos was a Phoenician city noted for export of payrus. Nashville, TN. is a sort of a modern Byblos because of the millions of Bibles produced there by the Thomas Nelson Company, the Baptist Sunday School Board, the Methodist Publishing House, and other Christian publishers. Emperors, wealthy people, and religious leaders collected roll books for their libraries. In ancient times most roll books, or scrolls, were bought from individuals and collectors. Some were "commissioned"; that is, writers were paid to produce books, in keeping with a production schedule, somewhat as they are today. One ruler, Ptolemy II of Egypt, sometimes locked scholars in cells and kept them there until they produced the books he wanted. The great library at ancient Alexandria, Egypt was said to have housed more than 700,000 scrolls. A good number of these were likely produced by imprisoned scholars.

The Bible is basically a collection, or small library of 66 scrolls, written over a period of 1500 years. A few of these books were composed in prison. No author, publisher, or editor ever planned the Bible.

No official committee sat down in Moses' time (when the first books of the Bible were written) to map out a production schedule for the next millennium and a half. The idea and schedule were conceived in the mind of almighty God.

Jehovah, the great I AM, the Alpha and Omega, the beginning and the end, inspired over 40 different authors and editors to produce, over this 15 century span, the autograph texts of this great book we call the Bible.

The Greek word for "inspire" is theopneustos—theo, meaning "God," and pneustos, "breathed." The same God who breathed life into man when He created man in His own image, breathed His revelation and will into the written Word. Only the Lord of the universe could have conceived and carried through such a project with His servants, the writers of the books of the Bible. Truly, "Holy men of God spoke as they were moved" by God, the Holy Spirit (2 Peter 1:21). The Greek word for moved is literally "borne along." The Divine Spirit directed these authors in penning the Word of God as the Bible grew through the centuries.

Nor did God sit at a writer's side and dictate into his ear.

To be sure, some parts of the Bible were directly spoken by God to His messengers, just as He spoke to Moses on Mt. Sinai. But for the most part God chose and inspired ordinary penmen to write without error in the language and literary techniques of their times. Consequently, there is much use of figurative and symbolic language. Jesus said, "I am the door of the sheep." (John 10:7). Paul urged Christians to "put on . . . bowels of mercies" (Colossians 3:12). These statements were not meant to be taken in a literal sense, but as symbols of a larger reality.

From "in the beginning" of Genesis 1:1 to the last "Amen" of Revelation 22:21, kings and rulers, nations and empires rose and fell across the Bible's pages. The Bible grew portion by portion, century by century into a progressive record of God's dealings with mankind, flowing into the redemptive gift of God Himself, incarnate in Jesus Christ, for man's salvation, then climaxing with the birth and growth of the church, and the promise of a new heaven and a new earth where sin and suffering will be known no more and God's redeemed people will live in His presence in perfect joy and peace forever.

For hundreds of years God's people, the Jews, had only the Pentateuch, the first five books of the Bible, which they called "The Law." "The Earlier Prophets," which included the historical books from Joshua to Kings," came next; then "The Later Prophets" (Isaiah, Jeremiah, Ezekiel, and the Twelve Minor Prophets); and finally "The Writings" (Psalms, Proverbs, Job, Song of Songs, Ruth, Lamentations, Ecclesiastes, Esther, Daniel, Ezra, Nehemiah, and Chronicles). By about 90 A.D. these 39 books were accepted by Jewish scribes and scholars as the canon (meaning rod, or carpenter's rule) of their Bible. The Jews did not accept as canonical a group of books, known as "The Apocrypha," which dealt with Hebrew history in the centuries just before the coming of Christ.

The 27 New Testament books fall into three groups. The historical group includes the four Gospels and the Acts of the Apostles. The second group is composed of The Epistles. The third is The Revelation, a book of prophecy also called The Apocalypse. These books were written after Christ's resurrection and ascension, but well before the end of the first century.

A number of other books were written about Christ and the apostles during the early centuries of Christianity. They reported as truth certain nonsensical Christian heresies then circulating through the Roman Empire. The "Gospel of Thomas," for example, told of a five-year-old Jesus miraculously creating a dozen live sparrows from clay. The "Acts of Paul" had the apostle John exorcising a plague of bedbugs from a bed. The "Acts of Paul" showed the apostle baptizing a lion. The "Acts of Peter" told of a dry sardine being made to swim again.

Early church leaders sought to separate authentic New Testament books from obviously spurious ones. By 350 A.D. there was general agreement that only the 27 books, which we now have in the New Testament, were fully inspired and of permanent value to the church. These were brought together in a canon. In A.D. 367 the noted theologian Athanasius declared: "In these alone is the teaching of godliness heralded. Let no one add to these. Let nothing be taken away." These 27 books were added to the 39 Old Testament books, already accepted by Jews and Christians as inspired, to make the Bible as we have it today.

Consider that the writers of the Old and New testaments never held an editorial conference or planning meeting. Matthew, Mark, Luke, and John, for example did not confer in a Jerusalem "Hilton" and agree that Matthew should focus on Christ as King, Mark depict Him as Son of Man, Luke present Him as the Servant Worker, and John emphasize His divinity. Nor did Paul and James meet over lunch in the Jericho Inn and decide that Paul should emphasize doctrine, and James, practical Christian living.

God, as Holy Spirit, allowed the human authors to express their own unique personalities and write, for the most part, within their own background and experiences. So Solomon in Proverbs reflected on practical lessons learned from life. David sang in Psalms of deep spiritual feelings and emotions, and Luke graphically recorded in Acts the expansion of the first century church as he observed it on missionary journeys with Paul.

"The personalities of the human authors are everywhere apparent," notes Dr. Jerry Vines, president of the Southern Baptist Convention, the largest evangelical body in America. We see the burning sarcasm of Isaiah and the moving pathos of Jeremiah. We witness the deep philosophy of John and the crisp logic of Paul. Amos writes like a farmer, Simon Peter like a fisherman. Luke writes like a doctor, James like a preacher. Each writer was sovereignly prepared by the Holy Spirit to be the ideal penman for that portion of Scripture. Does God want a selection of Psalms like David's? He prepares a David to write them! Does He want a series of letters like Paul's? He prepares a Paul to write them. But all "spoke" from God.

Scripture declares in hundreds of places, "The Lord said," "God spoke," "These are the words of the Lord," and "The Lord commanded." Evangelist Billy Graham observes: "Either God did speak to these men as they wrote by inspiration, or they were the most consistent liars the earth ever saw."

The most important church leaders and theologians through the ages agree that the Bible is uniquely and truthfully inspired by God.

Clement, the leader of the church at Rome and a contemporary of most of the apostles, wrote: "The Scriptures are the true words of the Holy Spirit."

Tertullian, the leading defender of Christianity during the second and third centuries, said: "The Scriptures are the writings of God."

Augustine, the most influential Christian writer since the apostle Paul, declared: "Not one of the authors [of Scripture] erred in writing anything at all."

Martin Luther, the spearhead of the Reformation noted: "No other doctrine should be proclaimed in the church than the pure Word of God, that is, the Holy Scriptures."

Sir Isaac Newton, discoverer of the law of gravity and the greatest scientist of his time, as well as being a theologian, wrote: "I find more sure marks of authenticity in the Bible than in any profane history whatsoever."

Edward J. Young, renowned Old Testament scholar of the 20th century, testified: "These Scriptures possess Divine authority and trustworthiness and . . . are free from error."

B. H. Carroll, founder of the world's largest theological seminary, Southwestern Baptist in Fort Worth, declared: There were no shorthand reporters in those days, and there is not a man on earth who could, after a lapse of 50 years, recall verbatim et literatim what Christ said, and yet John [for example], without a shadow of hesitancy, goes on and gives page after page of what Christ said. . . . Inspiration in that case was exercised in awakening the memory so that John could reproduce these great orations of Christ.

Consider four great witnesses that attest to the inspiration and truth of Holy Scripture. First, there is the witness of unity among diversity.

A book with many authors today usually calls for the writers to be educated in the same field and share similar experiences. Not so the Bible. Kings and peasants, priests and soldiers, scholars and professional men served as God's instruments in writing the Bible. "God "spoke" to them "in many ways" (Hebrews 1:1 NASB), as they wrote in three different languages—Hebrew, Aramaic, and Greek.

These divinely guided human authors followed different styles and presented God's revelation in such different types of literature as biography, philosophy, theology, poetry, prophecy, ethnology, genealogy, romance, and adventure.

Yet a beautiful unity envelops and entwines all this diversity. A marvelous progression of history unfolds, from Genesis to Revelation, clearly pointing toward the end of history as man knows it and a date with divine destiny.

At the center of this marvelous unity is God's love gift of Himself, "the Word" who "was made flesh, and dwelt among us" (John 1:14). So the New and Old testaments are complementary rather than contradictory. The Old Testament predicts and prepares the way for His coming. The New Testament proclaims the Savior's birth, ministry, death, resurrection, and promised return. As an unknown poet wrote:

> *The New is in the Old concealed*
> *The Old is in the New revealed:*
> *The New is in the Old contained;*
> *The Old is in the new explained.*

In the Old Testament, the Hope of Israel and the image of the Messiah shines from each book in reality and in symbol. In Genesis, He is the Seed of the woman; in Exodus, the Passover Lamb; in Ruth, the kinsman Redeemer; in Job, the living Redeemer; in Psalms, the Good Shepherd; in Proverbs, the personification of wisdom; in Ecclesiastes, the meaning of life; in Isaiah, the Child of a virgin, "Wonderful Counselor," and "man of sorrows . . . wounded for our transgressions"; in Amos, the Judge of nations; in Zechariah, the King riding upon a colt.

In the New Testament, the "Hope of Israel" is revealed in Matthew as the King of the Jews; in Acts as the Spirit that empowers the church; in Romans as the Justifier of all who accept His redemption; in Colossians, as our "hope of glory"; in 1 Peter as the Chief Cornerstone of the church and in The Revelation as the Victor over Satan, sin, and death, and finally and triumphantly as the King of the heavenly city.

Second, there is The Witness of Fulfilled Prophecies. Hundreds and hundreds of Biblical predictions have been perfectly and exactly fulfilled, while many others have partially come to pass, with the rest of their fulfillment yet to come. Biblical prophecies compass thousands of years and relate to individuals, cities, nations, empires, the earth, the universe, cataclysmic events, destructive judgments, cleansing revivals, the kingdom of God, and Jesus Christ, King of Kings. "Futurists" of today cannot begin to equal the Bible in its exactness of fulfilled prophecies.

Take predictions of the future of the once great city of Tyre on the Mediterranean Sea. The walls of ancient Tyre towered 150 feet and were just as broad. Built before Israel entered the Promised Land, Tyre stood for centuries as one of the world's greatest trading ports. But Tyre rejected God and practiced idolatry. The Lord spoke through Ezekiel in the sixth century B.C.: "Behold, I am against you, O Tyre, and I will bring up many nations against you, as the sea brings up its waves. And they will destroy the walls of Tyre and break down her towers; and I will scrape her debris from her and make her a bare rock. She will be a place for the spreading of nets in the midst of the sea . . . and she will become spoil for the nations" (26:3-5 NASB).

This and other Biblical prophecies about Tyre literally came true. Nation after nation besieged the seaside metropolis. Egypt captured and held the city for a short time, then as Ezekiel had predicted, Babylon launched an attack and destroyed the fortress. Many inhabitants fled to an island a half mile from the mainland and built a second Tyre.

The new Tyre became a great port city and endured until Alexander the Great laid a stone and timber causeway from the ruins of the old city to the island and conquered all. Today only the causeway stones remain to tell us that a great city was once there. Lebanese fishermen dry their nets on these stones, just as God predicted they would.

And what of Nineveh, built by Nimrod, the great-great-grandson of Noah? The prophet Nahum warned: "Whatever you devise against the Lord, He will make a complete end of it . . . . 'Behold, I am against you,' declares the Lord of hosts. 'I will burn up her chariots in smoke, a sword will devour your young lions . . . '" (1:9; 2:13, NASB). The prophet Zephaniah predicted: "He will make Nineveh a desolation, parched like the wilderness . . . . This is the exultant city which dwells securely, who says in her heart, 'I am, and there is no one besides me.' How she has become a desolation, a resting place for beasts! Everyone who passes by her will hiss and wave his hand in contempt "(2:13,15 NASB).

When these and other prophecies were written, Nineveh was the queen city of the most powerful empire in the world. Hundred-foot walls, punctuated by 1500 towers, each 200 feet high, encircled and protected the city sixty miles around. It seemed incredible that Nineveh should fall. But it was destroyed by invading hordes in 612 B.C. The attackers cleverly diverted the Khoser River into the city, where it dissolved the sun-dried brick buildings. Nahum precisely predicted just this. "The gates of the rivers are opened. And the palace is dissolved" (2:6 NASB).

I have not space to tell of prophecies fulfilled in the destruction of Babylon and other once-great nations. Even more remarkable are predictions of happenings among the Jews, hundreds of years before they occurred. The birth of the promised nation, the victories in Canaan, the fall of Israel into idolatry, the destruction of Jerusalem and the temple, the captivity, and the return of remnants of people from exile to rebuild Jerusalem and the temple were all declared in Scripture long before they occurred. And in the New Testament, our Lord foretold incredible judgments on Jerusalem which were fulfilled when the Roman army under Titus besieged and starved the Jews into submission. The gruesome results were graphically predicted in Luke 19:43,44 and Matthew 24:2, some 40 years before they happened.

The wonder of the rebirth of the modern state of Israel is a marvel to Christians who point to Bible passages which they believe predicted this amazing event. Who could have believed that after over 2,000 years of wandering among the nations and indescribable persecutions, Israel would be re-established as a nation?

"Give me a single, definitive proof that the Bible is true," Frederick the Great of Prussia asked his chaplain.

"The Jews, your Majesty, the Jews," the clergyman replied. This answer was given two centuries before Israel again became a nation.

Most amazing of all are the Old Testament prophecies about the Lord Jesus. Scores of details about his life and ministry were put down by Biblical writers many centuries before He was born. Predictions include His ancestry (Isaiah 9:7), birthplace (Micah 5:2), manner of birth (Isaiah 7:14), infancy (Hosea 11:1), manhood (Isaiah 40:22), character (Isaiah 9:6), career (Isaiah 35:5,6), reception (Zechariah 9:9), rejection (Micah 5:2), death (Psalm 22:16), burial (Isaiah 53:9), resurrection (Psalm 16:10), ascension (Psalm 68:18), and many other events that could not possibly have been known by human means in the centuries before.

Dr. E. Schuyler English, editor-in-chief of the Pilgrim Bible, notes the fulfillment of over 20 Old Testament predictions relating to the death of Christ alone.

A college class in Pasadena [California] City College applied the laws of probability to the fulfillment of eight Old Testament prophecies concerning the coming of Christ. The class concluded: (1) birth in Bethlehem (Micah 5:2)—one chance in 280,000; (2) a forerunner or messenger would announce His coming (Malachi 3:1)—one chance in 1,000; (3) the Messiah would make a triumphant entry into Jerusalem upon a colt (Zechariah 9:9)—one chance in 10,000; (4) He would be betrayed by a friend and suffer wounds (Zechariah 13:6)—one chance in 1,000; (5) the betrayer would receive 30 pieces of silver (Zechariah 11:12)—one chance in 10,000; (6) the silver would be thrown to a potter (Zechariah 11:13)—one chance in 100,000; (7) the Savior, though innocent, would be oppressed and afflicted; He would make no defense (Isaiah 53:7)—one chance in 10,000; and (8) He would die by crucifixion (Psalm 22:16)—one chance in 10,000.

Based on these estimates, the class figured that the chance of all eight of these prophecies being fulfilled by one person would be the equivalent of 280,000 X 1,000 X 10,000 X 1,000 X 10,000 X 100,000 X 10,000 X 10,000.

Is it any wonder, then, that thousands of Jews have accepted Christ as their Messiah? One is Joe Finkelstein of Philadelphia. When Joe was a teenager, his coach, George, showed him Messianic prophecies in the Jewish Scriptures that seemed to be amazingly fulfilled in the New Testament. After checking them all, Joe concluded that Jesus "was the promised Jewish Messiah, yet I couldn't see myself as a believer since all I had ever seen of 'Christianity' was outright hypocrisy. I was also afraid of how my family would respond."

Later when Joe was a senior at Drexel University, he introduced his girl friend Debbie to George. Debbie recalls: "George really got me mad. I started reading the passages in context to prove he was wrong. To me, Jesus was just part of the Gentile religion—a Jew whom Gentiles had made into God." It took Debbie a year and a half, but she, too, became convinced that Jesus was the Messiah. She called Joe and told him she had put her faith in Jesus. Joe then accepted Jesus as his Messiah-Savior also. His unhappy parents asked him to take Debbie and visit a rabbi. The rabbi, according to Debbie, "told us God was abstract and impersonal and couldn't be known . . . . He only made us stronger in our new beliefs."

Debbie and Joe are now leaders in a growing church of Jewish believers in Philadelphia, called, "The House of the Messiah."

Third, the witness of archaeology to the life and times of the sacred people of antiquity provides a remarkable authenticity to details in the Bible.

As a tribal boy I was fascinated by picture carvings on the tombstones of long-departed Hmars in jungle cemeteries. On a wooden figure representing a great man, relatives would carve pictures of his many slaves and the heads he had taken in battle. If he was a great hunter, they carved pictures of the elephants, tigers, and other animals he had killed. Some of the wood slabs were taller than a man in order that all the accomplishments of a great warrior and hunter might be shown. Most people in India at that time didn't know the Hmars existed, for we weren't on the census rolls. But the evidence was there in plain sight to any visiting archaeologist, even if he never saw one of us in the flesh.

Around the time of the American Revolution, it was popular in European and American intellectual circles to sneer at the historical record of the Bible, especially the Old Testament. Unbelievers argued that since only the Bible mentioned certain names, places, and events of ancient history, the record must be mythical. Relics had been found, but no one had been able to decipher the strange hieroglyphics (picture language). Many people assumed that these had nothing to say about the historicity of the Bible.

Then Biblical names, dates, places, and peoples began coming alive. In 1799 a French soldier found a huge basalt slab near Rosetta, Egypt, covered with inscriptions in hieroglyphic, Demotic, and Greek languages. I've seen this marvelous Rosetta Stone in the British Museum. By comparing the parallel texts, Jean Francois Champollion discovered the key to understanding hieroglyphics.

With this and additional discoveries, the ancient civilizations described in the Bible came to be verified. The sites of Babylon, Nineveh, Ur of the Chaldees, and other long-lost cities were uncovered. The great Code of Hammurabi, which predated the Ten Commandments, was found and translated. Stories from many cultures of the creation, the fall of man, and a great flood were unearthed.

The Babylonians, for example attributed creation to a group of warring deities. The earth, they held, was formed from a leftover carcass on the battlefield.

The most critical skeptics stood amazed at the astounding similarities between some of these stories and Biblical events. The likeness of a Babylonian tale of sin in "the garden of God" and the Genesis record of Adam and Eve's transgression was especially striking. The Babylonian version read in part: "In sin one with another in compact joins. The command was established in the garden of God. The Ansantree they ate, they broke in two. Great is their sin. Themselves they exalted."

Those who rejected the Bible said such similarities merely indicated that the Genesis writer had copied from pagan stories. Bible believers said the evidence indicated just the reverse.

Unbelievers were set back further when Abraham's ancestral city of Ur was unearthed. Skeptics had been saying that the stories of the Genesis patriarchs were myths, that people in the time claimed in the Bible for Abraham didn't even know how to write. Archaeology shattered these claims. The evidence showed Abraham's home town to have been a thriving metropolis long before the biblical time of the father of the Jews. Ur had well planned streets and shops. Urites excelled in penmanship, math, geometry, grammar, and the fine arts. They played harps, flutes, trumpets, lyres, drums, and cymbals.

The Hittites were another favorite laughing stock of skeptics. That the Bible mentioned them over 40 times was not sufficient reason to believe they had ever existed. Then the archaeologist's spade began turning up Hittite inscriptions. Even the Hittite capital of Hattusas (modern Boghaykoy) was uncovered. By 1900 the most stubborn unbelievers were forced to admit that the biblical record was correct. Indeed, the Hittite kingdom had once been as powerful as the Egyptians and Assyrians. Once more the Bible was proven right and the naysayers wrong.

The story of Jericho's walls falling down flat at the trumpet blasts of Joshua's soldiers was another source of amusement. Doubters pointed to the existing city of Jericho, which had been reliably dated only to the time of Christ. There probably never was another Jericho, they said.

Then Dr. John Garstang found "old" Jericho about a mile north of the Jericho of Jesus' day. Scientific dating established that old Jericho had been destroyed about 1400 B.C., the approximate time of Joshua's victory. Evidence showed the city was surrounded by double walls, connected by beams at the top, on which houses had been built as described in Joshua 2:15. There was also a single gateway to the city as noted in Joshua 2:5-7.

Furthermore, it appeared the outer wall had toppled backwards and slipped down an incline, dragging the inner wall behind. This could have happened when the Hebrew priests blew their trumpets and the people shouted (Joshua 6:16). The underlying layer of earth remained undisturbed, indicating that the walls had not been undermined. The city had been destroyed by fire as reported in Joshua 6:24 and had not been looted before being set aflame, supporting Joshua 6:18. Finally, no other city had been built on the site for centuries, a fact agreeing with Joshua 6:26 and 1 Kings 16:34.

Dr. Robert Dick Wilson was professor of Semitic languages at Princeton Theological Seminary for many years. He was considered the greatest biblical linguist of modern times. To answer the critical assaults on the Bible, he learned 45 languages and dialects, including the languages in which the Bible was written, plus Egyptian, Syrian, Latin, French, and German. He read all of the available ancient literature of the biblical period. He studied every criticism of the Bible he could find up until modern times. He collected over 100,000 citations. This was his conclusion: "After 45 years of scholarly research and Biblical textual studies and language study I have come to the conclusion that no man knows enough to assail the truthfulness of the Old Testament."

Many more witnesses of archaeology, from the late 19th and early 20th century, that testify to the authenticity of the Old Testament, as well as the New Testament, could be cited. I will mention just a few examples which support the historical integrity of the New Testament.

Peter's house—where Jesus stayed, taught, and performed healing miracles, including that of Peter's mother-in-law—has been found in Capernaum. Dr. James H. Charlesworth, chairman of the biblical department at Princeton Theological Seminary, calls it an "authentic relic." The house dates to about 60 B.C. and contains etched crosses, a boat, and fishhooks. A rock under the Church of the Holy Sepulchre has been shown to be a rejected quarry. This appears to fulfill and explain the double meaning in I Peter 2:7, " . . . The stone which the builders rejected, this has become the head of the corner." The official residence of the Roman governor during Jesus' time has been unearthed in Jerusalem.

Double gates and passageways to Solomon's Stables have been discovered under the Temple area. This confirms that the area was larger than had previously been thought and included stalls for large animals, thus lending authenticity to the biblical account of Jesus cleansing the Temple of the money changers.

These and other discoveries cause Dr. Charlesworth to say: "Jesus did exist, and we know more about Him than about almost any other Palestinian Jew before 70 A.D.

Let us move quickly to the Book of Acts.

About a century ago, a young English scholar named William Ramsay went to Asia Minor to prove what he had been taught—that Dr. Luke's history as recorded in Acts was full of errors. After years of painstaking study, Ramsay declared that his teachers had been wrong. His study of inscriptions and other evidence showed Acts to be completely trustworthy in every historical and geographical detail. Furthermore, Ramsay said that partly as a result of his findings, he had become a Christian.

In more recent times archaeology has brought forth the testimony of the famous Dead Sea Scrolls, about which I will say more later. Another startling discovery is the Ebla Tablets. Sixteen thousand and five hundred of these tablets, along with many fragments, were uncovered at Ebla, Syria by Italian archaeologists during the last decade. The inscriptions were published in detail in 1981, with the archaeologists crediting the Old Testament with much greater historical accuracy than ever thought possible by secular scholars.

The witness of archaeology has not "proven" everything in the Bible. We must be careful not to claim too much. However, it has verified many, many details of the biblical record. Furthermore, Dr. Nelson Glueck, one of the greatest men of the spade of the 20th century, states, "No archaeological discovery has ever controverted a biblical reference.'

Fourth, there is the witness of science. Although the Bible is not a textbook on science, it contains hundreds of scientific facts, as up to date as tomorrow's newspaper.

Some 3,000 years before William Harvey proclaimed his theory of the circulation of the blood, the Bible declared, "The life of the flesh is in the blood . . . " (Leviticus 17:11). Medical science was a long time accepting the view of Harvey and the Bible. As late as George Washington's time, the draining of blood from the bodies of the seriously ill was still believed to be a curative for many diseases. While phlebotomy (bloodletting) is still practiced today in a few instances, physicians now know that excessive loss of blood weakens the body and can only make the patient much worse.

It was also once commonly thought that the earth was flat. The Flat Earth Society today perpetuates this myth and rejects pictures made from space as propaganda. The Bible is in agreement with the photos made by astronauts. Isaiah 40:22, for example, speaks of the Lord sitting on the circle of the earth.

Many ancients also thought that the earth was held in place by an under-support. But Job declared, "He stretches out the north over empty space, and hangs the earth on nothing" (26:7, NASB).

Job said, "The morning stars sang together" (Job 38:7). Scoffers once dismissed this as impossible. We now know there is a beautiful unity and harmony in light and sound. Light properties can have wave motion. If we could hear at the proper frequency, our ears might pick up the melody in the color coming from stars of different temperatures.

Jeremiah declared that "the host [stars] of heaven cannot be numbered" (33:22). The Greek astronomer Hipparchus, who lived hundreds of years after Jeremiah, stated dogmatically that there are only 1,056 stars in the heavens. "I have counted them," he said with certainty. Centuries later the scientist Ptolemy confirmed Hipparchus's count as correct. Not until A.D. 1610 did Galileo, a devout Christian, peer through a telescope and proclaim, "There are more stars out there than we can count." Now we know that billions of stars hang in our Milky

Way galaxy alone and that uncounted trillions are suspended in billions upon billions of other galaxies." Truly, as the inspired writer said, the "host of heaven cannot be numbered."

The Bible records numerous miracles. Miracle is defined by the Random House Dictionary as, "an event that surpasses all known human or natural powers and is ascribed to a divine or supernatural cause." Doubters say that some Biblical events merely appeared to be miraculous because the observers were living in a pre-scientific age. Such happenings, the doubters assert, would not be considered miraculous by knowledgeable observers today.

Another explanation frequently given is that the events took on a miraculous and supernatural aura as they were told and retold in following centuries. The stories then became a part of the religious history of the people. Theologian Eric Rust declared in an article titled "Biblical Faith and Modern Science": The miracle or wonder was not characterized by being unusual or abnormal, for even normal happenings could be wonders. What characterized a miracle was that the divine activity was especially evident in it to the man of faith and that it significantly furthered the accomplishment of the kingly power of God in redemptive mercy.

In other words, the miracle was in the perception, not in the actual happening.

This is merely an attempt to make the record of the supernatural Book subject to human judgment. Astronaut Jack Lousma put it right: "Miracles . . . are perfectly possible because God is capable of doing anything, even that which science can't explain."

In numerous instances, skeptics set out to disprove a biblical miracle and ended by becoming believers. Gilbert West and George Lyttelton, prominent English authors of the 18th century, each agreed to write a book exposing the falsity of a New Testament event. West wrote *Observations on the Resurrection*, and Lyttelton penned *Observations on the Conversion of Paul*. They worked independently and did not meet until finishing their books. In the process of research and writing about their subjects both became Christians.

A few years ago a brash young college student was challenged by his professor to disprove the resurrection of Christ, as proclaimed in the Bible. The result of the investigation was that the young man became a Christian. Josh McDowell is today one of the foremost defenders of the faith.

"Heaven and earth shall pass away," said Jesus, "but my words shall not pass away" (Matthew 24:35). Only God's Word is unchanging amidst the flood of new information now engulfing us. At Princeton University Dr. Walter Stewart asked several students coming out of a seminar, "How did it go?" "Wonderful," one cracked. "Everything we knew about physics last week isn't true." That will never be said of the Bible.

Chapter 3

"The Book of Almost 2,000 Languages"

English readers are of all people most fortunate. They have dozens of translations and paraphrases of the Bible from which to choose. But, of course, the Bible was not written in English. Neither Moses nor Paul wrote in "King James" English, but in languages understood by the people of their times. Almost all of the Old Testament was written in Hebrew. (Only Ezra 4:8-6:18, 7:12-26; Jeremiah 10:11; and Daniel 2:4-7, 28 are believed to have been penned in Aramaic.) Biblical Hebrew before the Babylonian exile was written right to left, without vowels, and without spacing between words and paragraphs. Using English letters and reading right to left,"The Lord is my shepherd" would appear as, DRHPHSDMSDRLHT.

Furthermore many of the Hebrew consonants looked very much alike, fairly begging for copying mistakes. R and DH looked almost alike in the Hebrew, as did H and T, N , and G. How difficult it must have been to avoid slips in copying on animal skin parchments.

The Hebrew scribes were called sopherim, literally meaning "the counters." They deserved this title because they counted every letter of every book of Scripture to make sure that nothing was left out. Then they counted the number of times a particular word appeared in a book and checked each letter that appeared in the middle of each book and in the middle of each major section of the book. The Hebrew Bible was literally copied jot by jot, tittle by tittle, dot by dot.

None of the biblical autographs in Hebrew and Aramaic are believed to have survived because of the scribal practice of destroying deteriorating manuscripts after they were copied. Up until the discovery of the famous Dead Sea Scrolls, the oldest Hebrew scriptures extant dated only to the tenth century of the Christian era, although Greek versions are preserved from a much earlier time. The Dead Sea Scrolls were found to contain the texts of many Old Testament books, including a complete copy of Isaiah, written before the birth of Christ. Comparison revealed only minute differences between the Scrolls and later copies, and in no case was any major doctrine or event contradicted.

Writing skills and materials were more advanced by the first century A.D. when the 27 books of the New Testament were written. These books were probably penned on papyrus paper in Greek, although a few scholars think the original writing might have been in Aramaic. They were passed from church to church, with copies made by hand for further study by the congregations. Because papyrus soon grows brittle with age, the Greek New Testament originals are likely lost forever.

Not considering the Old Testament, over 24,000 Greek and Latin manuscript copies of all or part of the New Testament have been preserved. The oldest manuscript yet discovered, known as the Rylands Papyrus, contains only John 18:31-33, 37, 38 but dates to around A.D. 200. Almost complete New Testament manuscripts are preserved from the third and fourth centuries A.D.

It was during this period that the canon of the New Testament, as we know it today, gained acceptance by most church leaders. Since the second century there had been general agreement upon most of the New Testament. The major test of canonicity was authorship by an apostle or someone closely associated with an apostle. The historian Eusebius in A.D. 324 thought at least 20 books (of the New Testament as we have it today) could be called inspired. The delay in accepting James, 2 Peter, 2 and 3 John, Jude, Hebrews, and the Revelation was caused by questions of authorship. But in A.D. 367, the highly respected Bishop Athanasius declared these to be canonical. His recommendation was accepted by most church leaders and the New Testament, as it appears in our Bibles today, was complete.

No other ancient book has as much manuscript evidence as the Bible. Only a single manuscript preserves the famous history by the Roman writer Tacitus. Only a handful of copies exist of the writings of such acclaimed literary greats as Homer, Cicero, Virgil, and Sophocles.

The agreement of the canonical New Testament manuscripts, which come from all parts of the Greek and Roman world and date to the early centuries of the Christian era, is amazing. Dr. A.T. Robertson, the foremost biblical Greek scholar of the 20th century, found notable variances in only one one-thousandth of the New Testament texts, with none of the differences being of any real significance.

The scholar Jerome first translated the entire Bible into Latin. His Vulgate appeared in A.D. 405 and became the authorized version for much of the organized church. After the breakup of the Roman Empire, Latin became a dead language. Jerome's Latin translation was understood only by scholars and clergy. During these "Dark Ages" the Bible became virtually lost to the common people and the established church became corrupt.

Still the Bible continued to be studied. In the year 1250, Cardinal Hugo divided the books of the Bible into the chapter division which is generally followed today. Verses were not marked out until 1551 by Robert Stephanus. A story goes that Stephanus did much of his work while riding a horse; thus the grammatical awkwardness of some divisions.

The great pioneer of English Bible translation was John Wycliffe, born around the year 1320. At 16 he entered Oxford to be educated for the priesthood. He noticed that teachers and fellow teachers regarded the Bible as an "elementary" book, not worthy of teaching. Wycliffe decided to examine the Latin Bible for himself and determine if it was worthy of sharing with his countrymen.

While Wycliffe was still a young man, the dreadful Black Plague swept across London and 100,000 people perished. The deadly scourge caused Wycliffe to seek a new rest and confidence in God based on his study of Scripture. Shortly afterwards he wrote, "So when we were sinful and the children of wrath, God's Son came [and] died for us . . . Now we are made righteous through His blood."

Wycliffe was such a brilliant scholar that after graduation he was made master of one of Oxford's five colleges. He also lectured on the Scriptures. Students crowded into his classes to hear him declare, "The Bible is our final standard of appeal—not the Pope." For his love and knowledge of the Bible, Wycliffe became known as the "Gospel Doctor."

Relations between the English monarchy and the Vatican hierarchy were ruptured at the time by England's discontinuance of paying tribute. When the Pope demanded that the payments be resumed, King Edward

III and the Parliament refused to respond. Wycliffe, a most influential theologian, supported Parliament.

As the rebellion grew, Wycliffe charged that church prelates "are so occupied in heart about worldly lordships that they are not found studying and preaching the Gospel."

The church hierarchy ordered Wycliffe to stop preaching. Wycliffe refused. There were now two "popes" contesting the headship of the Roman Catholic church. The pope in Rome ordered Wycliffe's arrest. Wcyliffe declared his Biblical faith by posting 12 theses at Oxford. A council met at Oxford and condemned his "opinions."

An officer of the council marched into Wycliffe's classroom and demanded, "Either be silent or go to prison."

Wycliffe appealed to the King and Parliament.

The bishop of London demanded that the king stop the spread of Wycliffe's heresy. Buffeted by political pressures, the King ordered the imprisonment of anyone caught teaching the condemned beliefs.

Wycliffe was forced to retire to his church parish. There he began the greatest work of his life: translation of the Bible into English for the common people. A clergymen wailed that "the pearl of the Gospel" would be "scattered abroad and trodden under foot by swine," while "the jewel of clerics is turned to the sport of the laymen."

Wycliffe responded, "Though there were a hundred popes, and all the friars were turned into cardinals, yet should we learn more from the Gospel than we should from all that multitude." Wycliffe completed the New Testament by himself. A friend then translated the Old Testament and gave it to Wycliffe for revision. There was no printing technology yet, so Wycliffe enlisted 100 scribes to make copies. Each "Wycliffe Bible" took about 10 months to copy by hand and cost at least $200. Few people could afford to buy one. Many paid just to hear Scripture read for one hour in their native English. Some copies were sold page by page.

The English church hierarchy stepped in and banned further distribution of the Wycliffe Bible. An archbishop charged Wycliffe with doing the work of the Antichrist. The angry cleric called the translation Wycliffe's "crowning act of wickedness."

Wycliffe died on the last day of 1384 and was buried by friends in a church cemetery. In 1415 the Council of Constance ordered his bones dug up and removed from the "consecrated" ground. This was the same council which had earlier sentenced the leading Bible preacher of Bohemia (now Czechoslovakia), John Huss, to be burned at the stake.

Not until nine years later were Wycliffe's bones exhumed and burned, and the ashes cast into a nearby stream. From there they were swept into a river and carried on to the ocean, symbolizing the spread of a wave of Bible translation which has never stopped.

Wycliffe's translation was based largely upon Jerome's Vulgate. William Tyndale, a Cambridge educated scholar who was born 60 years after Wycliffe's ashes were cast into the water, determined to make a better translation. Greek New Testament manuscripts, older than the Vulgate, were now available to scholars. Religious oppression had eased and Tyndale thought his church superiors might give him permission to both translate and use the technology developed by the German printer Johann Gutenberg (1397-1468), who was the first to print with movable type.

Tyndale pleaded in vain for permission from authorities to do the translation. After a year Tyndale left England and went to Germany where the preaching of Martin Luther had opened new windows of freedom. There he completed the New Testament and was printing the first run of 3,000 when a clerical enemy of Luther's learned of the project and obtained sanctions against distribution. Tyndale and his assistant escaped to the more friendly city of Worms and completed 3,000 copies each of two different editions of the translation.

Enemies came after Tyndale from both Germany and England. The great English scholar was forced to flee with his books and manuscripts from one hiding place to another until finally, on orders from the King of England, he was caught and imprisoned in the dungeon of a Belgium castle. One of his last letters was a plea to the master of the castle where he was confined. Be kind enough to send me from my goods . . . a warmer cap, for I suffer extremely from cold . . . a warmer coat also . . . . Kindly permit me to have my Hebrew Bible, my Hebrew grammar, and Hebrew dictionary, that I may spend my time with that study.

But like the apostle Paul who made a similar request while in prison (2 Timothy 4:13), Tyndale's life race was done. On the morning of October 6, 1536, the great translator was strangled. With his last breath, he gasped, "Lord, open the King of England's eyes."

It was Tyndale's translation rather than Wycliffe's that became the basis for future English editions of the Bible. My friend and neighbor in Wheaton, Kenneth Taylor, who gave us the famous Living Bible, chose to name his publishing house for the great William Tyndale.

Tyndale was fortunate to have the use of the Gutenberg printing press (1450) on which the first book printed was the Bible. One copy of Gutenberg's Bible, now in the United States Library of Congress, is valued at well over one million dollars. Printing was invented by the Chinese centuries before Gutenberg built his press. But it was in Europe that printing technology caught on. More books are believed to have been produced in the last half of the 15th century than in all previous human history. Almost half were Bibles or on biblical themes, with more than 150 editions of the Bible published. "Printing," said Martin Luther, who himself translated the New Testament into German, "is God's latest and best work to spread the true religion through the world."

The march of the Bible was just beginning. One edition after another, derived largely from Tyndale's translation, appeared in England. In haste to satisfy the thirst of the masses, some editions were a little less than perfect. Psalm 119:161 read in one translation: "Printers (instead of princes) have persecuted me without a cause." Another difficulty was rapidly changing definitions and spellings. In the Taverner Bible a messenger described a battle to King David as "a great hurlee burlee" (2 Samuel 18:29).

Every new edition and translation brought improvement. Most notable was the Bible commissioned by King James I in 1611. King James hoped that a new Bible would heal divisions within the English church. The greatest biblical scholars of that day were appointed as translators. The King James Bible is still the most popular Bible in the world. At least 90 percent of this translation is based upon Tyndale's.

The public demand for Wycliffe's and Tyndale's Bibles was fueled by the great Reformation that swept across Europe during the 16th century. But the Reformation could not have spread as it did without the translation and printing of Holy Scripture into the common tongues of the people.

Martin Luther was the great translator in Germany. While a theological student, Luther punished himself in penance for his sins. He went without food for days at a time. He cast off his blankets and almost froze in winter. He went to Rome and on his knees climbed the steps of the Scala Sancta, reputed to be the staircase from Pilate's palace in Jerusalem. "Surely if I ascend the steps Jesus climbed, I will be accepted by God," he told himself. But peace did not come.

He turned to the Latin Bible in desperation. Slowly the light dawned as he grasped that God's righteousness is attained as a gift through the atoning death of Christ. Finally he was able to say with conviction, "The just shall live by faith!"

As Wycliffe and Tyndale had done, he began lecturing on the Bible. Some of Germany's keenest minds heard him declare: "We cannot merit the forgiveness of sins by our own works . . . . Jesus bore our sins and His favor is to be received by faith alone."

Luther's posting of 95 theses on the Castle Church door in the city of Wittenburg is an epochal event in history. His positions boldly challenged traditional beliefs on important doctrines. Multiplied by printing, they "spread through Christendom as though angels were the postmen," one observer noted.

Luther's challenge to clerical selling of indulgences for the forgiveness of sin triggered charges of heresy. Refusing an order to appear in Rome for a hearing, he challenged his opponents, "Show me my errors from Scripture. Only the Bible is infallible. Even [church] councils may err, and have erred."

The German emperor's priestly adviser ordered Luther to appear before the emperor, the German princes, and the church hierarchy in the city of Worms "to give information concerning [your] books and doctrine." Speaking to a huge throng, Luther declared, "Show me my errors by proofs from the Bible, and I shall be the first to throw my books in the fire. But unless I shall be convinced by the testimonies of the Scriptures, I cannot recant anything, since I cannot act against my conscience. Here I stand! I cannot do otherwise!"

The emperor was caught between the popularity of Luther among the masses and pressure from the corrupt church establishment. He first gave Luther a safe-conduct pass to travel about the city. Then he ordered Luther's arrest. But by this time Luther had slipped away and was securely hidden in a castle by the powerful Prince Frederick.

While in hiding, Luther set to work translating the New Testament into German. Two years later it was on the black market. Five thousand copies were snapped up in less than three months. More copies were printed. Luther's work spread to surrounding countries until all of Europe was aflame from the teaching of the Bible.

By the end of the 16th century, all of the great leaders of the Reformation—Tyndale, Luther, Calvin, Zwingli, Knox and others—were dead. "Christian" Europe was wracked by religious wars. Formalism enveloped Lutheran and Reformed churches on the Continent, while in England a deadly anti-missionary fatalism gripped Baptist and other evangelical Dissenter churches.

Some two centuries after Luther's death God raised up a poor shoemaker named William Carey to launch a new wave of Bible translation.

Too frail to do agricultural work, Carey apprenticed himself to a shoe cobbler and studied languages after work hours. "Why should you, a poor boy cobbler, need to know so many languages?" a customer asked. Replied Carey: "I want to be able to speak other languages so as to understand other men."

When Carey became a Christian he could not learn enough about the Bible, even if it meant starving himself to buy books. For his morning devotions he read a portion of Scripture in three languages—Greek, Latin, and Hebrew.

After completing his apprenticeship in the cobbler shop, Carey became a Baptist minister. A few weeks later he was at a ministers meeting when someone requested a topic for general discussion. Carey rose and suggested, "Whether or not the Great Commission is binding upon us today to go and teach all nations." Immediately he was rebuked by an older minister: "Sit down, young man. When God pleases to convert the heathen, He will do it without your aid or mine."

Carey was silenced but only for the moment. Six years later, on May 30, 1772, his time came when he was invited to preach at the Baptist Ministers' Association at Nottingham, England. Taking as his text Isaiah 54:2,3, he gave two burning challenges: "Expect great things from God. Attempt great things for God." The next morning he proposed the formation of a missionary society. The following October, Carey and 11 other ministers, a student, and a layman met in Widow Wallis' house, popularly known as the "Gospel Inn." Spurred on by Carey, they banded themselves together into a missionary society on capital of less than $100.

The very next year Carey and his family boarded a Danish ship for India, even though an act of the English Parliament declared, "British subjects found in the East Indies without a license are subject to fine and imprisonment." Carey had no license to do missionary work, but when the ship arrived off the coast, the Danish captain allowed the missionary party to board a native boat which slipped them into Calcutta unnoticed.

Carey obtained a job managing an English indigo factory and settled down to study the major languages of India. He translated the New Testament into Bengali, the majority language of India. This was the first time Bengali had been put in written form.

Carey worked amidst great personal difficulties. His wife went insane and had to be secluded. A missionary doctor also became mentally ill and had to be institutionalized. Not until seven years after arriving did Carey baptize his first convert.

But the British governor-general of India liked the ex-shoemaker's work so well that he appointed him Professor of Bengali and Sanskrit at Fort William College near Serampore. Carey used his salary to continue Bible translation and other missionary work. In time he translated the entire Bible into the four leading languages of India, and guided others in translating the Bible into 32 more Asiatic languages.

This "father and forerunner of the modern missionary movement" made the Bible available and readable to 300 million people in their own languages. On his deathbed he whispered, "What hath God wrought!" Friends chiseled his life motto on his gravestone: "Expect great things from God. Attempt great things for God."

William Carey is reverenced by millions of Christians in India today. When I went to college in Calcutta, I attended the Carey Baptist Church. his church commissioned me as their missionary to the west. When I was living in Wheaton, Illinois and translating the New Testament into Hmar, I often thought of Carey's determination to give the Word of God to so many of my countrymen.

What Carey did for India, the great Adoniram Judson did a few decades later for Burma, the hilly Asian country which lies not many miles south of my Hmar area.

The son of a pastor in Plymouth, Massachusetts and a brilliant student, Judson was led into unbelief by Jacob Eames, his closest friend at Brown College in Providence, Rhode Island. After graduation Judson kept up a pretense before his parents. But when his father mentioned studying for the ministry, the young man blew up and said, "I can no longer believe the Bible."

Young Judson left home in a huff. A few weeks later he stopped at a village inn and was given a room next to one occupied by a man who was critically ill. Through the night he heard low voices and people moving about on the creaking floor. The sounds made him think of death and how he would face it. He did not fall asleep until the wee hours.

The next morning the innkeeper told him the sick man had died during the night. "Too bad," Judson replied respectfully. "Who was he?"

"He registered as Jacob Eames from the college in Providence.

Stunned, Judson rode away along a country road, wondering, "Where is Jacob, now that he is dead." Suddenly he had the feeling that his parents were right. The Bible was true. He whirled his horse around and galloped towards Plymouth where he dedicated his life fully to God.

Judson joined "The Brethren," a band of dedicated young men who banded themselves together to prepare for foreign missionary work. The newly organized American Board of Commissioners for Foreign

Missions appointed four of them to mission service. Judson married the beautiful Ann Haseltine and they embarked for Asia with instructions to baptize "credible believers and their households." Bible study aboard ship convinced Judson that it would be unscriptural to baptize unconverted servants and children who would be part of an Asian household. After arriving in India, he and Ann switched to the American Baptist Mission and took a ship to Burma. Their baby died on board while they were enroute to Rangoon.

The Judsons worked six years before seeing a convert. Adoniram was at work translating the Bible into the major Burmese language when war broke out between Britain and Burma. He and a fellow missionary were arrested as spies and tortured in prison. Ann Judson, now a mother again, worked bravely for their release. Six months after Adoniram was let out of prison she died, leaving him with their infant daughter.

Though deeply depressed, Judson plodded on with his translation. He gave his life savings of $6,000 to the mission. Finally, on January 31, 1834, at the age of 46 and seven years after Ann's death, he completed his first draft of the Burmese Bible.

The following April Judson married Sarah Boardman, whose own missionary husband had died of consumption. Sarah gave him six children, then died on the ship that was taking them home for a rest—Adoniram's first trip back since he left 33 years before.

Judson married again and returned to Burma where he finished the revision of the Bible into the Burmese language. He had completed most of a Burmese-English dictionary when he became ill and consented to take a sea voyage for his health. He died quietly at sea and was buried in the Indian ocean.

More than 7,000 baptized Burmese converts mourned the great American pioneer missionary's death. A century later almost 200,000 believers were counted in the country. Missionaries are not allowed in Burma today, but the church is still thriving—primarily because Adoniram Judson translated the Bible into the native language.

Time and paper would fail me to tell even a small part of the story of Bible translation during the past century and a half. In England and America a giant step came in 1881 with the publication of the Revised New Testament made from three major manuscripts and some others not available to translators of the King James Bible.

One of these major manuscripts was Codex Alexandrinus, which scholars date to the fifth century A.D. It contains almost the entire New Testament. A second, Codex Vaticanus, was discovered in the Vatican Library in Rome where it had lain unnoticed for many centuries. Codex

Sinaiticus, the oldest of the three, is believed to have been written in the fourth century A.D.

Siniaticus was discovered by a German professor named Tischendorf. On a trip through the Bible lands in 1844 he came to a monastery at the foot of Mt. Sinai. He happened to notice a basket full of old parchments and asked a monk about them. "Oh, we use them to start fires," he said. They were the most ancient New Testament "leaves" that Tischendorf had ever seen.

Fifteen years passed before Tischendorf was able to return to the monastery to look for the rest of the manuscript. After several days of fruitless searching, he was ready to give up and return home. Then a man living at the monastery invited him into his room and took from a shelf a bulky volume wrapped in red cloth. Tischendorf unrolled the wrappings and "discovered to my great surprise, not only those fragments which fifteen years before I had taken out of the basket, but also other parts of the Old Testament, and the New Testament."

Trembling with excitement, Tischendorf asked "for permission to take the manuscript into my sleeping chamber. . . . There by myself I could give way to the transport of joy which I felt. I knew that I held in my hand the most precious biblical treasure in existence.

By a great deal of effort, Tischendorf persuaded the monks to part with the treasure. Named Codex Sinaiticus for the place where it was found, the precious manuscript wound up in the Russian Imperial Library at St. Petersburg. It was later purchased by the British Government in 1933 for a half million dollars.

These three codexes provided the foundation for the major translations of the New Testament during the past century.

Translation of the Bible into tribal languages is another exciting story. The most important person in this monumental 20th century enterprise is William Cameron Townsend, founder and long-time general director of the Wycliffe Bible Translators. More than anyone else, "Uncle Cam" Townsend deserves the title, "Apostle to the small tribes."

In 1917 Cam went to Guatemala to sell Spanish Bibles and discovered a large tribe of Indians called the Cakquichels who spoke only their mother tongue. Cam set out to learn the language and translate the Bible into it. Thousands of Cakquichels became Christians after they learned that "God speaks our language, too."

Cam was amazed to learn of hundreds of other tribal groups in underdeveloped countries who had no Scripture in their mother tongues. In 1934 he and a preacher friend, L.L. Legters, started a summer training camp for prospective Bible translators in an old barn in the Arkansas Ozarks. That first year they had only three students. The next year six came. One was a young greenhorn named Kenneth Pike who had been turned down by the China Inland Mission for missionary service.

Everybody worked at the camp. Pike's job was to gather firewood from the forest. Instead of picking up dead limbs off the ground, Pike climbed a tree and began breaking off green branches. Spotting him in a treetop, Cam moaned, "Oh, Lord, is this the best you could send us."

From Cam Townsend's pioneering work with the Cakchiquels and the training camp grew the 6000-member Wycliffe Bible Translators, who have translated Scripture into scores of languages during the past 60 years. As for Pike, he became one of the most brilliant linguists of modern times. He and his wife Evelyn translated the New Testament for a tribe in Mexico, then he obtained a doctorate in linguistics. He then became the leader of the training schools for aspiring translators which now enroll hundreds every year. Today, Kenneth Pike is recognized as one of the greatest linguistic scholars in the world.

Wycliffe translators pursue essentially the same method which Carey and Judson did. First, they must learn the language of the people. As anyone who has ever learned a language "foreign" to his culture knows, this is not something you just get from a book. Tribal languages are not "primitive" at all. Some are much more complex than English or one of the major European languages. Aided by his Cakchiquel language helper, Cam Townsend worked up a chart on which he could move different word stems, prefixes, and suffixes around to make up 100,000 possible forms for a single verb.

If you happen to be an English speaker trying to learn French, for example, you have the benefit of grammars and dictionaries in both French and English. A Wycliffe Bible Translator has neither grammar nor dictionary when he begins. He must make his own. For some languages he must learn how to make sounds in different ways, like making his Adam's apple rise to compress air in the throat for releasing a "whoosh" or drop to make a "cork-popping" sound. For tonal languages he must develop an extremely sensitive ear. The same word, spoken in five different tones, can have five different meanings!

Bible translators to so-called "primitive" tribes find that the Bible cannot be translated word for word since a single word in one language may represent a long phrase in another or even a sentence. For example, *tsiyatamparshataniya* in the Candoshi Indian language of Peru means, "we do not talk enthusiastically then." *Papigpinagwinulowitik* means in the Umiray Dumagat language of the Philippines, "he threw something or other repeatedly without intending to, here and there, habitually."

It is essential that the right idiom be used to make the Bible word or concept understandable to the native speaker. Translator Bob Eastman, for example, wanted to put Mark 10:35 into the Iquito Indian language of Peru. The verse reads in English: "It is easier for a camel to go through the eye of a needle, than for a rich man to enter into the kingdom of God." Eastman threaded a needle and asked his Iquito language assistant, "What did I do?"

"You put the string through the needle's ear," the Iquito replied.

Eastman questioned him further and learned that needles had ears, not eyes in the Iquito language. So he translated: "It is harder for a camel to enter a needle's ear than for a rich man to enter God's country."

"Heart" means the center of one's emotions and desires in many languages. But "stomach" is used by the Mantjiltjara aboriginal people of western Australia. One day a young Mantjiltjara told translator James Marsh, "My stomach sits with yours." Further investigation convinced Marsh that he meant, "I believe you." This proved to be a good concept for "faith" in the Mantjiltjara language.

One more example: Mark 12:38,40 warns, "Beware of the scribes . . . which devour widows' houses." First century Jews understood this to be a symbolic way of saying, "Beware of those who exploit and defraud poor widows." Translator Philip Baer found that the Lacandon Indians of Mexico couldn't understand a literal translation. "Here where animals eat palm roofs and jungle termites devour houses," he wrote, "can you imagine what a Lacandon would think of a scribe who eats a poor woman's home? He can only conclude that a scribe is either an animal or an insect." So Baer chose to simply write in Lacandon: Beware of the scribes . . . who take the possessions of widows and use them up."

Bible translation into the language and idioms of tribal people has resulted in thousands of tribal people becoming Christians. Whole societies have been lifted out of superstition and degradation to become productive, God-loving citizens of their native countries. It is the story of the Hmars, after they received the Bible, over and over.

These "nieces" and "nephews" of the famous Uncle Cam have received recognition from many national and international leaders for their dedicated, sacrificial work which enables tribal peoples to advance into full citizenship in their native countries. Both Townsend and Pike were nominated for the Nobel Peace Prize. "Uncle Cam" lived to be 85, still dreaming, still calling for the translation of Scripture into every tongue on earth. Ken Pike still travels the earth in his service as a consultant to much younger Bible translators.

The history of Bible translation is an amazing story. Translations are now being produced at the fastest pace in history. Thanks to computers and other advanced technology, a Bible translator can now complete a New Testament in a previously unwritten language in less than one third of the time it once took.

Altogether, Scripture has been translated into almost 2,000 languages during the past 180 years, with over 500 translations coming in the past century. Currently a portion of Scripture is appearing in a new language on the average of one every fourteen days. Wycliffe Bible Translators, with over 6,000 members, are now working in over 600 additional languages, and the United Bible Societies are involved in translation projects in more than 500 languages around the world.

If Bible translation continues at the present pace, by the year 2,000 more than 2,000 language groups will be singing:

> *O for a thousand tongues to sing*
> *My great Redeemer's praise*
> *The glories of my God and King,*
> *The triumph of His grace.*

Chapter 4

"The Book That Triumphs Over Its Enemies"

We saw in the last chapter how the Bible has been transmitted through translation until it now has the largest circulation of any book on earth. This is remarkable because no book has been hated and feared as much as the Bible. From ancient times to the present, mobs have burned the Bible in public squares, and soldiers have ransacked homes to find and destroy the Book of the ages. Through many centuries, kings and emperors, corrupt churchmen and pagan warlords, Fascist and Communist governments, terrorists and religious fanatics have sought to keep the Bible from the eyes of seekers.

Assaults on the Bible and moral wickedness walk hand in hand. Manasseh, son of the godly Hezekiah, came to the throne of Judah in 687 B.C. when he was only 12 years old. Royal courtiers persuaded him to do away with the religious reforms Hezekiah had made. He brought a host of heathen practices into the life of the nation. He worshipped the sun, moon, stars, and planets, and built altars to them in the courts of the temple where the God of the sacred Hebrew Scriptures had been honored before. He even put a heathen altar into the sacred temple which his father had held sacred to Jehovah. He had children sacrificed to the heathen god Molech. He persecuted God's prophets, and according to Jewish tradition had the prophet Isaiah sawed asunder.

Yet 10 years after Manasseh's death, his grandson, Josiah, found the lost books of Moses in the temple and called for public reading and observance. A powerful religious revival swept the land.

Jehoiakim, second son of the godly Josiah, was every bit as oppressive and godless as his ancestor, Manasseh. The prophet Jeremiah boldly warned Jehoiakim: Woe to you, King Jehoiakim, for you are building your great palace with forced labor. . . . But a beautiful palace does not make a great king! Why did your father Josiah reign so long? Because he was just and fair in all his dealings. That is why God blessed him. He saw to it that justice and help were given the poor and the needy and all went well for him. This is how a man lives close to God. But you . . . . are full of selfish greed and all dishonesty! You murder the innocent, oppress the poor and reign with ruthlessness. (22:13,15-17, Living Bible)

When Jehoiakim sought to silence Jeremiah, the princes hid the prophet and his secretary Baruch. Jehoiakim found the written prophecy, cut up the scroll on which Jeremiah's prophecies were written, and threw it into the fire. Upon learning what had happened, Jeremiah predicted: His family will not weep for him when he dies. His subjects will not even care that he is dead. He shall be buried like a dead donkey—dragged out of Jerusalem and thrown on the garbage dump beyond the gate! (22:18,19, Living Bible)

Jehoiakim was treated just as Jeremiah said. The inspired prophecies of Jeremiah, which the king had ordered cut from the roll book, were rewritten and enlarged with other prophecies. They remain in the Bible to this day.

Some 500 years later the Syrian despot, Antiochus Epiphanes seized control of the land of the Jews. He plundered the sacred temple, sacrificed swine on the altar, and ordered his inspectors to ferret out every copy of Hebrew Scripture in the land. Anyone found possessing a copy of the Old Testament was killed on the spot.

The massacres, sacrilege, and Bible burnings by Antiochus ignited a revolution among the Jews. The patriotic Maccabee leaders raised a guerilla army and defeated the foreign ruler. Three years after ordering the Hebrew Bible destroyed, Antiochus died in humiliation. The temple was repaired, worship reinstituted, and Scripture was again taught publicly.

The Romans were in control of Palestine when Jesus was born. The emperors were called Caesar, after Julius Caesar, who reigned during much of the century (102-44 B.C.) before Christ. The title reappeared later as the German "Kaiser" and the Russian "Czar," or "Tsar."

Incidentally, the term "Caesarean Section" is derived from Julius Caesar because he was supposedly born this way.

The ruling Caesar was held to be a god. But enforcement of emperor worship was sporadic, depending on the whims of the ruler in power. For many years the Romans paid little attention to the Jewish holy book. They generally allowed Jews and other sectarian groups to follow their religion so long as they did not foment revolution or publicly refuse to acknowledge Caesar as divine and offer incense on altars dedicated to the worship of the emperor.

Julius Caesar made the Roman Empire a reality by bringing order out of disorder. After he proclaimed himself Emperor for Life, in 44 B.C., a palace conspiracy rose against him and he was stabbed in the House of the Senate.

Julius Caesar's grand nephew Augustus succeeded him and was the reigning Caesar when Jesus was born. Caesar Tiberius (A.D. 14-37), a stepson of Julius, was on the throne when Jesus was crucified. In his old age Tiberius became mentally ill and was murdered.

The murder of Tiberius made way for the evil Caligula (A.D. 37-41). Caligula, whose name meant "little boots," became insane shortly after coming to power. Ruthless and cruel, he exercised autocratic power at the trials of dissenters. He would merely nod his head or point his finger and the executioner killed the accused instantly. Caligula carried a box of deadly poison in a snuff-like box for more distinguished citizens. Anyone taking a pinch of the fatal drug died as a traitor. Caligula was murdered by an officer of his personal guard.

Caligula's successor, Claudius (A.D. 41-54), was outclassed only by his fiendish wife's depravity and brutality. The Christian movement probably took root in the city of Rome during the reign of Claudius. The first persecutions of Christians may have begun under him.

Claudius despised both Jews and Christians, whom he lumped together as one sect. His appointee Herod beheaded "James The Just," the brother of our Lord. Yet it was during Claudius' rule that the Romans invaded and brought Britain under the power of the Roman Eagle. The message of the Bible was probably brought to the newly conquered territories by Roman soldiers and merchants who were Christians. When the famous Patrick arrived in Ireland three centuries later he found some Bible believers already there.

The greatest persecution of Christians and Jews to date took place under the monster Nero, who took the throne in A.D. 54, when he was only in his late teens. Much of the New Testament was written during this terrible time. The Apostle Paul wrote to the suffering Roman believers: ". . . What can separate us from the love of Christ? Can affliction or hardship? Can persecution, hunger, nakedness, peril, or the sword? We are being done to death for thy sake all day long, as Scripture says; 'we have been treated like sheep for slaughter'—and yet, in spite of all, overwhelming victory is ours through him who loved us"(Romans 8:35-37, NEB).

The Apostle Peter may have already been a captive of Nero's at this time. Paul was sent to Rome as a prisoner in the year 60. After arriving, he sent greetings to the Philippians from "the saints . . . that are of Caesar's household" (4:22). How angry the wicked Nero must have been to learn that Christianity had infiltrated into his household." I can almost hear this egomaniac shouting an order to a crusty old general: "Round up every Christian in the city and demand that they sacrifice to me." And the general's reply, "Even those in your own household, Young Majesty?" I can see the Emperor's face redden and hear him sputter: "Who . . . ? How . . . ?"

Nero's legions burned every scroll of Jewish and Christian scripture they could find. When the Christians in Rome refused to sacrifice to him and other gods, he had Rome set afire and blamed the Christians. His crimes against Christians are almost too horrible to describe. Tacitus, dean of Roman historians, wrote: "Various forms of mockery were added to enhance the dying agonies of Christians. Covered with the skins of wild beasts they were doomed to die by the mangling of dogs, or by being nailed to crosses; or to be set on fire and burned after twilight by way of nightly illumination." Nero offered his own gardens for this show, and gave a chariot race, mingling with the mob in the dress of a charioteer, or actually driving among them.

Dean Farrar described the terrible persecution in his book, *The Early Days of Christianity*: "Along the paths of those gardens on the autumn nights were ghastly torches, blackening the ground beneath them with streams of sulphurous pitch, and each of those living torches was a martyr in his shirt of fire. And in the amphitheater hard by, in sight of 20,000 spectators, famished dogs were tearing to pieces some of the best and the purest of men and women, hideously disguised in the skins of bears and wolves. Thus did Nero [in Rome] baptize in the blood of the martyrs which was to be for ages the capital of the world."

Many Christians survived only by going underground and holding their services in underground vaults and galleries used for the burial of the dead. I have visited these catacombs and seen the inscriptions left by these believers on walls.

Nero is believed responsible for the death of the apostles Peter and Paul. According to tradition, Peter asked to be crucified upside down because he did not deem himself worthy to die in the manner of his Lord. It is a divine twist of history that some parents took to naming their sons Peter and Paul and their dogs Nero! And, of course our calendar dates not from the reign of Nero or any other Roman emperor, but from the birth of our beloved Lord.

Caesar Nero died in the year 68 at age 32, in fear and screaming horror at the hands of one of his own attendants. Even as the infamous Nero was carried away to be buried, Christians were huddling in the catacombs underneath the city and making plans to speed the message of the Bible with greater fervor to every corner of the Empire. In the providence of God, the Romans had, by abolishing national borders and laying out trade routes across the Empire, unwittingly opened the way for the advance of the Biblical faith. All the powers of Caesar and the zeal of his bloodthirsty legions could not stop these brave soldiers of the cross.

The emperor who followed Nero committed suicide. The next died from gluttony. In A.D. 70 the Roman legions, under General Titus, besieged and burned Jerusalem. The sacred temple was destroyed and the blood of thousands of slain Jews choked the conduits of the holy city.

Domitian (A.D. 81-96) eclipsed Nero in blood-letting. His hirelings brutally massacred thousands of Christians, mostly in Rome and surrounding towns. Domitian rewarded persons for spying on family and neighbors until it was said, "There was a spy in every house and an executioner at every door."

Domitian must have been infuriated to find that Christianity had infiltrated into his own family. Flavius Clemens, the Roman consul, was his cousin. Flavius' wife Domitilla was Domitian's niece. Next to the Emperor himself, Flavius Clemens and Domitilla held the highest rank in the Empire. Their two sons had been designated by the Emperor as his heirs. Both the consul and his wife were accused of "atheism" and of "going astray after the customs of the Jews." Flavius was put to death. Domitilla was banished for "confessing Christ." What happened to their sons remains a mystery. Perhaps they were killed also.

The tradition of "St. John Before the Latin Gate" credits Domitian with ordering the apostle John thrown into a caldron of boiling oil, "which to him was no place of torture, but as a refreshing bath, in which the old man seemed to renew his youth .... Seeing him come forth full of life and strength, [Domitian] attributed his deliverance to magic, but nevertheless was so far restrained by fear . . . that he dared not inflict any further sufferings on him, but banished him to Patmos, where he remained until the Emperor's death, when he returned to Ephesus."

As for the fate of Domitian, his wife Domitia had him murdered.

Trajan, Emperor from A.D. 98-117, was the first to formally declare Christianity an illegal religion and a threat to the Empire, although it had been treated as such for several decades. Christians held allegiance to a Lord, other than Caesar. Christians refused to burn incense to the Emperor on altars. They prayed with closed eyes to no visible idols. That is why the Romans called them "atheists." They took bread and wine in the "Lord's Supper" as representative of Christ's broken body and shed blood. This led many to believe the story that the Christians killed and ate infants as a sacrifice to their God.

Is it any wonder that 11 of our Lord's 12 apostles, excluding only the Apostle John, are believed to have died a violent death?

There were great secular writers during this first century. Such authors as Livy, Ovid, Strabo, Seneca, Lucian, Petronius, Pliny, and Tacitus have since faded into obscurity. Their works are familiar only to scholars and students of Roman classics. While they have great value to human culture, none are read and cherished as are the Bible books written by Matthew, Mark, Luke, John, Peter, and Paul. One does not turn to Pliny or Seneca for solace in sorrow, but to the Bible, and in particular to the New Testament, which was born during a time when the greatest power on earth sought to wipe Christianity from the earth.

The second and third centuries brought more persecutions and the death of untold thousands of Bible believing martyrs. I will note only Pastor Polycarp who laid down his life in the middle of the second century.

Polycarp had been a disciple of the Apostle John and was now pastor in Smyrna. A heathen sports spectacle was held there in A.D. 155 or 156 and a number of Christians thrown to hungry lions to appease the bloodthirsty crowd. A cry went up for Pastor Polycarp.

Friends spirited him outside the city, but a young slave was found who knew where he was. Under torture the slave disclosed the pastor's hiding place. When the police came for Polycarp, he asked only for a little time to pray. Then he said, "I'm ready to go."

They rode back to Smyrna in the carriage of the chief of police. The officer pleaded with Polycarp to worship the Emperor. "What harm is there to say 'Lord Caesar' and offer incense?"

"I will not do it," the aged saint declared resolutely. The police chief led Polycarp into the arena that rocked with loud laughter, curses, and drunken shouts. The Roman proconsul looked at him sorrowfully. "You are an old man. It is not necessary that you die. You have but to curse Christ, swear by Caesar, and say to the Christians, 'Away with the atheists,' and I will gladly release you."

Pastor Polycarp replied, "Eighty and six years have I served Him, and He never did me wrong. How can I blaspheme my King who saved me."

"Deny Christ," the Roman officer urged, "or I shall have to throw you to the wild beasts."

"Call them," Polycarp said calmly.

"I shall have you consumed with fire, if you despise the wild beasts."

Polycarp answered, "The fire you threaten burns but an hour and is quenched . . . . Come, do what you will."

The crowd began screaming, "Burn him alive! Burn him alive!"

Quickly a fire was prepared. When the executioner came to nail Polycarp to a stake, the pastor asked calmly, "Leave me as I am. He who grants me to endure the fire will enable me to remain on the pyre unmoved, without the security you wish from the nails."

The gentle, fearless pastor raised his voice in prayer, praising God that he was "deemed worthy to die." The fire was lighted and a sheet of flame flashed upward about his body. When his body did not immediately crumble in the flames, an executioner stabbed him with a dagger.

Diocletian became Caesar in the year 284. For the first 19 years of his reign Christians had rest from persecution, probably because of Diocletian's wife and daughter who were followers of the Savior from Nazareth. Many Christians rose to high positions in government. A number of large churches were built in major cities.

Then, under the influence of his cruel son-in-law, Diocletian issued four harsh edicts.

The first called for the destruction of all places of Christian worship and the burning of all Christian books. This order also stripped Christians of all honors and civic rights.

The second called for the imprisonment in chains of pastors and church officers.

The third, issued on the eve of Diocletian's 20th anniversary as emperor, offered a cruel kind of amnesty. The Christian prisoners would be released if they would sacrifice to the Emperor and other Roman gods.

The fourth, issued in A.D. 304, ordered every person in the Empire to sacrifice and make offerings to heathen gods, or suffer torture and death.

Churches were destroyed all over the Empire. All Bibles and writings of the church fathers that could be found were burned in public gatherings. Christian men, women, and children were tortured, thrown to wild beasts, and burned to death. Diocletian had a monument erected at the site of one Bible burning, bearing the inscription, *Extincto nomine Christianorum*—"Extinct is the Name of Christians."

Less than 10 years later the tide dramatically turned. Constantine, the illegitimate son of a military leader and a beautiful Christian Oriental woman, seized power. His change of heart toward Christianity is said to have occurred at the Battle of Milvian Bridge. When enemies were about to overwhelm his soldiers, the Emperor reportedly saw a flaming cross in the sky, declaring, "By This Sign Conquer." Taking this as a sign of Christ's favor, Constantine adopted the cross as his symbol, attacked, and won a decisive victory.

Constantine's proclamation of toleration marked the beginning of a new era for Christianity. He ordered the rebuilding of destroyed churches and an end to all persecution of Christians and burning of Bibles. He urged his subjects to be baptized, declared Sunday a day of worship, and gave special privileges to pastors and church officers.

In his zeal to advance Christianity, Constantine commissioned the great church historian Eusebius to assemble a battery of scholars to prepare 50 magnificent Bibles, "easy to read and conveniently portable." The writing was to be in Greek, the language of the common people. If even one of these 50 Bibles ordered by Constantine should come to light today, it would be a priceless manuscript find.

Constantine also convened the great Council of Nicea to deal with doctrinal issues that were plaguing the church. It was the first great church council in the history of Christendom to which church delegates came from all over the Empire.

Yet Constantine was far from a saint himself. He murdered several members of his family and was not baptized until hours before his death. Yet his favors were hailed as a triumph for Christians and the Bible. For the first time Christians could worship openly and hold church councils without fear of persecution. It was during this period of good will and religious freedom that the canon of the New Testament, as we have it today, was formally accepted by most leaders of the Church.

One of the great preachers during this time was Bishop Ambrose of Milan. Great crowds flocked to hear his sermons. One was a pagan professor named Aurelius Augustine who had been following a pagan cult that proclaimed its doctrines as "pure truth." Augustine's mother was a devout Christian and he had become attracted to her faith.

Sick of his own dissolute life style, Augustine heard Ambrose tell of King David's sin: "That David sinned is human, that he repented is exceptional. Men follow David into his sin; but they leave him when he rises into confession and repentance."

Augustine's immoral past rose to haunt him; David had repented, but he had not.

Augustine became convinced that the Bible was an inspired book. He wanted to become a Christian, yet he feared he could not control his passions.

One day he was in such despair that he burst out weeping in a garden. "O Lord," he cried, "make an end of my vileness." At that moment he heard a child crying, "Tolle lege! Tolle lege! Take and read! Take and read!"

"Is this God's way of telling me to open the Bible and read?" he asked himself.

He opened a scroll book of Romans which he had left in the garden and read the first passage his eyes fell upon: "Not in rioting and drunkenness, not in chambering and wantonness, not in strife and envying. But put ye on the Lord Jesus Christ, and make not provision for the flesh, to fulfil the lusts thereof (13:13-14, King James Version).

He joyously ran to show a friend the passage. "I have put on Christ!" he declared. "My heart is glowing with the light of peace."

Augustine became the greatest Christian writer of his time. He wrote more than 70 books, two of which rank today among the world's great literature, *City of God* and *Confessions*. Many acclaim him the greatest Biblical theologian since the Apostle Paul.

Momentous political and religious changes were now taking place which would deeply affect the future of Christianity and the availability of the Bible. Constantine moved the capital of the Empire from Rome to Byzantium, the location of modern Istanbul, Turkey. After 395 the Empire became permanently divided between east and west and Rome rapidly lost its political importance. In 476 the last Emperor of the West, Romulus Augustulus, was deposed by the Goths. This marked the end of the Western Roman Empire. The Eastern Empire would continue until the 15th century.

Islam arose as a heresy of Christianity during the sixth century after the fall of Rome and advanced across Christian North Africa and into

Spain. North African Christianity virtually disappeared, mainly because the Bible was not available in the native tongues.

As the old Roman Empire was breaking up, Western Christians began looking more and more to the bishop of Rome for leadership and guidance.

Bishop Gregory (called "The Great," 540-604) was the catalytic personage in this development. He had been a rich nobleman who gave up his fortune and became a monk because he thought this was the way to glorify God. When Pelagius, the bishop of Rome, died of the plague in 590, Gregory was chosen to take his place.

Gregory was a man of deep humility who considered himself the "servant of the servants of God." More than anyone else he was responsible for winning England to Christianity. Yet his greatest work was to establish the Roman bishopric as the most powerful office of organized Christianity. Though he refused the title of "pope," he exercised the power of later popes and appointed bishops over the churches of Gaul, Spain, Britain, Africa, and Italy. From the time of Gregory the Great, Western church leaders virtually took their orders from the "Holy Papa" in Rome.

Rome was now the seat of the "Holy Roman Empire." It became a tradition for heads of state, to come to the "Holy City" for crowning by the "Holy Father."

This period of the Middle Ages extended roughly from Gregory the Great to Martin Luther. "Christian" kings, crowned by the pope, exercised both political and spiritual authority over "Christian" nations. Yet, despite many great accomplishments, this was also the period of the "Dark Ages" for the Bible.

The Bible became a closed book to the common people. It was available only in Latin and only the clergy were held wise enough to read, interpret, and apply God's Word. Kings were fearful that mere reading of the Bible, without interpretation by a recognized spiritual authority, could put bad ideas into their subjects' heads.

In 1229, a Catholic synod in Toulouse, France, actually forbade the laity to even possess the Scriptures, except the Psalms and a few verses contained in prayer books. Other church synods followed suit, especially in Spain. But there was never universal denial of Bible reading during the Middle Ages.

As you might expect, there were groups who sought to return to the pure religion they saw in the Bible. The Waldensian movement was one.

The Waldensians were named for Peter Waldo, a rich merchant in Lyons, France. Waldo, in the year 1176, read the New Testament and was so impressed with the call of Christ that he gave all his property to the needy, keeping back only enough to feed his family. He recruited a band of lay preachers, known as the "Poor Men," who taught that every person should have the Bible in his own tongue and that it should be the final authority for faith and life. Following the New Testament example, these Poor Men went out by twos, dressed in simple clothes, and preached to the poor in the local vernacular. They administered the Lord's Supper and baptism and elected their own clergy and deacons. The Poor Men quickly attracted the attention of clerical and civic authorities who saw them as a threat to their authority. Ex-communicated from the Catholic Church and ordered to stop preaching, the Poor Men went underground and continued their spiritual work. Their descendants exist today as a church of about 35,000 believers in northern Italy.

The Waldensians and other groups outside the official church were forerunners of the great Protestant Reformation which would burst forth in the 16th century. They took the Bible—not bishops or church councils—as their absolute spiritual authority.

One of the many who paid with their lives for holding this doctrine was John Huss, the Bible preaching pastor of Prague. "The Bible," he declared, "not the Church, is the Christian's sole authority." For this, Huss was summoned before a council of cardinals and denounced as "a mind reader, a magician, and a vile heretic."

At his trial, Huss tried to defend his teachings from the Bible. His pleas were shouted down. After being taken back to prison to wait for the verdict, he wrote friends, "Pray that God will give me steadfastness."

On June 23, 1415, Huss's books were condemned to be burned. On July 6, he was sentenced to the stake.

Thousands trailed behind his death procession. When they stopped at the place of execution, Huss prayed, "In Thee, O Lord, do I put my trust; let me never be ashamed."

The chief executioner shouted, "Stop!" But Huss cried joyfully, "Lord Jesus Christ, gladly and in humility will I bear this shameful and cruel death for the sake of thy holy Gospel. Forgive my enemies."

"Will you recant, Master Huss?" a stern voice asked.

"No," declared Huss in a firm tone. The beloved pastor of Prague was chained to the stake and the fire lighted. While the flames rose up around him, those standing close by heard him singing, "Jesus Christ, Son of the Living God, have mercy upon me."

When it was certain he was dead, the executioners crushed his head with a club and threw his remains into the nearby Rhine.

That night his Bohemian followers dug up the earth beneath the stake and reverently carried the sacred dirt back to Prague. There the influence of Huss burned brighter than ever as hundreds of Hussites defied the authorities and proclaimed the Bible as God's highest message to man.

The Anabaptists were another much persecuted group for placing the Bible above churchly authority. From their study of the Bible, the Anabaptists insisted on baptizing adult believers as a sign of personal faith, though they had once been baptized as infants.

Over a hundred were killed in one massacre near the Netherlands seacoast. The brother of Menno Simons was one. After his brother's death, Menno Simons found a New Testament. This led him to decide: "No human authority can bind souls to eternal death." Then he received news of the beheading of a poor Dutch tailor, Sicke Freerks. "He was an Anabaptist and guilty of rebaptism," fellow clerics told him.

Through his own study of Scripture, Simons became convinced that the Anabaptists were right. He became the most noted of the "outlaw" preachers and was so influential that Emperor Charles V issued an imperial edict: "No one is to receive Menno Simons in his house on his property. No one is to give him shelter, provision, speak with him, or read his books." The penalty for violation was loss of life and property.

For the next quarter century, Menno Simons and other Anabaptist preachers crisscrossed Europe, declaring that the Bible was man's only supreme authority and that every man's conscience should be free to follow his own convictions. Today, at least 200,000 Mennonites, along with millions of Baptists and other "free church" Christians salute Menno Simons as a champion of the "truth that sets men free."

In the previous chapter I cited the role of Bible translation by Luther, Wycliffe, Tyndale, and others in fueling the mighty Protestant Reformation. As this world-changing Bible awakening swept across Europe, the decadent state church establishments took a harder line against lay possession and reading of the Bible. Some monarchs, notably "Bloody" Queen Mary of England, ordered Bible printing and distribution stopped at the price of blood.

Benjamin Franklin wrote of his great-great-grandfather fastening a Bible under a stool. When he wanted to read to the family, he simply turned the stool upside down. As he read, one of the children stood at the door to watch for "Bloody" Mary's soldiers.

The Bible in Reformation times was not unlike the Irishman's wall which was built four feet wide and three feet high. When asked why he had been so foolish as to build a wall wider than it was high, the Irishman replied, "I built it so if a storm should come and blow it over, it will be higher afterwards than it was before."

Queen Mary's five-year reign of terror finally ended with her death in 1558. The storm of persecution finally blew over. Her half-sister Elizabeth came to the throne and quickly reversed royal policy toward the Bible. The Bible was "higher" than before.

Queen Elizabeth ordered a Bible placed in every court office and called the Bible "the jewel I love best." Ninety editions of the Geneva Version and 40 editions of other versions of the Bible were published during her long reign. For the first time, the Bible became the best selling book in Europe.

The Reformation, Bible translation, and the speed of the printing press made the Bible available to the masses. No longer could the Bible be confined in musty monasteries and bishops' palaces. The Bible, however, was not destined to be free from future attack. A new foe of the Bible emerged from a rationalism that placed the Bible in subjection to man's reason.

Rationalism was the ill-begotten child of the European Renaissance, a movement which somewhat paralleled in time the Reformation. The Reformation brought spiritual light and freedom, the Renaissance emphasized individual expression, literature, science, and the arts. Like the Reformers, leaders of the Renaissance rejected the Catholic papacy as final authority. Unlike the Reformers, some Renaissance figures questioned the authority of the Bible. In this they were joined by German and French philosophers.

The most influential German philosopher, Hegel, held there was no absolute right or wrong, black or white, but only a mixture of gray coming together in synthesis produced by the opposites of thesis and antithesis. Only God was absolute and His will cannot be known, he said.

French romanticism rejected the Biblical doctrine of sin and affirmed the innate goodness of man. Philosopher Jean Jacques Rousseau said man had been corrupted, not by the Biblical Fall but by ownership of property.

German "higher critics" regarded the Bible as an imperfect human book. They denied the Mosaic authorship of Scripture, advanced prophecies past the Biblical record of fulfillments, and saw miracles as natural events perceived by credulous, pre-scientific people who wanted to believe in the intervention of God into human affairs.

Voltaire (1694-1778) was one of the most caustic critics of the Bible. He boasted: "One hundred years from my day there will not be a Bible in the earth except one that is looked upon by an antiquarian curiosity-seeker."

Two hundred years later a first edition of one of Voltaire's works sold in Paris for eleven cents. That same day the British Government paid Soviet Russia $500,000 for the famous New Testament manuscript, Codex Sinaiticus. Voltaire's rationalism served him poorly on his deathbed. He wailed to his doctor: "I am abandoned by God and man! I will give you half of what I am worth if you will give me six months of life. Then I shall go to Hell, and you will go with me. O Christ! O Jesus Christ!"

In the next century Ernest Renan (1823-92) led rationalistic attacks against the Bible and the divinity of Christ. However, the brilliant Renan turned to the Bible for guidance in his closing years and left this testimony: "O man of Galilee, Thou has conquered. Henceforth no man shall distinguish between Thee and God."

During the latter part of the 19th and early 20th centuries, higher criticism and Darwinian evolution weakened the foundations for Biblical authority in many theological schools on both sides of the Atlantic. We are still reaping the bitter fruits of these onslaughts on the Bible, even though many scholars have ceased to accept some of the dogmas once held as virtually infallible by Darwinists. Darwin's theory of survival of the fittest in the evolutionary process, for example, is now rejected by some of the greatest biologists of modern times.

The 20th century brought fresh attacks on the Bible by dictators and godless nations. Hitler set out to exterminate the Jews and destroy faith in the Bible and supernatural Christianity. The German Fuhrer predicted that his *Mein Kampf* would become the Bible of a "Master Race" and he would be the savior. Now Hitler is held only in infamy and dedicated German missionaries are going to distant nations to translate the Bible.

Emperor Hirohito of Japan joined Hitler in attempting world conquest. Japanese militarists encouraged the people to worship Hirohito as a god. Allied victory demolished Hirohito's myth of deity. No longer held in reverence by most Japanese, he withdrew into his palace and lived until 1989. In a touch of irony, Captain Mitsuo Fuchida, who led the attack on Pearl Harbor, became a preacher of the Bible.

Communism came to dwarf all other foes of the Bible. Lenin and Marx both predicted that the Bible would become only a relic in a new classless, atheistic society. Adjoining countries were annexed into the Soviet Empire, religious freedom denied, missionaries banished, Bibles confiscated, and churches turned into museums or closed. Millions of citizens, including many Christians, died in Stalinistic blood purges in the 1920s and '30s. In village after village, residents were called to mass meetings and asked, "Are you with the Marxists or the believers?" Those who said "believers" were shoved into cattle cars for shipment to Siberia.

After Stalin, who died in 1953, came Malenkov, Bulganin, Khrushchev, Brezhnev, Andropov, Chernenko, and now Gorbachev. All, except Gorbachev (about whom I will say more later), were militantly opposed to distribution of the Bible.

Georgi Vins, the great Baptist preacher who was banished from the Soviet Union, recalls that for five years after he became a Christian, he couldn't obtain a Bible. Finally he was able to buy one for a whole month's wages.

Since all printing presses belonged to the government, which refused to permit the printing of Bibles needed, Vins and his Baptist friends built and designed their own presses to print Bibles. They used a motor from a washing machine and took other parts from bicycles and motorcycles. They built each press so it could be disassembled into several pieces, slipped into suit cases, and carried from city to city across the Soviet Union. On this type of press they were able to produce during the next 12 years (1968-1980) over 500,000 Bibles.

All of the Bibles printed were distributed free of charge. Some of the printers, when caught, paid with their lives. Others lost their freedom.

One of the Bible-printing "criminals" arrested was a young woman named Luba Kosachevich. She could have been released if she had denied Christ and pledged not to help print any more Bibles. She said, "I love life. I love the blue sky. I love the flowers. But more than life I love Jesus Christ. And I will give my life to serve him." She went to prison.

Vins himself spent eight years in prison, including four years in the far northeast of Siberia where the temperature dropped to as low as 64 degrees below zero. Some of the officers who guarded him in Siberia had never seen a Bible and asked Vins questions about it. One officer began secretly listening to Christian broadcasts in the Russian language from South Korea. He told Vins privately that he had "no objection" to the "convincing power of the Gospel."

Another officer who was openly opposed to the Bible urged Vins to deny God while he was still young. Otherwise, he said, "when you finish this term, we'll give you another."

Vins was put in a cell of 20 murderers. Their first questions were, "Why are you here? Whom did you kill?"

"I didn't kill anybody," Vins said. "I'm here only because I preached the Gospel."

They asked to see a Bible as proof that he was a Christian. Fortunately Vins had a Gospel of Mark hidden in some rags in his bag. He showed it to the murderers. Because the prisoners had shed blood, they hesitated to take it. Finally one did and began reading it.

Noticing that Vins was exhausted, one of the prisoners gave him his cot. Vins immediately fell asleep. He awoke the next morning to find one of the prisoners reading the Gospel aloud to the other prisoners who were seated in a circle.

"I have killed five men. Can God forgive me?" one asked Vins.

"Yes," Vins assured him. "Jesus Christ forgave the thief hanging on the cross next to Him. He will forgive you if you repent, if you leave your criminal life."

Vins spent a week with the murderers, sharing with them the redemptive promises of the Word of God. Word had spread to Christians in the West about Vins' imprisonment. Many wrote letters to Soviet officials protesting his imprisonment. His release came very suddenly. He was taken to a prison in Moscow and the next day given a suit, a white shirt, and tie, and told he was being stripped of his Soviet citizenship and exiled to the United States. "You are now a man without a country," the officials said.

Hardly. His brothers and sisters in the Soviet Union appointed him to be the official representative of the Evangelical Christian Baptist Church in the West. His headquarters is now in Indiana from which he maintains contact with fellow believers in the Soviet Union. His message to Christians in the West is to "value the freedom you have, love Jesus Christ, and cherish the Bible."

Millions perished in Communist countries other than the Soviet Union. Here too, Bibles were destroyed. It was a rerun of the hate-filled persecutions under the old Roman emperors, except that many, many more have died for the Christian faith and an authoritative Bible in the 20th century than in all of the bloody vendettas by the Caesars of Imperial Rome.

Yet the Bible and Christian faith remain triumphant. At present momentous changes appear to be taking place in the Soviet Union and

Communist Eastern Europe under President Gorbachev's glasnost. Communist Party officials recently celebrated the 1,000th anniversary of the coming of Christianity to Russia. Some churches closed for decades are being allowed to reopen for worship. More religious freedom is being allowed. Hundreds of thousands of Bibles are being allowed to be brought into the country. One well-known Bible smuggler says he was told by Soviet officials, "Bring in all the Bibles you wish." A leading Soviet magazine is reported to be considering printing the New Testament in full. Another Soviet magazine called for publication of the Bible, arguing that atheistic education cannot be complete without some knowledge of opposing beliefs. Arrangements have been made by the Slavic Gospel Assocication to print Bibles on government presses.

In another development, a government publishing house has signed a contract with an American Christian publisher to print 500,000 copies of Christian psychiatrist Dr. Ross Campbell's Bible-based book, *How to Really Love Your Child.*

Two Soviet scholars recently admitted, in a letter to a Soviet journal, that atheist literature has done little to attract followers to its doctrines. One of the two, Dr. S.I. Zhuk, a teacher of scientific communism, noted: "The word 'Bible' has been excised from the history syllabus in schools as though this work never existed . . . . It is imperative to publish a secular edition of the Bible, . . . understandable to the general reader." While claiming that much of the Bible is legend and myth, Atheist Zhuk admits that without the Bible as "a historical source," it is "impossible to gain an adequate understanding of ancient history" and "the history of mankind's development."

Dramatic new winds are also blowing in China. During the radical Cultural Revolution almost all Chinese churches were closed, religious leaders attacked and imprisoned, and their Bibles burned. The Christians simply began meeting in small house churches to share testimonies and pray and quote from memory encouraging passages from God's Word. They took precious Bibles, kept hidden from Communist militants, and divided portions among themselves. One believer would copy a few pages, return it, then receive another. Some learned Bible passages by heart and went from group to group dictating Scripture to fellow believers who wrote it down.

The Cultural Revolution is now labeled a dismal failure. Bibles are actually now being printed in China again; however, the number is limited and the demand is far greater than the supply. Christians in China are currently believed to number from 30 to 50 million. Billy

Graham estimates there were only about 700,000 Christians when the Communists captured China in 1949 and expelled all foreign missionaries.

Many, many individual stories testify to the triumph of the Bible over Communism in modern times.

Remember the Pueblo? The capture, in 1968, of the American electronics "spy" ship and its 81-member crew by Communist North Korea made headlines around the world. But the most significant part of the Pueblo story—the story of the "Pueblo Bible"—may never be told in secular history books.

The Pueblo Bible was begun by Lieutenant Commander Stephen Harris, commander of the ship's intelligence group. Harris had been the lay worship leader aboard ship. A graduate of Harvard University, he had previously memorized dozens of Bible verses as part of the Navigators' Scripture memory program.

In his book, *My Anchor Held* (Fleming H. Revell Co.), Commander Harris tells how the Bible got started: "One morning I used a piece of leftover 'confession' paper to write down a Scripture verse, 'I can do all things through Christ which strengthenth me' (Philippians 4:13). This was the beginning of our Pueblo Bible."

As day after dreary day passed with hopes waning for release, the Pueblo Bible grew as members of the crew contributed verses. They recalled the 23rd Psalm, portions of the Sermon on the Mount, John 3:16, and about 20 other passages. They made a complete list of the New Testament books, but couldn't recall all of those in the Old Testament.

They wrote the verses and lists of books on sheets of paper left over from "confession" sessions with captors. They had to keep the verses and book lists in their pockets because their rooms were searched frequently. "Unauthorized writing" was a severe offense.

After several months the men were permitted to write to their loved ones. Harris wrote his wife Esther: "The Lord never fails to give continuing comfort. My faith never wavers; it's only stronger than it has ever been. I'm certain I shall return."

When the men were finally released two days before Christmas, 1968, every one attended a prayer and praise service led by Harris. They found that not one had been brainwashed!

The American Vietnam POW's also compiled their own "Bible" from memory. The 23rd Psalm was their major means of Scriptural support. The Beatitudes, Romans 12, and 1 Corinthians 13 were also of great solace.

When finally released, the American prisoners told of holding worship services, forming choirs, and meeting for secret Bible studies. Favorite hymns included, "In the Garden," "You'll Never Walk Alone," "What a Friend We Have in Jesus," and "Holy, Holy, Holy!"

Attacks on the Bible continue even in "Christian" America. Not very many years ago certain Protestant "theologians" were proclaiming that God is dead. The "God-is-dead" fad has withered away, but many so-called intellectuals continue ridiculing God and the Bible in college classrooms and in the media. And in many public schools, students and teachers are not allowed to bring Bibles to the classroom, while curriculum is used which undermines Christian morality under the guise of "values education."

Many American school administrators are afraid of the Bible. Some have actually pulled Bibles from their school libraries in fear that they are breaking the law. In Charleston, West Virginia, during a dispute over textbooks, Bibles were secretly burned in a public school incinerator. Even so, some educators are now beginning to admit, "We over reacted. The Bible can legally be studied as literature, history, and philosophy." Yes, it can, no matter what anyone tells you. Furthermore, the Supreme Court has said in an "equal access" ruling that students may meet before or after school to study the Bible as a group. They have just as much right to do this, the Court said, as student groups who meet for other purposes. So while many American Christians may wish for a return to the time when the Bible was honored as "The Book" in public schools, the Bible has not been banned from public education. It is just regarded as merely another "human" book.

The year 1988 marked the release by Hollywood of the blasphemous film, "The Last Great Temptation of Christ." If we are to believe the reviews, it is unbelievably sacrilegious. Yet many theater owners showed it and thousands paid to see it—out of curiosity, perhaps, because Christian and Bible bashing has been interesting to unbelievers since the days of Rome.

Attacks and the undermining of God's Word will continue, right up to the instant when, as the Bible predicts, our Lord returns and takes His people to their eternal home.

The Bible will never be banished from the earth. It will be victorious over all enemies. Hear the great preacher John Jewell: "Cities fall, empires come to nothing, kingdoms fade away as smoke.... Where are their books? and what has become of their laws?"

The Book of the ages endures because it is the Book that stands. Barring the return of our Lord, I expect the Bible to be the Book of books a hundred years, yea, a thousand years from now.

Allow me one more illustration of this truth. I was only a lad in a mission school, far back in the Indian jungle, when the New York World's Fair was held in 1939. I did not even know the great event was going on. I certainly did not know that a time capsule of items was buried at the fair, not to be dug up for 5,000 years when archaeologists of another time could learn about the 20th century.

Only one full-size book was stuffed into the capsule—the Bible. When asked why the Bible had been chosen, an official said: "The Holy Bible, of all books familiar to us today, will most likely survive through the ages. Therefore the Bible that we placed in the time capsule will be a sort of connecting link between past, present, and future."

The Bible, above all books, is the Book that endures and triumphs over all its enemies. Our Lord put it best: "Heaven and earth shall pass away, but my words shall not pass away" (Matthew 24:35).

Chapter 5

"The Book That Is Incomparable to All Other Scriptures"

We've been talking about the greatness of the Christian Bible. But how does the Bible stand against the holy books of other religions?

Not many years ago Christians in the West were content to leave this question to missionaries whom they sent abroad. Now some non-Christian faiths are aggressively pursuing converts in other lands, including "Christian" America. Dr. John T. Seamands tells of a Buddhist priest in Sri Lanka coming to a Christian missionary to borrow some books on Christianity. "I didn't know you were interested in Christianity," the missionary said.

"I am not," the Buddhist replied, "but my job is to train young monks who will go as missionaries to the West; and I think it's a good idea that they should know something of the religion of the natives before they get there."

Buddhist leaders are adopting many methods used by Christian missionaries. They are translating Buddhist scriptures into major world languages. They hold youth rallies and scripture quizzes. They organize Sunday schools and branches of their YMBA (Young Men's Buddhist

Association). They even sing, "Buddha Lover of My Soul," and "Buddha loves me, this I know; for the Dhamma tells me so."

Islam is the most aggressive of the non-Christian religions. *Eternity*, an American Christian magazine, headlined a report: "The Muslims Are Coming.... Is That a Mosque in Your Neighborhood?" The writer told how Arab petrodollars were advancing Islam and estimated that "there may be two million Muslims on the North American continent."

The Islamic Council of Europe is establishing a mosque in every major city of Europe. The $7.5 million Central Mosque in London, which seats 2,900 people, is now open. Islam is growing in Britain at a rate of over ten percent each year, while only 18 percent of the people in "Christian" England are attending church each week. In Rome, Muslims are building a $20 million mosque that they claim will rival St. Peter's Cathedral in splendor. In France, Islam has become the second largest religion.

Then there are the cultish bizarre offshoots of non-Christian religions which have invaded the west.   The first time I saw in an American airport two young men in saffron robes, peeled heads, and flopping pigtails, I thought for a moment I must be back in India. "Hare Krishna, Hare Krishna," they chanted. "If you can't make a donation, will you please say, 'Hare Krishna?'" I noticed that a number of people did both, not realizing they were calling Krishna, "Lord." My friend Pat Boone knows better. When they stop Pat in an airport and ask him to say "Hare Krishna," he replies, "No, but I'll say, 'Jesus is Lord.'"

Krishna Consciousness, the Divine Light Mission, and Transcendental Meditation are among the best known outcroppings of Eastern religions in the West. Soka Gakkai (Value Creation Society), a Buddhist export from Japan, is led by a man named Ikeda who claims to be a reincarnation of the god Nichiren. The Integral Yoga Institute is another. It asserts, "There are not many gods, there is only One. And that One has no name.... but is everywhere, neither he, nor she, nor it, ... and is both evil and good." There is also The Healthy Happy Holy Organization, the Self-Realization Fellowship, the Inner Light Foundation, and many others.

American children are being taught about non-Christian religions in public school. Concepts and words from these religions are becoming lodged in western culture. The "New Age" movement, which is now sweeping America, is basically an export of Hinduism. Every day we hear such terms as consciousness raising, reincarnation, karma, self-realization, yoga, mantra, and—thanks to Shirley McClaine—reincarnation. New Age concepts are even being taught in business seminars and college courses on creativity.

Christians in the West cannot just send missionaries abroad any more. They are now faced with questions about these religions at home: Are the non-Christian scriptures as divinely inspired as our Christian Bible? Can you find the way to God in non-Christian scriptures?

A distinguished Hindu diplomat took me aside at a reception in New Delhi. "Dr. Pudaite, I can see where the Christian Bible is an advancement over the ancestral religion of your Hmars and other animists. They have only the oral tradition passed down from one village fire to another. But as you very well know, Sir, we Hindus, like you Christians, have our own sacred books, as do the Buddhists and other great religions. Each religion is but one slice of the whole loaf of God's revelation. As the noble Mahatma Gandhi said, 'All religions are springs running from the same source, and nourish different soils and different peoples.'"

As I travel from one country to another, I hear similar analogies expressed: "Just as the many rivers flow into one ocean, so the many faiths led to the one God." "There are many mountain climbers scaling the peak to God. Eventually all will reach the top."

The syncretistic or union approach is very popular today. It is taught in university classrooms and proclaimed in ecumenical gatherings of liberal Christians. An evangelism which proceeds from the premise that the Bible is unique and Christ the only way to God is said to be arrogant and disrespectful of the sincere beliefs of others. Syncretists argue that God is too great and too unknowable to reveal himself in a single once-for-all revelation.

Instead of seeking to assert the superiority of one "Bible" over others, they say, let us strive to understand one another in our common search for truth. So historian Arnold Toynbee called on Christianity to "purge" itself "of the tradition that Christianity is unique" and abandon any claim that the Bible presents the only saving revelation of God to mankind. So the liberal Christian theologian Albert Schweitzer urged a "moving toward a way of thinking which shall . . . eventually be shared in common by all mankind." So the Hindu mystic Ramakrishna proclaimed himself to be the same soul that was born before as Krishna, Buddha, Jesus and others. So the Hindu Swami Vivekananda declared to a World Parliament of Religions: "May he who is the Brahama of the Hindus, the Ahura Mazda of the Zoroastrians, the Buddha of the Buddhists, the Jehovah of the Jews, the Father in Heaven of the Christians, give strength to you to carry out your noble idea."

The religion of Bahaism is founded on this concept. The great Bahai temple in Wilmette, Illinois has nine doors which represent nine major religions of the world. Seekers enter through the different doors to seek from the Bahai faith the essence of one's own religion encompassed in the highest divinely revealed reality.

Mahatma Gandhi, however, said, "The need of the moment is not one religion, but mutual respect and tolerance of the different religions . . . The soul of religions is one, but it is encased in a multitude of forms. The latter will persist to the end of time . . . . Truth," Gandhi declared, "is the exclusive property of no single scripture . . . Jesus is as divine as Krishna or Rama or Mahomed or Zoroaster."

I was raised and educated among animists, Hindus, and Buddhists. I understand the seductiveness of this appeal, especially to those who have never really compared the Christian Bible to other holy books.

I hear just the opposite from some Bible-believing Christians. George, a pastor in Wisconsin told me, "Christians should avoid these false religions. They're all of the devil and the depravity of man. There's no truth in any of them."

I tried to calm him. "George, is it fair to say that the other religions are void of any truth? The Muslims believe as we do that there is one God. The Hindus say the spiritual should take precedence over the material."

"Oh, I suppose there is a little good in them," he conceded. "But the good is so closely mixed with error that it can only lead the naive into a trap."

I have seen a few missionaries in India like George. As soon as they step off the plane, they go on the attack. The people get defensive and will have nothing to do with them. They usually burn out after a year or two and come back to America blaming their problems on the devil."

I know some other Christians who see the non-Christian religions as possessing a considerable amount of truth, while falling short of the highest truth which is proclaimed in the Bible. The Christian message is the final and absolute truth, they say. It goes all the way and fulfills all that is best in the other religions.

I propose that we simply compare the similarities and dissimilarities of teachings of the Bible to the sacred books of the seven major living non-Christian religions: Hinduism, Buddhism, Confucianism, Taoism, Shintoism, Zoroastrianism, and Islam. I am excluding Judaism, because its "Old Testament" Scripture is contained in the Christian Bible.

Before doing this, allow me to present a brief introduction to each of the seven major non-Christian religions.

Hinduism is rooted in the ancient religion of Babylon. The name *Babylon* is derived from the tower of Babel (Genesis 11:4) meaning "gate of God." The Babylonians built ziggurats or cosmic mountains in hopes of bringing together heaven and earth.

The belief that all is God and God is all was brought to India around the time of Abraham by Aryan colonizers from Persia and Afghanistan. Aryan ideas were combined with the beliefs of forest gurus (spiritual teachers) of India and passed along through oral tradition and incorporated in written form as sacred lore known today as the *Vedas*, meaning "revealed wisdom." The *Vedas* are the basic scriptures of Hinduism.

Hinduism's divine allness includes an innumerable number of gods who incarnate themselves in living things. The three major gods form a kind of Trinity: Brahma (a word meaning "sacred knowledge," the Creator Vishnu, the Preserver, and Shiva the Destroyer. After the world was formed, myriads of *jivas* (souls) emanated from Brahma and entered the simplest forms of life and began transmigrating and reincarnating into higher forms Hindus believe that this process will continue until all souls are fully absorbed into the Divine Essence.

Buddhism was founded in northern India in 563 B.C. by Siddhartha Guatama, who at 29 left his wife and infant son to seek truth about suffering. From his belief that seekers could escape this material world and find a better life, he became known as *Buddha*, meaning "Enlightened One."

Buddha took many of his ideas from Hinduism. He taught that existence is a continuing cycle of death and rebirth. One's well-being in life is decided by *karma*—the effect of behavior in the soul's previous existences. Eventually, through this cycle, the soul breaks free from all worldly desires and enters into a state of peace and happiness called *nirvana.*

Confucianism is a moral philosophy that fused with nature worship in ancient China. Founder K'ung-fu-tzu (meaning "Great Master K'ung; Confucius in Latin) was born about a hundred years before Guatama the Buddha. He never claimed to be a religious leader or a prophet and was indifferent to religious rites. The greatest blessedness, he said in true humanistic fashion, is found in pursuing duty and honor, not in a future life. As proof that this was possible, he pointed to ancient records which described a primeval Golden Age that once existed when people were truly dutiful to one another.

The Chinese made him into a sort of god. When Mao took control of China, sacrifices and worship were being rendered to Confucius in 1500

temples. The Communists have been only partially successful in per-
suading the Chinese people to revere Confucius only as a wise man.
Worship of him continues today. The Confucian holy books, known as
"*The Analects*," were written mostly by Confucius himself and, along
with some other books by his disciples, are held in great reverence today
by followers.

Taoism is loosely based on the teachings of Lao-Tze, born about 50
years before Confucius. Tao apparently knew Confucius and urged him
to search for the mystic Tao principle of the universe which alone can
help one understand religion and life. The Tao ideal was quite different
from the wisdom of Confucius. Lao-Tze and his disciples urged
avoidance of conventional social obligations and the pursuit of a simple,
spontaneous, and meditative life close to nature. In other words, be
yourself and follow your natural urges. It is not hard to understand why
Tao was revered by many of America's "flower children" during the
1960s and '70s.

Modern Taoism focuses more attention on the supernatural and
makes use of sorcery and divination in making spirits do what the
worshiper desires.

The basic scripture of the Taoist religion is a little book of 81 short
chapters which counsel readers to attain spiritual contentment by
emptying themselves of material desires. Avoid setting your heart on
specific ambitions, Taoist scripture advises, and the ambitions will not
escape you. It will be as though you actually realize them because if
you do not live for Self, your self will achieve perfection.

Shintoism is the state religion of Japan. Shinto means "the way of
the gods."These gods were originally nature deities, of which the
Sun-goddess,   Ama-terasu (the Heaven-Shining-One), is the most important. Shinto Scripture says the islands of Japan were the first divine
creation and the first Mikado (Emperor) was a literal descendant of the
Sun-goddess from Heaven.

Shinto gods are called *kami. Kami* is the basic force in nature, human
growth, disease, healing, and creativity. Shinto shrines, where *kami* are
venerated, range from wayside god-houses, to large national temples,
to god-shelves in Shinto homes on which are placed the names of
beloved ancestors. Shinto parents expect that their children will pray
for them after death. Shintos who perform brave deeds for the Emperor
may become gods after death. That was the hope of the *kamikaze*
("divine wind") suicide pilots who flew planes loaded with explosives
into American ships.

Shinto's two holy books, the *Ko-ji-ki* ("Records of Ancient Matters") and the *Nihon-gi* ("Chronicles of Japan"), were written in the eighth century A.D. They present the deeds and conversations of the gods before there were any human beings.

Zoroastrianism, unlike the religions of the Orient that worship many gods, acknowledges only one worshipful god, Ahura Mazda, whom Zoroaster, the Persian founder, prayed to "as friend to Friend." This one god has six names: Good Thought, the Beauty of Holiness, Righteousness, Perfect Health, Dominion, and Immortality. His counterpart is Angra Mainyu, the arch spirit of evil.

Cyrus and other Zoroastrian kings of Persia are mentioned in the Old Testament. The Magi who followed the star to see the infant Jesus were probably Zoroastrian priests. The sacred scriptures of Zoroastrianism are known as *The Avesta,* meaning "knowledge." Zoroaster's only attributed writings, the 17 *Gathas,* or psalms, are included in the Avesta.

Islam (Arabic for "submission"), the best known non-Christian religion in the West, is also monotheistic. Islam was founded in the seventh century A.D. by Muhammed ibn Abdallah-Mutallah ibn Hashem el-Quaraysh, who believed he was divinely called to lead his people out of paganism to worship Allah (the Arabic word for God). Adherents prefer the name Muslim ("one who submits to God"). They resent "Mohammedanism," because it gives the impression that they worship Mohammed.

Companions of Mohammed preserved his "visions" and "revelations" by writing them down—with Mohammed's approval, Muslim scholars say—during his lifetime. These writings were later combined to form the *Koran* ("recitation"), the holy book of Islam. Large portions of the Bible, including some misquotations, are included in the Koran. Muslims believe that Allah sent down a succession of books to include the Taurat ("The Law") to Moses, the Zabur ("The Psalms") to David, the Injil ("The Evangel") to Jesus, and the *Koran* (to Mohammed).

Twenty-two of the 28 prophets of Islam are Biblical personages. Among them are Adam, Noah, Abraham, Moses, David, Elijah, Jonah, John the Baptist, and Jesus. Mohammed, according to Islam, is the final prophet and authority on knowing God's will.

Any intelligent Muslim can quickly state the major theological beliefs of Islam: 1. Belief in Allah as the one true God. 2. Belief in angels as the instruments of God's will. 3. Belief in the inspired books, which include most of the Bible and the Koran, which is the final and complete revelation of God. 4. Belief in the 28 prophets of Allah, of whom Mohammed is the last. 5. Belief in a final day of judgment.

There you have the seven major non-Christian religions. Each, like Christianity, has divisions and a number of offshoots. There are several other significant religions, such as Sikhism and Jainism in India—both combining elements of Hinduism and Islam—which we do not have space to discuss. Now let us compare the scriptures of these religions with the Bible on several key points:

Relationships with Fellow Man

Here is how the Golden Rule appears in six of the seven major non-Christian religions and the Christian Bible:

Hinduism: "This is the sum of duty: Do naught unto others which would cause you pain if done to you" (*Mahabharata* 5, 1517).

Zoroastrianism:"That nature alone is good which refrains from doing unto another whatsoever is not good for itself" (*Dadistan-i-dinik*94, 5).

Confucianism: "Is there one maxim which ought to be acted upon through one's whole life? Surely it is the maxim of loving-kindness: Do not unto others what you should not have them do unto you" (*Analects* 15. 23).

Buddhism: "Hurt not others in ways that you yourself would find hurtful" (*Udana-Varga 5, 18*).

Taoism: "Regard your neighbor's gain as your own gain, and your neighbor's loss as your own loss" (*T'ai Shang Kan Ying P'ien*).

Islam: "No one of you is a believer until he desires for his brother that which he desires for himself" (*Sunnah*).

Bible: "All things whatsoever you would that men should do to you, do you even so to them: for this is the Law and the prophets" (Matthew 7:12).

In many other respects, there are vast differences between the non-Christian religions and the Bible. Let us explore the most important divergencies.

God and gods:

Confucianism speaks of the divinity as a "Supreme Ruler," or impersonally as "Heaven." Before the Communist takeover in China, the Chinese emperor was worshiped as this being. Confucianism also encourages the worship of nature spirits and the spirits of deceased ancestors.

The God of the Bible is Lord of heaven and earth, righteous, holy, merciful, a just judge of the world, and the King of kings. His first commandment is, "Thou shall have no other gods before me" (Exodus 20:3).

Hindu holy books pay homage to Brahma as the supreme cosmic being of Hindu holy books. Yet Brahma, who emerged from the Hindu pantheon of gods as the chief god of 330,000,000 deities, did not exist in the beginning. The 10th book of *Rig-Veda* speaks of a time when "there was neither being nor non-being. There was no air or firmament beyond it .... until the power of warmth produced the Sole One. Then in that One, Desire stirred into being; Desire ... was the earliest seed of Spirit .... The gods came later than the earth's creation."

The God of the Bible existed from the beginning: "In the beginning was the Word (Phillips translates this "personal expression") and the Word was with God, and the Word was God" (John 1:1). He is entirely self-existent: "Thus says the Lord: ... I am the first, and I am the last; and beside me there is no God" (Isaiah 44:6).

The Hindu Brahma god and the Taoist Tao deity are impersonal and more to be meditated upon than worshiped. The Muslim's all-powerful and all-knowing Allah is personal, but He is also capricious. The *Koran* says that Allah both leads and misleads, punishes and forgives, according to his own good pleasure. The Allah of the *Koran* is like an opulent, irresistible, cosmic Arab sheikh. This Allah is not the same as the God of the Bible.

Zoroastrianism's supremely worshipful cosmic Power, Ahura Mazda, shares his power with the eternally existent, opposing evil cosmic Power, Angra Mainyu.

The God of the Bible shares his power with no one: "The Lord is a great God, and a great King above all gods" (Psalm 95:3). He is sovereign over all:

"The earth is the Lord's, and the fulness thereof; the world, and they that dwell therein" (Psalm 24:1). He is infinite in power: "Great is our Lord, and of great power: his understanding is infinite" (Psalm 147:5). He is all-powerful: "Thine, O Lord, is the greatness, and the power, and the glory, and the victory, and the majesty" (1 Chronicles 29:11). Satan, the personification of evil, is only a created fallen being, who will ultimately be vanquished completely: "... The God of peace shall bruise Satan under your feet shortly.... [God] has delivered us from the power of darkness, and has translated us into the kingdom of his dear Son" (Romans 16:20; Colossians 1:13).

Unlike the gods of other religions, the God of the Bible is always faithful: "He will not forsake you, neither destroy you, nor forget the covenant of your fathers, which he sware unto them" (Deuteronomy 4:31). He is the ideal father: "A father of the fatherless, and a judge of the widows, is God in his holy habitation" (Psalm 68:5). He is absolute good: "The earth is full of the goodness of the Lord .... O taste and see that the Lord is good" (Psalms 33:5, 34:8). He is holy: "There is none holy as the Lord" (1 Samuel 2:2). He is just: "Just and true are your ways, thou King of saints" (Revelation 15:3). He is longsuffering, "not willing that any should perish, but that all should come to repentance" (1 Peter 3:9). He is loving: "I have loved you, saith the Lord" (Malachi 1:2). He is merciful and compassionate: "The Lord is gracious and full of compassion; slow to anger, and of great mercy" (Psalm 145:8). He is righteous: "O Lord, righteousness belongs to you. . . . The Lord our God is righteous in all his work which he does" (Deuteronomy 9:7, 14).

Man

Only Islam and Zoroastrianism approach the lofty teachings of the Bible that man is an eternal being with infinite value.

In Hinduism man is only an emanation or temporary manifestation of impersonal deity. Man is of no more inherent or permanent worth than any other being.

Hinduism is unique among world religions for its four castes whose members must follow their hereditary vocations and are forbidden to marry or even eat with members of other castes. The Brahmans are the priestly and intellectual class; the Kshatriyas, the rulers and the warriors; the Vaisyas, the common agriculturists and artisans; and the Sudras are the lowest. This subdivision is further broken down into over 2,000 mutually exclusive sub-castes. In addition there are millions of untouchables or "outcastes," who are the servants of the higher castes.

Hindus—strange as it may seem to Christians—venerate the cow more than human beings. A Hindu writer says, "The cow is of all animals the most sacred. Every part of its body is inhabited by deity." The ground where a cow leaves its wastes is considered hallowed.

In Buddhism's contradictory world humanness is worthlessness. The supreme value and power in the world is not a person, but an impersonal non-substance. The human body and bodily activity are worthless. The goal of this non-existence is to escape from the illusion of personhood and become absorbed into the common good of nirvana.

Contrast this with the doctrine of man in the Bible. God created man in his own image (Genesis 1:26), just a "little lower than the angels" and "crowned him with glory and honor" (Psalm 8:5). He made man to "have dominion" over the lesser creation and "put all things under his feet" (Hebrews 2:8). He made him a spiritual, as well as a physical being (Job 32:8). He gifted man with moral nature, intelligence, free will, and the capacity to know and love his fellow man and his God.

Biblical Christianity has no caste system, although it is true that some of the early Christians thought Jews were favored more than others by

God. Peter held this mistaken idea before God showed him a vision of a variety of creatures descending in a sheet from heaven. When a Voice commanded, "Kill and eat," Peter said, "Not so, Lord; for I have never eaten anything that is common or unclean." The Lord quickly assured Peter, "What God has cleansed that call not thou common" (Acts 10:10-15). Peter later realized that God was telling him that there are no "castes" or other distinctions among God's people. "Of a truth," Peter said, "I perceive that God is no respecter of persons" (Acts 10:34).

Many, many Biblical passages express this great truth. The apostle Paul wrote by divine inspiration: "For there is no difference between the Jew and the Greek (Gentile): for the same Lord over all is rich unto all who call upon him" (Romans 10:12). "[In the Christian fellowship] there is neither Jew nor Greek, there is neither bond nor free, there is neither male nor female: for you are all one in Christ Jesus" (Galatians 3:28).

These were revolutionary statements in the first century when women were regarded as little more than burden-bearers and reproducers of a man's children, when slaves could be abused as a master desired, when Romans divided the world into citizens and the conquered, when Jews saw all Gentiles (non-Jews) as unclean, and when "wise" Greeks looked down their noses at the unlettered "unwise."

Some of my Hindu friends try to defend their caste system by saying, "In America, a Christian nation, you have discrimination against blacks and other minorities." I remind them that the civil rights "revolution" in America was born in black churches and that the laws against discrimination which followed were voted by legislators elected by the people of America. I tell them that any Christian who takes the Bible seriously must realize that discrimination against another human being is wrong, whether it is against the civil law or not.

Sin

The power of free will is a part of being created in the divine image. From the beginning, according to the Bible, God gave man the power to choose between obedience and disobedience (Genesis 2:16,17). Other created things respond only by physical necessity or instinct. Man obeys or disobeys as he wills.

The Bible says man was created in perfect fellowship with God. God placed him in a disease-free environment (Genesis 2:28-31). Man was then tempted by Satan and he deliberately chose to corrupt himself by disobeying the clear command of God not to eat of the tree of knowledge of good and evil (Genesis 2:17).

According to the Bible, man is a sinner by nature (because of his sin nature received from the fallen Adam and Eve) and by choice (because all men choose to follow their "natural" inclination and willfully sin). Sin is universal. "Wherefore, as by one man sin entered into the world, and death by sin; and so death passed upon all men, for that all have sinned" (Romans 5:12). Sin is in man's race, nature, and actions.

The Bible defines sin a number of ways. Sin is unbelief, rejection of God's revelation, rebellion, trespass of God's law, self-centeredness, and "missing the mark" of the glory of God. Sin brings guilt. Unlike the animals, man knows deep down when he has sinned. Because he knows he becomes guilt-conscious and seeks to shift the blame to others.

Sin also brings moral and spiritual blindness and degradation. A graphic picture of this is found in the first chapter of Romans. They "became vain in their imaginations, and their foolish heart was darkened. Professing themselves to be wise, they became fools." So "God gave them over to a reprobate mind . . . " (vs. 21, 22, 28).

In Hinduism there is no real sin, but only defects of ignorance which keep one from rising to a better incarnation. In Buddhism there is only bad behavior which can lead to rebirth as a poor or sickly man or as a prisoner in a place of punishment.

In Confucianism there is only poor conduct which impedes the development of good character and an orderly social life.

In Taoism there are only unnecessary social obligations which prevent one from leading a simple, satisfying, and meditative life close to nature.

In Shintoism there is only impurity which can be cleansed by confession and offering prayers and gifts to the *kami* (gods). In Zoroastrianism there are only bad thoughts, words, and deeds.

The Islamic doctrine of sin is close to the teaching of the Old Testament. The *Koran*, like the Old Testament, forbids worship of pagan gods, dishonoring of parents, mistreatment of servants and neighbors, lying, stealing, adultery, and murder. Punishment is by the law of retaliation, "an eye for an eye and a tooth for a tooth."

Redemption and Hope of Eternal Life

There is no hope for individual survival in Hinduism. Non-material mind and soul rest in the high god, Brahma. Maya, the Hindu term for the material realm, is an illusion. One can only seek to rise higher, through reincarnation, into the mystical world of supreme higher consciousness. This can only be done by obeying the law of *karma*, the Hindu cosmic power or principle of justice which rewards or punishes every person for his deeds. *Karma* wills that every action, no matter how small, influences how the soul will be born in the next reincarnation. If you live a proper life, your soul will be reborn into a higher state. If you fall short, your next reincarnation will be lower. You could even be reincarnated into a worm. There is no Savior in Hinduism.

In Buddhism you also work out your own salvation without a Savior. Your only hope is to break out of the cycle of death and rebirth, and become free from pain and suffering by faithfully following the Middle Way and the Noble Eightfold Path. Following the Middle Way calls for avoidance of control by human desires while avoiding extremes of self-torture. Following the Noble Eightfold Path requires (1) knowledge of the truth; (2) intention to resist evil; (3) saying nothing to hurt others; (4) respect of life, morality, and property; (5) doing work that does not injure others; (6) striving to free your mind of all evil; (7) controlling thoughts and feelings; and (8) practicing right forms of concentration.

If you faithfully follow these guidance systems, eventually you will overcome all worldly and material desires and attain the Buddhist nirvana.

Confucian scriptures have nothing to say about an afterlife. Like Western humanism, Confucianism offers no hope beyond this life and can only promise a good life within the confines of good relationships. Shintoism also provides no hope of eternal life.

Taoists seek eternal life through magic, special diets, breath control, meditation, and reciting scriptures. The possibilities are not pleasant to consider. Taoism has numerous heavens and hells where good is rewarded and evil punished. Zoroastrianism teaches that even the wicked will finally be saved. The righteous go immediately to paradise at death. The unrighteous go to hell for purification before being admitted to the better place.

The Muslim *Koran* teaches that earthly life is a time of testing and preparation for life to come. Heavenly angels record the good and bad deeds of everyone. At the final judgment everyone receives the record of his earthly works. If the record book is placed in your right hand, you can expect immediate entrance to paradise. If it is placed in your left hand, you have hell to fear. The Muslim paradise is a lovely garden of flowing streams, delicious fruits, richly covered couches, and beautiful nubile maidens for faithful men to enjoy.

It is easy to sum up redemption in the non-Christian religions. There is none. Man must work out his own salvation. Whether Buddhist nirvana or Muslim paradise, attainment to some higher realm depends upon man's behavior. There is no divine rescue, no deliverance from the power of evil, no God coming down from heaven. You must always be striving to ascend higher by your own will and deeds. Buddhism, Hinduism, Zoroastrianism, Islam, Shintoism, Taoism, and Confucianism all have one common lacking: there is no Savior.

Here is the great difference between the Christian Bible and the scriptures of the world's other great religions. The God of the Bible is the Savior who seeks man. In the non-Christian scriptures it is just the other way around—man seeks God in a variety of confusing ways.

When I was a student at Allahabad College in India, my teacher in comparative religions termed Christianity a topsy-turvy religion where God seeks after man. "The truth is man seeks after God," the professor said. "Man needs a god to believe in, so he conveniently creates one and seeks after the creation of his mind. The Christian God need not seek man, if he is God. That's where Christianity is wrong."

I studied the Bible and found my non-Christian teacher wrong about my Heavenly Father. From Genesis to Revelation, He is the seeker.

For awhile I puzzled over the question why God seeks after man. I had difficulty with that until one day I lost my prize pen with my initial R carved on it. I searched for that pen for a week, then while returning from a sports meet I happened to look under a hedge where I had once picked up a shuttlecock during a badminton game. There was my valued pen with the big R on it.

Suddenly I realized the answer to the question about why God seeks after man. I had been seeking my pen. The pen had not been seeking me, though it was lost. I, the owner who had carved my initial, had been seeking it. Man is lost. Until he reads or hears the message of the Bible, he does not realize that God is seeking him, because he—God's most valued creation—is mired in sin.

The Bible presents God as a loving Heavenly Father seeking his lost offspring, created in the image of the Divine. The idea of God as Father is not unique to the Bible. Zoroaster speaks of the Father of Justice and Right and the Father of Good Mind. In the earliest scripture of Hinduism, *Rig Veda*, the deity Indra is worshiped as the "most fatherly of fathers." (Yasna, 44:3; 47:2, and Yasna, 31:8; 45:4) Yet Indra is represented elsewhere in that same document as a drunk braggart, who boasts of his utter indifference to human supplicants. In contrast, the Father God of the Bible is a consistently loving Heavenly Father, who is always the same.

Only the Bible gives us a divine Father God who came as Savior, seeking lost man. This God came "to seek and to save that which was lost" (Luke 19:10).

Our loving Father God of the Bible came into our world of time and space to find and redeem his beloved. This is no myth passed down by forest gurus. Biblical and secular history attest to his birth, atoning death, and resurrection. Non-Christian records of Jesus the Christ are found in the writings of Josephus (born about 37 A.D), Pliny the Younger (who wrote about the year 112), Tacitus (who wrote about 117), and Suetonius (who wrote about 120).

God became "flesh and dwelt among us, . . . full of grace and truth" (John 1:14). God stepped into human history when he was divinely conceived and born of the Virgin Mary. "She shall bring forth a son, and you shall call his name Jesus: for he shall save his people from their sins" (Matthew 1:21).

He came not as some strange emanation of an unknown deity, but as an identifiable Person. God's act of redemption is described beautifully in the fifth chapter of the Epistle to the Romans: "For when we were yet without strength, in due time Christ ("Messiah") died for the ungodly. For scarcely for a righteous man will one die: yet peradventure for a good man some would even dare to die. But God commends his love toward us, in that, while we were yet sinners, Christ died for us. Much more then, being now justified by his blood, we shall be saved from wrath through him" (vs. 6-9).

This was not the end of Messiah God. Three days after his death, in the year 29 A..D., he rose again. The resurrection of Christ is an event in history attested to by eye witnesses and other writers of the first century. Says noted scholar Edwin Gordon Selwyn of London: "The fact that Christ rose from the dead on the third day in full continuity of body and soul—that fact seems as secure as historical evidence can make it." Many more such statements are available from historians.

Contrast two very different declarations: (1) Jesus Christ, the principle Figure of the Bible, was born, lived, died, and rose from his tomb on the third day after internment. (2) The founders and apostles of all other world religions died as all other humans do.

No one knows exactly when or how Hinduism, Shintoism, and Taoism began. No one disputes the fact that the founders (whoever they were), the builders, and all other influentials in the histories of these religions are dead. Shinto's god emperors, including Hirohito, who inspired the sneak attack on United States forces at Pearl Harbor, are in their graves. The successor of Hirohito has yet to declare himself a god.

Few details exist about the death of Siddhartha Gautama, the Buddha (meaning "Enlightened One") of Buddhism. He was born about 563 B.C. in the foothills of the Himalayas in northern India. He lived until about 80 when he became ill and died. His disciples held no illusions that he would be resurrected. They gave him an elaborate funeral, burned his flesh, and distributed his bones as sacred relics.

Confucius died before he became well known throughout China. His disciples spread his teachings.

The Persian prophet Zoroaster is believed to have been killed at the age of 77 by invaders of Persia.

Muhammed, the great prophet of Islam, came down with a fever and lapsed into a delirium. Near noon of the next day, his wife Aishah felt his hand go limp in her own. She heard only the soft whisper, "God forgive me, have compassion on me, and take me into the highest heaven." An instant later the prophet of Islam was dead. Muslims claim no resurrection for their Prophet.

Jesus the Christ is a different story. He is alive and will return to bring his own into a place prepared for them from before the foundation of the world. No other holy book makes such a claim of any other religious leader.

I close this chapter with a true story of the life and death of a Christian convert from Hinduism.

Pishak Singh came from the Metei tribe, the dominant tribal group in our Indian state of Manipur. The Meiteis adopted the Hindu religion over 300 years ago. After his graduation from college, Pishak found a copy of the New Testament which we had sent. The book became his constant companion and within a year he became a Christian. "My mother had taught me that there are 330 million gods in the world," he told us. "I was in great confusion and had no peace in my mind."

In the Meitei culture it is not unusual for families to even murder converts to Christianity. Neighbors and family members did not kill Peshak, but some openly persecuted him. His father also resented Pishak's conversion at first, but later tolerated it.

Pishak married a Meitei girl named Memcha who lived only five miles from a Hmar mission station and had become a Christian. Knowing Pishak's need for Christian fellowship and for employment, we asked him to teach mathematics in our Christian high school at Senvon, the place where Watkin Roberts first brought the Gospel to our people. Pishak quickly gained the friendship of the local people and became an active leader in the Senvon church.

Pishak and Memcha were blessed with two boys. Then after two miscarriages, she became pregnant again and he brought her to our Christian hospital at Sielmat for a checkup. After she gave birth to a beautiful girl, they decided that she should stay a few days with her parents while he returned to his teaching duties in Senvon.

Pishak preached at a Hmar mission station near Sielmat on Sunday morning and spent the afternoon with a little flock of new Meitei Christians. At 4:30 he told his friends, "I must rush to catch the bus back." A few of them walked with him to the road to await the bus. When they saw the bus coming, Pishak moved out and raised his hands to stop it.

The Hindu Meitei driver suddenly swerved toward the group, hit Pishak head on, and dragged his body 23 feet from the point of impact. His friends rushed his broken body to the hospital, while the driver ran frantically to the police station. Whether it was a brake failure, a deliberate attempt, or a freak accident, no one knows for sure.

I was in the area at the time and preparing to leave for the Sunday evening church service when messengers brought the terrible news. A young man quickly drove me to the hospital. The attending physician told me sadly, "Your friend is dying. I cannot help him."

Pishak's parents arrived at midnight. His elderly father looked at me in helpless silence, then grasped my arms and wept. I held him and let him cry on my shoulder. I asked the Lord to use my arms as His own. I wanted Pishak's father to experience God's amazing peace. After an hour, I asked him, "Will you give us the honor of providing a Christian burial for Pishak?" According to the Meitei custom, nothing could be done without the father's consent.

"Doctor Sahib," he said respectfully, I give you permission to do as you wish. But please allow us to bid him goodbye."

We arranged for a bus to bring Pishak's mother and the rest of the relatives. By the time they arrived the grave was dug and the coffin prepared.

The Hindu Meiteis have different customs regarding death. One custom calls for the Hindu priest to build a funeral pyre. The corpse is placed on the pyre and a relative ignites the fire. The priest chants and pokes the corpse with a spear-like device to turn the body so it will burn better. In the process, the priest demands something from the bereaved family—food, clothes, money, or furniture. If his demands are not met, he abruptly stops, covers the body with dirt, and leaves it for the vultures and jackals. The deceased spirit is then believed to hover aimlessly for eternity.

This funeral was different from any that the Meitei Hindus had ever seen. Over 500 Christians came with Pishak's wife and their little children to bid Pishak farewell. They brought clothes, money, and other tokens to express their love to the deceased's family. A moving graveside service was conducted by my aged father Chawnga Pudaite and Pastor Nipamacha, himself a Meitei Hindu convert through the reading of the New Testament.

My father looked first at the coffin, then at the bereaved family. "Dear friends, there is only one way for us to see Pishak Singh again. Pishak is not dead. He is in Heaven! He is alive! The way to Heaven is through Jesus Christ. Jesus has prepared a mansion for us in Heaven. The Lord Jesus said, 'He that hears my word, and believes on Him who sent me, has everlasting life, and shall not come into condemnation, but is passed from death unto life.' No, the real Pishak is not in the grave, not in the body you see. He is in Heaven with Jesus. If you want to see Pishak again, you must come to Jesus and receive Him as your Savior. He will also take you to Heaven where there will be no more sorrow or tears."

Pastor Nipamacha invited the people to receive Jesus as their Savior. Then the body of Pishak was lowered into the grave.

The Christians sang and gave their gifts to the family. At the close of the service, four Hindus declared their desire to receive Christ. During the week, 22 of Pishak's relatives and friends also declared their decision to follow Jesus.

Pishak's father asked my father and Pastor Nipamacha, "Venerable Sirs, will you please come to our village and visit us. Give the same message you gave at the grave of my son to a thousand of our people. Tell our people where Pishak is now and how we may see him again."

As I was about to leave, my father, now past 90, whispered to me, "I have already engaged a bus to take 50 Christians to help as singers and counselors. The hour is come for the Hindu Meiteis to turn from idols to the true and living God."

I fondly embraced my father and we said our farewells. He reminded me, "When I was sick and dying last January, I told the Lord I could not meet Him now because the Hindu Meiteis have not had a chance to hear the Gospel like our people. God restored me to life after the doctors thought I was dead. He lends me life for the Meitei Hindus."

On the airplane back to the United States, I reflected on the death and homegoing of young Pishak. I saw that it was not a tragedy, but a triumph. How he must be rejoicing to know that his family and friends are coming to the Lord Jesus, so that they can be with him in Heaven.

I thought again of the difference between the Bible and the books of the non-Christian religions. They proclaim no resurrected Savior. They offer no salvation and abundant life that opens to a daily walk with the loving Lord. They provide no real hope that we will see our loved ones again.

I challenge you to read and compare the Bible to any and all of the scriptures of other religions. I believe you will discover that none can compare with the Bible.

Chapter 6

"The Book That Meets Our Deepest Needs"

The first book I ever saw was the New Testament in the Lushai language. Our Hmar language had not yet been written. Oh, how my father Chwanga treasured that book. I noticed that he kept it in a special place, away from where it might become soiled or stolen. When a visitor came, he always had the Book handy for witness. When he left on a journey, the Book went with him, and when he went to preach the Book was in his hand. Several years later I walked into the library of a mission school. There standing before me was a whole wall of books. I was filled with awe. There were probably no more than 500 or 600 volumes, yet at 16 I thought they must contain all the wisdom of the world. If the librarian had let me, I would have slept and taken all my meals beside those books.

At that time I had no idea of the vast number of books in the world. I had never heard of the United States Library of Congress, which now houses over 12 million books and pamphlets in two buildings covering thirty-six acres of floor space. Two copies of every new book published and copyrighted in the United States have been filed there since 1870. Among them is two copies of this book and of my biography, *God's Tribesman.*

Over 40,000 new books will be published this year in the United States alone! Over 600,000 will be published in the world. Books on every conceivable subject, from asteroids to zephyrs. The author of Ecclesiastes was right: " ... of making many books there is no end ... ' (12:12).

Only about one in 200 among the new books published in the United States will make any best seller list. Only one of ten best sellers will remain in that category for as long as ten weeks. Only one-half of one percent of all books published will still be for sale in bookstores seven years from now. Go to the library and look at the best sellers listed a year ago in the *New York Times, Time, Publisher's Weekly*, and *Christianity Today*. Copy the lists and take them to a nearby bookstore. See how few are still in the store.

The eminent literary critic Clifton Fadiman has been a "judge" for the Book-of-the-Month Club since 1944. In 1986 he listed the books "which I'm glad we chose" during the past 20 years: *The Rise of Theodore Roosevelt* by Edmund Morris. *Sophie's Choice* by William Styron. *A Flag for Sunrise* by Robert Stone. *The Collected Stories* by Isaac Bashevis Singer. *The Years of Lyndon Johnson: The Path to Power* by Robert Caro. *The World Is Made of Glass* by Morris West. *The Discoverers* by Daniel J. Boorstin. *The Day of the Jackal* by Frederick Forsyth. *Burr* by Gore Vidal. *Pilgrim at Tinker Creek* by Annie Dillard. *Memoirs: 1925-1950* by George W. Kennan. *Fire from Heaven* by Mary Renault. *The Myth of the Machine* by Lewis Mumford. *Ragtime* by E.L. Doctorow. *Humbolt's Gift* by Saul Bellow *Daniel Martin* by John Fowles. *The First Circle* by Alexander Solzhenitsyn. *Bullet Park and Collected Stories* by John Cheever. *Glory Speak; Memory; King, Queen, and Knave* by Vladimir Nabokov. The final volumes of *The Story of Civilization* by Will and Ariel Durant. *The Spy Who Came in from the Cold* and four other books by John Le Carre.

How many of these books have you read? Can you write a 50-word summary of each one you remember? How many, if any, do you think will be talked about, except by literary historians, 100 years from now?

Writer Alice Payne Hackett listed all the books on the major best sellers' roster in the United States for the period 1895-1965. She found that only 633 titles in both hard cover and paperbck had sold over a million copies. *The Pocket Book of Baby and Child Care* by Dr. Benjamin Spock topped her list, selling over 19 million copies.

Although Hackett does not include the Bible, she says: "Any discussion of such a list must start with the Bible. The general public probably asks more questions of libraries and trade specialists about the Bible than about any other book. The most familiar question is, 'Is the Bible the best seller?' The answer is unequivocally in the affirmative."

Here are the top ten in literary authority according to Horace Shipp's *Books That Moved the World*: 1. The Bible. 2. *The Republic* by Plato. 3. *The City of God* by St. Augustine. 4. *The Koran*. 5. *The Divine Comedy* by Alighieri Dante. 6. *Plays* by William Shakespeare. 7. *Pilgrim's Progress* by John Bunyan. 8. *Areopagitica* by John Milton. 9. *The Origin of Species* by Charles Darwin. 10. *Das Kapital* by Karl Marx.

Heading the list is the Bible. Four of the remaining nine are directly related to the Bible. *The City of God* is a Biblical account of the city of man, as well as the city of God. *The Koran* is packed with historical material from the Bible, but with many significant differences. *The Divine Comedy* is a medieval interpretation of the Bible. *Pilgrim's Progress* is a divine allegory based upon the Bible.

Shakespeare's Plays are infused with Biblical ideas. John Milton's *Areopagitica* builds a brilliant defense of freedom of the press upon biblical concepts. Milton also penned the Bible-centered classics, *Paradise Lost* and *Paradise Regained.*

The three remaining books in Shipp's top ten deal with themes which are highlighted—though from a contrasting perspective—by the Bible. *The Republic* unfolds Plato's ideal society under the rule of a human elite; the Bible proclaims the kingdom of God under the rule of God. Darwin says man evolved through a process called the survival of the fittest; the Bible says God created man "in his own image" (Genesis 1:27). The atheist Karl Marx argues in *Das Kapital* that the primary determinant of history is economics. Marx views the history of society as the history of class struggle in which the capitalist (bourgeoisie) class, which replaced the feudal nobility, will inevitably be swept away by the working class striving for the common good of all. The Bible says history is under the sovereignty of God.

Why, among the myriads of books published, is the Bible the all-time best seller and most influential among all of them? The primary reason, I believe, is that the Bible is the Book most able to meet man's deepest needs. It is, above all books, the Book for humanity that is always up to date.

Marketing experts say modern publishing has moved sharply toward specialization. Most nonfiction books are written, edited, and promoted with special interest groups in mind. Have you noticed all the diet books in the bookstores recently? Books on running and physical exercise? Books telling us how to balance budgets and make good investments?

Books about the single life? About the married life? About improving marriage and getting along better in the family? Each is addressed to a special interest and readership.

Not everybody is interested in dieting or in investments. But enough people are to justify publishing books in these areas. The Bible, however, is a universal book, with something for everyone. It is even the book most frequently stolen from libraries.

Almost every person asks these questions: Why am I here? What is the ultimate meaning of my life? Will I have an identity after death? Will I know my loved ones in the after-life? How can I satisfy the deepest longings of my heart? How can I be rid of the burden of guilt? How can I learn to love others? How can I find happiness in my family? Such questions cannot be answered by science or philosophy. Only the Bible gives fully satisfactory—and eternally significant—answers.

Declared the great American writer, Henry Van Dyke: "Born in the East and clothed in Oriental form and imagery, the Bible walks the ways of all the world with familiar feet and enters land after land to find its own everywhere. It has learned to speak in hundreds of languages to the heart of man. It comes into the palace to the monarch to tell him that he is a servant of the Most High, and into the cottage to assure the peasant that he is a son of God.   Children listen to its stories with wonder and delight and wise men ponder them as parables of life. It has a word for the time of peril, a word of comfort for the time of calamity, a word of light for the hour of darkness. Its oracles are repeated in the assembly of the people, and its counsels whispered in the ear of the lonely. The wicked and the proud tremble at its warnings but to the wounded and penitent it has a mother's voice. The wilderness and the solitary place have been made glad by it, and the fire on the hearth has lit the reading of its well-worn page. It has woven itself into our dearest dreams so that love, friendship, sympathy and devotion, memory and hope put on the beautiful garments of its treasured speech, breathing of frankincense and myrrh. No man is poor or desolate who has this treasure of his own. When the landscape darkens and the trembling pilgrim comes to the valley of the shadow, he is not afraid to enter; he takes the rod and the staff of Scripture in his hand, he says to his friend and comrade: 'Goodbye, we shall meet again,' and comforted by the support, he goes toward the lonely pass as one walks through darkness into light."

When translated into a native tongue, the Bible is as relevant and life-changing for the Aucas of the rain forests of eastern Ecuador as it is for the Nafanra people of Ghana, the Tinputz tribe of Papua New Guinea, or the Tzeltals of Mexico.

Here is what Juan Lopez Mucha, a ruling elder of the Tzeltal church, said when the first printed copies of the New Testament in his own language were delivered:

"Our hearts are happy because today we have received in our own hands the Word of God translated into our language in order that we may be able to understand it. The Word of God is powerful. It makes the hearts of the people turn in the other direction (repent). It is like a fist and like a fire—very powerful. It makes our hearts upright before the Lord. The heart of every believer will be upright because of it. God is the One who uses the Word to reach our hearts. It is He who makes it remain in our hearts. By means of the Book of God we can have eternal life. I want His Word to be written in my heart and remain there. I want it to work in my heart and put an end to all evil there and in my life."

The Bible is just as relevant for "civilized" people also, no matter how many academic degrees they may have. My good friend Dr. Paul Krishna was raised a Hindu. As a child he prayed daily with his brothers and sisters at a little shrine. But in college he lost confidence in his religion and became enamored with Marxism.

When Marxist theory left him empty, he sought satisfaction in law practice. When this did not fill the vacuum, he went back to school for a Ph.D., then took a post as head of the Department of Oriental Studies at University College in Durban, South Africa. He enjoyed the life of a teacher-scholar for a while, then the old emptiness returned. Surely there must be something more, he thought.

One morning when driving to the university he picked up a laborer hitch-hiking to his job. The man shared his Christian faith. Paul envied the man's peace and contentment. Later three students from a nearby Bible college stopped at Paul's house and left a New Testament.

"A verse from Matthew startled and sent an electric thrill through me," Paul recalls. "I read these magnificent words from God: 'Come unto me, all ye that labor and are heavy laden, and I will give you rest'" (11:28).

Paul couldn't get enough of the Bible. Often he read until the early hours of the morning. He asked for Christian baptism and two days later boarded a plane for the United States. This lawyer and distinguished professor entered Trinity Evangelical Divinity School to prepare for a new career of preaching and teaching the Word of God. Every time I see Paul Krishna, I marvel at the glow on his face.

I was sharing Dr. Krishna's story with a good friend when he told me about a former Russian officer he knew who had found spiritual rest and purpose for living from the same Bible verse.

Captain Nikolai Alexandrenko, my friend said, was a student in a Russian military academy when World War II erupted. Commissioned an officer in the paratroops, Nikolai was made commander of a company and dropped into the front lines near the Dnieper River where the Germans were advancing toward Moscow.

The company was advancing on a nest of German riflemen when German tanks roared down upon them. Nikolai felt a sudden sharp pain in his left leg. He looked and saw blood and knew he was hit. The standing order to Russian officers was "suicide before capture." Nikolai started to swing the barrel of his gun toward his temple, then hesitated and threw the gun away. He hopped toward an approaching Nazi tank, hands high in surrender.

The Germans shoved him into a railroad cattle car with 19 other captured soldiers. As the train was moving out, Russian planes swooped in and bombed their own soldiers. Only Nikolai and one other survived.

Nikolai was put in a prison camp in Munich. His wounds went untreated and he almost starved on a diet of grass soup. Hundreds of his fellow prisoners died from hunger.

When the war ended in 1945, the Germans told him he was free to return home. "If I go back, they'll send me to Siberia for surrendering," he pleaded. "Let me stay in Germany."

His new home was a displaced persons camp. As month after weary month passed, questions came to him for which atheism had no answers: "Why was my life spared during the war? Why did I survive in the prison camp when so many others died of starvation?"

One morning, while in a despondent frame of mind, Nikolai noticed the fire had gone out in the barracks' stove. Apparently someone had stuffed the door full with waste paper, cutting off oxygen to the fire. He tossed a lighted match into the rubbish. When the flame failed to catch, he bent over to shove the trash back into the stove. That's when he noticed two Bible verses on a torn, dirty slip of paper. One was Matthew 11:28, the same verse which had touched Dr. Paul Krishna. The other was Revelation 3:20: "Behold, I stand at the door and knock: if any man hear my voice, and open the door, I will come in to him."

The paper said the words were from Jesus Christ, whom Nikolai had been told in school was only a character from Christian mythology. "What if He really is the Son of God?" the weary war refugee asked himself. "Could He give me the rest I so desperately need?"

"Oh, God, if you exist, help me," Nikolai finally cried. "If Christ truly be Your Son, give me rest. Show me the way."

Warm tears trickled down his cheeks. He had not cried since he was a child—not even when his mother died, not when hit on the battlefield, not when tortured by hunger pangs in the prison camp. Now as he wiped away the new tears, a strange warmth and tender calmness enveloped his heart.

A few days later he ran into an old friend from the Russian army. The friend said he had also become a Christian and offered to get Nikolai a Bible.

Nikolai read the Bible through in a month. He was baptized and began preaching to Russian refugees. Many responded to the biblical message from the former atheist.

Now here—as my friend related it and as Paul Harvey would say—is "the rest of the story." Within ten years Nikolai earned a doctor of theology degree in the United States and was teaching the Bible in a Christian college. He is still doing so today.

World War II, from which Nikolai Alexandrenko was only one of millions of refugees, was supposed to end all wars. It didn't. Over 130 bloody regional wars have come since. That doesn't include the many internal wars which continue to rage within many nations. In my native India there is sporadic fighting between the Sikhs and the central government; in Iraq, the Kurds stage raids against the government soldiers; in Nicaragua, the Contras seek to overthrow the ruling Communist Sandinistas; in the Sudan, the animists and the Christians in the south battle for human rights against Muslims in the north. These are only four examples.

The most intractable conflict is in ancient Palestine, the land in which most of the Bible was written. For 40 years there has been no peace on the West Bank of the Jordan between Palestinians and Jews.

Is there no healing for this bitter animosity between these modern Semites? The best diplomats in the world have not found any permanent answers. My friend Anis Shorrosh says the only solution is in the Bible.

Anis, an Arab Palestinian, calls himself a "member of the new PLO—Palestinians Loving Others." But he was, in his own words, "as hateful as a man could be, before I found in the Bible the way to love."

One winter afternoon in Chicago, Anis shared his gripping personal story with me. He was a lad of 15 in Nazareth, the home town of Jesus, when Israel proclaimed itself a state and fighting broke out with the Arabs. Anis's father and uncle were killed in that war. He fled with his mother, brother, and sister across the Jordan river."

"Ro, you can't imagine how revengeful I felt. Our family had to live in just one room. I couldn't get a job or go to school. My only identity was a ration card issued by the United Nations, allowing me nine cents worth of food each day. "Oh, how I hated. I hated the British because they had exploited my people and then abandoned us to the Jews. I hated the Jordanians and Syrians for not coming to our aid. I hated the Jews for killing my loved ones and forcing my family to flee. If I could have gotten a gun, I would have gone back and killed every Jew in sight until they killed me."

After months of brooding and despair, Anis ran out into the desert and lay down on the rocky ground, waiting to die. "I thought, if I didn't starve to death, the heat would kill me. Or if not that, wild animals or a poisonous snake would end my miserable life.

"As I lay there in the desert, boyhood memories flashed before me. I thought of my selfish life. I remembered the time when I had piled stones on a railroad track, almost causing the train to wreck and endangering hundreds of people. Never had I felt so wretched."

Morning came and the sun and dryness sucked at his body moisture. His mouth became parched, his lips split, and he became delirious from fever. By afternoon his vision was blurred. By sunset he was incoherent, alternately laughing and crying, mocking himself.

"Ro, I thought this is what hell must be like. I knew if there was such a place, I was a good candidate. Not wanting to take that chance, I got up and stumbled home to Mother in our tiny refugee quarters. She welcomed me with open arms."

The next morning was Easter. Anis spent the day reading his mother's Bible.

"I read for three days. Finally, I paused where Jesus said, in the Sermon on the Mount, 'Seek ye first the kingdom of God, and His righteousness; and all these things shall be added unto you" (Matthew 6:33). I knew God was real and that if my life was ever to change I would have to put Him first. I knelt beside my sleeping mat and gave Him the rest of my life."

When Anis believed this Bible promise, things began to happen. He got a job. Missionaries arranged for him to attend college in the United States. Today, Dr. Anis Shorrosh is a worldwide evangelist, proclaiming the love of God to Arabs, Jews, and thousands of others around the world.

Anis makes his headquarters in a little town near Mobile, Alabama, but twice a year he makes a trip back to his shattered homeland. On one occasion he was accompanied by a choir from a church in Florida.

The choir was invited to sing for wounded Israeli soldiers before television cameras. After the program, Anis recalled for the soldiers the killing of his loved ones by Israelis and the loss of his home in Nazareth. "I hated Jews with all the intensity of my being for what had been done to my family," he said. "But now, I want to tell you that I love you because of Jesus."

Another time he was escorting a group of Christian pilgrims to Nazareth. As they neared the home town of Jesus, the tour guide recalled to the Arab—Anis Shorrosh—at his side that he had been commander of the tank company that had taken Nazareth in the 1948 war. Anis listened, struggling to control his emotions. When the Israeli finished Anis looked at him and said tensely, "I am a native of Nazareth. My father and uncle were killed there, probably by your men. By all the traditions of my people, I ought to kill you and take revenge. I cannot. I can only say, 'I love you,' because of my Savior, Jesus of Nazareth. May I show you what the Bible says about His love?"

When Anis finished telling me his story, he pointed to the Bible. "That Book, Ro, which tells of the ancestry of both Jews and Arabs, provides the only blueprint for lasting peace between the Jews and their neighbors, the Palestinians."

The reason man cannot find peace with fellow man is that without God he has no peace within himself. "From whence come wars and fightings among you?" the Biblical writer James asks? "Come they not hence, even of your lusts (or desires) that war in your members?" (James 4:1).

There is no peace within ourselves when the God of the Bible does not fill the emptiness in our hearts. St. Augustine expressed the deepest longing of every man's heart when he wrote: "Thou hast made us for Thyself, O Lord, and our hearts will never rest until they find rest in Thee." The great French mathematician, Blaise Pascal declared: "There is a God-shaped vacuum in the heart of every man which only God can fill through His Son, Jesus Christ."

Only the Bible, among all the books held sacred in the history of mankind, tells us of the One who can fill this vacuum. Only the Bible tells us that we are made in the image and likeness of God. Only the Bible tells us that we have marred that image by rebellion and sin. Only the Bible tells us how to find cleansing and forgiveness and become a new creation of peace and love in Christ.

Nothing else can quench this thirst. The famed historian and philosopher H. G. Wells rejected the Bible as inspired truth. He lamented at age sixty-one, "I have no peace. All life is at the end of its tether." England's great poet Lord Byron, who disdained Christian morality and rejected the Bible as a life guide, wrote, "My days are in the yellow leaf, the flowers and fruits of life are gone, the worm and the canker and the grief are mine alone."

King David cried in the wilderness; "O God, thou art my God; early will I seek thee: my soul thirsteth for thee, my flesh longeth for thee in a dry and thirsty land . . . " (Psalm 63:1). Only the Bible tells how this thirst can be satisfied. Said Jesus to the woman at the well: "Whoever drinks of the water [believes in me] that I shall give him shall never thirst; but the water that I shall give him shall become in him a well of water springing up to eternal life" (John 4:14 NASB).

Young Francis Bernardone discovered this living water and became one of the most heroic figures of history. As a young man, Francis was a playboy in Italy's Tiber Valley. Son of a wealthy cloth merchant from the town of Assisi, Francis spent his days and nights in revelry. Then war broke out and Francis was captured. After a stay in prison and a grave illness, he began seeking a deeper meaning in life.

Francis found the secret of true meaning in the Bible. He vowed to serve Christ for the rest of his life, but he did not know what he was to do until he read these words from the Bible: "As ye go, preach, saying, The kingdom of heaven is at hand. Heal the sick, cleanse the lepers, raise the dead, cast out devils: freely ye have received, freely give. Provide neither gold, nor silver, nor brass in your purses, nor scrip for your journey, neither two coats, neither shoes, nor yet staves: for the workman is worthy of his meat "(Matthew 10:7-10).

"From this time on, my life will be one of Gospel poverty," Francis vowed. Leaving his wealth behind, Francis set out with 11 equally committed companions for a humble ministry of preaching and ministering to the sick and needy. The Franciscans, as they came to be called, left a greater mark for good on medieval Europe than many kings and popes. The great church historian Philip Schaff wrote of their noble leader, "Few men of history made so profound an impression as Francis of Assisi."

Biblical faith meets needs which cannot be met by any earthly pursuit. Ponder this statement from Dr. Wernher Von Braun, whose genius made possible man's flight to the moon:

"The materialists of the 19th century and their Marxist heirs tried to tell us that as science shows us more knowledge about the creation, we could live without faith in a Creator. But with every new answer from science, we have discovered new questions. The more we know about the nature of life, the master plan for the galaxies, and the intricacies of the atomic structure, the more reason we have found to marvel at the greatness of God's created works. But beyond awe, we know that man needs faith just as he needs food, water, or air."

The Bible is the Book for humanity at every stage of life, but it is particularly meaningful when life seems most fragile. When the Nazis overran Norway, the Bible was called "the Book of the day, the only weapon that can resist the tanks." When Communists overran part of Korea, murdering and imprisoning Christians, a pastor's wife fled with her baby, a bag of rice, and her precious Bible. Knowing that she might be killed if caught with the Bible, she was tempted to leave it behind, but she tucked it in her bosom and went on. Later she hid the Book of books in a cave. Each day at sunset she crept cautiously to the cave to read words that "made my heart leap!"

When the Communists came closer, she fled further south. Finding shelter in a village, she hid the Bible under a stone floor and sheltered the baby in a foxhole. When the fighting finally stopped, she still had her baby and her Bible.

A similar story comes to us from Vietnam. Wilson Chen, a South Vietnamese army officer, was sent to a "re-education" camp after the Communists took over South Vietnam. For five years he was forced to do excruciatingly hard labor and eat rats, locusts, lizards, frogs, snakes, and other living things just to stay alive. After work, he had to suffer through painful brainwashing sessions. To make his situation worse, he received news while in the camps that his brother had died and that his fiancee had married and fled the country.

Fortunately, Mr. Chen had several small Bibles in Chinese, Vietnamese, and English which he kept hidden in holes around the camp. When the guards were not around, he and his friends took turns reading and encouraging one another. "It was hope in the Lord Jesus that kept me alive," Mr. Chen said later. "I fed this hope by reading the Scriptures."

Eddie Rickenbacker is one of the great Allied war heroes of World War II. Rickenbacker and seven other American airmen were forced down in the Pacific about 600 miles north of Samoa. Day after fear-filled day they drifted on a rubber raft. Their food and water ran out. They were tortured by hunger and thirst. High waves tossed them about. Hungry sharks circled, waiting for the kill. Some men in the group became delirious. But Rickenbacker never lost hope. He had a Bible from which he gathered strength. When they were rescued after 24 days on the water, Rickenbacker said the Bible had saved them.

My friend Edward Lacaba grew up on the remote island of Cebu in the Philippines. In his teens he lost faith in the idol-worshiping religion of his family. The death of a beloved brother caused great anguish. Poor grades in school and his father's business failure dropped him deeper into the pit of despair. When the Japanese invaded, he fled with his family to a mountain hideaway. There he came across a tiny book, hidden in a dry nook by a departed American soldier. The book was olive drab in color, one of the millions of New Testaments issued to soldiers by the U.S. government.

In the Gospels Edward saw "a caring Man, a Man of love and righteousness, a Man so real and near that when I came to John 5:24 it was as though Jesus Himself was there and spoke to me: 'Verily, verily, I say unto you, He that heareth my word, and believeth on him that sent me, hath everlasting life. . . . '

"The impact of the words, 'hath everlasting life,' so overwhelmed me that it became the moment of my rebirth," he testified. "It ushered me into the world of reality. Before, there had been only darkness. Now I discovered Christ's world of light, life, and meaning."

He shared this good news with his parents, brothers, and friends. Many of them believed. Edward Lacaba is today a leading Christian of the Philippines, who "marvels" at the "genuine miracle which began when God's Word entered my life and I received His Son."

Christian leaders of all denominations agree that the Bible is the most important book in the world. Cardinal Sin of the Philippines declares: "Through reading the Bible we learn what God wants us to do. If we really want a new society where honesty and love for one another exists, then we should begin with the individual ... [and] conversion. ... When you are converted you listen to God's Word through reading the Bible and you would like to execute in your personal life what God wants you to do.

The Bible is a very old Book, but it is as up-to-date as tomorrow's newspapers. Not only is it a balm in time of sorrow, it is a guide to true success. Marion Wade, the founder and long-time chairman of the board of the Service-Master Company discovered this early in life. Until his death a few years ago, Mr. Wade was one of the finest citizens and most generous supporters of Christian causes in the Wheaton, Illinois area. Mr. Wade recalled: "I was especially drawn to Joshua 1:8, which says,'This book of the law shall not depart out of thy mouth; but thou shalt meditate therein day and night, that thou mayest observe to do according to all that is written therein: for then thou shalt make thy way prosperous, and then thou shalt have good 'success.' Later I found that this is the only place in the Bible where the word 'success' appears. The truth hit me that I could only succeed with God, my fellow man, and myself by living according to the Bible."

Marion Wade was very active in the Christian Businessmen's Committee, which once had offices not far from our Bibles For the World headquarters. Ted DeMoss, an insurance executive is the current president of the USA chapter of this world-organization of businessmen who try to live by the Bible. Mr. DeMoss tells in his book *The Gospel and the Briefcase* what happened when he heard the Biblical plan for a right relationship with God:

"I came to realize that religion and Christianity are entirely different. Religion, according to the dictionary, is man's best effort to find God. Christianity is the opposite: God's best effort to find man. You spell religion with two letters: 'Do!' Christianity is spelled with four letters: 'Done.' That is what Christ meant when He hung on the cross and said, 'It is finished.' On that night [when I became a Christian], I began a new life with purpose, direction, and values that I could never fully explain. For the first time, I understood that although I was not a perfect man, I was a forgiven man in God's sight. That night I also received some fantastic advice, namely that I should read the Bible every day. I've been doing that now for more than 40 years."

Another marvelous testimony comes from Charles Colson, the so-called "hatchet man" in the White House during the Watergate scandal. After resigning in the wake of damaging disclosures, Colson visited with a long time friend, Tom Phillips, president of the Raytheon company. Colson remembered Phillips as a hurrying, hard driving nervous corporate executive. Now, in Colson's words, "he was a totally different human being."

Phillips explained how that during a time of great inner turmoil he had attended a Billy Graham Crusade and had become a Christian. Colson reacted skeptically, saying that faith might work for some, but not in politics. "When the other guy hits you, you've got to hit him back."

Still, Colson was impressed and returned for another visit. This time, Phillips showed him passages from C.S. Lewis' book, *Mere Christianity*. A chapter about pride and arrogance really jolted Colson. He would later tell audiences, "Arrogance was the great sin of Watergate, the great sin of a lot of us, probably my greatest."

Before departing, he and Phillips prayed. On the driveway outside, Colson said he felt the need to pray again. There by his car he asked Christ to come into his life.

Phillips asked Doug Coe, a Christian worker in the Washington prayer group movement, to look after Colson. Coe introduced Colson to members of his own prayer cell: Iowa Senator Harold Hughes, Minnesota congressman Albert Quie, former Texas congressman Graham Purcell, and their wives. Hughes took Colson under his wing. Hughes and Colson had been on opposite sides of many issues in political life. Now they became close friends.

Colson pled guilty to one of the Watergate charges. After being sentenced to a one- to three-year prison term, he told the judge: "I have committed my life to Jesus Christ. I can work for the Lord in prison or out of prison, and that's how I want to spend my life."

Colson did just that. After release he organized Prison Fellowship which has grown into the largest and most effective ministry to prisoners in history.

Colson is only one of several Watergate figures whose lives were changed by the message of the Bible. Another is former White House aide G. Gordon Liddy who since childhood had venerated Nietsche's secular philosophy of the "will to power" as the highest of human goals. To overcome his fears of electricity, Liddy had climbed to the top of electrical towers. Because he was frightened of rats, he had eaten part of a rat.

Even as other Watergate figures crumbled, Liddy refused to be broken. When asked in court if he would swear to "tell the truth, the whole truth, and nothing but the truth," he responded bluntly, "No!"

Colson visited Liddy in prison and asked if he had "seen the light."

"(Expletive), no!" Liddy snorted. "I'm not even looking for the switch."

Liddy served four years and was released. Appearing on the David Letterman TV show, he was asked, "What happens after we die?" Liddy replied coldly, "We are food for worms."

Liddy and his wife moved to a new state, where they renewed friendships with former FBI colleagues they had known and respected for 30 years. When they asked him to study the Bible, he agreed, adding bluntly, "I'm an agnostic. I'm here because I'm interested in the Bible. Period. Please do not try to convert me. I don't want to be bothered."

Liddy's interest in the Bible was then only historical. But because of the respect he had for his friends and their example of Christian love, he thought he should take a closer look at the Bible.

He started by thinking about God. If God is infinite and we are finite, he reasoned, we cannot apprehend Him. So any communication must come from him.

His next step was to wonder if there was any communication from God:

"A light went on in my head: 'That's what the Bible is all about!' The Bible is not merely a historical record; it is God's means of communicating with finite man."

But a finite being cannot be worthy of the infinite, he reasoned further. There must be something more than communication. This was where Christ entered the picture for Liddy. In a "rush of reason," Liddy accepted Christ as who He claimed to be and became a Christian.

Indeed the Bible does speak to the needs of people in every walk of life.

The Music City Christian Fellowship gathers every Thursday at noon in Nashville. Singers, song writers, and other professionals in the music business attend. Marijohn Wilkins is one of their leaders. As a songwriter Marijohn made it big in Nashville, but she found that fame and success did not satisfy. After several personal tragedies, she saw no hope for living. Twice she tried to kill herself. Then she turned to the Bible, which she had loved in her childhood back in Texas. In God's Word she found joy and purpose for living. While wondering how she could be faithful to the commands of God's Word, a prayer came to her mind: "Lord, help me live for you one day at a time." The prayer became the most popular gospel song in history, "One Day at a Time." She wrote another much loved song that depicted the new life she had found in the Bible, "I Have Returned to the God of My Childhood."

The best known Christian musician in Nashville is probably Johnny Cash. Johnny was converted in a country church back in Arkansas when he was 12 years old. "A beautiful peace came over me that night," he recalls. "I felt brand new."

Like Marijohn Wilkins, he drifted away from his childhood faith. He gained a reputation for drinking, drug use, and crazy practical jokes. One night in Georgia he was arrested and jailed on a drug charge. The next morning the sheriff had him brought into his office.

"Tell me, Mr. Cash," he said solemnly. "Why would a man like you at the top of his profession let a little thing like this [he held up a pill] destroy his life?"

An uncomfortable silence hung in the room. The sheriff continued. "Mr. Cash, I'm not angry at you, just deeply hurt. I want you to know that my wife and I have followed your career for over ten years. We've bought every record you put out. You probably have no better fans than us. We've always loved you and we're hurt."

The sheriff handed the singer his drugs. "Here are your pills. Take them and go. It will be your decision to destroy yourself or save your life."

"Sheriff," Johnny finally said, "I give you my word that I'll never take another." Then he walked outside and threw the pills on the ground.

It wasn't easy for him to quit, but with God's help he finally did. He also determined to chart his life by the Bible. He read where the Bible said he should make restitution for past wrongs. He did. He read that believers should help widows and orphans. He did that, too. He read that a follower of Christ should not be ashamed to confess his Lord's name. When time came for the closing hymn on his next television show, he put aside the script and said, "I've sung lots of hymns and gospel songs, but this time I want to tell you that I feel what I'm about to sing. I'm a Christian."

The Bible is the best "medicine" for physicians and nurses. It worked for Dr. C. Everett Koop, the former surgeon-general of the United States and a long-time leader in the Christian Medical Society.

Dr. Koop's initial commitment to the God of the Bible came after he had become a doctor. He was a rising young surgeon of 28 when a nurse suggested that he would "appreciate the scholarly, Biblical preaching of Dr. Donald Grey Barnhouse, then pastor of Tenth Presbyterian Church in Philadelphia, PA. Dr. Koop slipped quietly into a service and immediately became interested in a sermon about the priesthood of Christ. Dr. Barnhouse's text was from Hebrews 7:21: "Thou [Christ] art a priest forever after the order of Melchizedec. . . . "

"What bothered me," Dr. Koop recalls, "was that I had read the Bible through and couldn't remember Melchizedec. Curious, I kept going back to hear Dr. Barnhouse, and discovered the relationship between the Old Testament priest and Christ. More important, I learned that Christ had the power to forgive my sins."

The counterpart of the Christian Medical Society for Bible-believing nurses is the Nurses Christian Fellowship. Professional, college, and high school athletes find direction for life in Bible study through the Fellowship of Christian Athletes and Athletes for Action. I've been told that every major league baseball and professional football club in the United States and Canada has a team chapel where Jesus Christ and His Word are proclaimed.

Chapters of the Christian Women's Club meet regularly in many cities across the United States. There is a Fellowship of Christian Companies for Bible believers in the corporate business world. In Washington, D.C. the Fellowship Foundation and the Christian Embassy ministers to believers in the diplomatic corps from many countries and to government officials. There are Bible study and prayer groups in the U.S. Senate, the House of Representatives, and many other federal agencies. There is a Fellowship of Airlines Personnel for pilots, flight attendants, mechanics, and others employed by commercial airlines. There is another goup known as the Fellowship of Christians in the Arts, Media, and Entertainment, with branches on Broadway, in Hollywood, and throughout the country. There is even an organization of policemen called Cops for Christ.

Bible study groups thrive on practically every college campus in the United States and Canada, under the sponsorship of churches, Campus Crusade for Christ, InterVarsity Christian Fellowship, and The Navigators. Hundreds of "Bible clubs," sponsored by Campus Life and other Christian youth ministries, meet in or near public and private high schools, before and after school.

There are a growing number of Bible study groups in prison. Converted Watergate figure Charles Colson, for example, held a Bible study seminar for 15 men on Death Row at the Holman Correctional Institution in Alabama—the first time condemned prisoners were ever permitted to congregate in groups larger than three or four. The condemned men asked such questions as, "How can I be sure I will go to heaven after what I've done?" The Bible provided the answer.

This is only in America. Countless other groups, not considering the hundreds of thousands of churches and Sunday schools, meet regularly all over the world to mine rich nuggets from God's Word. In some lands, believers must meet in secret to study the Bible, knowing that if discovered they may be arrested and sent to prison.

The depths of this marvelous Book, which appeals to the deepest needs of every person on Planet Earth, can never be fully tapped. After several days of reading the Bible, a Chinese scholar who had been engaged by the American Bible Society to help with a translation project, concluded: "The One who made that Book made me, for it tells me things about myself that no one else knows and some things I did not even know."

Woodrow Wilson, who served as president of the United States during the critical days of World War I, once observed: "Every time you open the Bible, some old text that you have read a score of times suddenly beams with new meaning." English poet Samuel Taylor Coleridge reflected: "In the Bible there is more that finds me than I have experienced in all other books put together." Dr. Charles Malik, the great Lebanese statesman and educator and former President of the

United Nations General Assembly, testified: "The Bible is the source of every good thought and impulse that I have."

The Bible is truly the Book for every man and woman of every race, culture, and nation to live by and to die by. It speaks to the young and old, the educated and uneducated, the poor and the the wealthy, to those of every class and vocation, to every tribe and nation. Each seeker finds God's Word to be Truth above all other truth, a precious guide for life, a light along the dark paths, and a sure anchor in the most stormy weather.

It is the Book of life for all humanity. When Sir Walter Scott lay dying, he called for "the Book." When asked, "What book?" the great English man of letters replied, "There is only one Book for this time, the Bible."

Indeed there is only one Book for all times, the Bible.

This is the Book that abides, for Jesus said, "Heaven and earth shall pass away, but my words shall not pass away" (Matthew 24:35).

Chapter 7

"The Book That Carries a Mandate for Caring"

I was once chided by an anthropologist: "Why do you keep pushing a western religion among tribal people. They're happy with the beliefs they have."

I had to tell him that the Holy Book of Christianity was written by Easterners and that as a tribal person myself, I knew that tribal people were not happy with a life controlled by superstitions and belief in dark spirits. I told him a bit of how life was before my people, the Hmars, accepted the Bible as their guide—all night drinking parties to dull the frustrations of life, fighting in families, killing and stealing, and pitiful poverty. "My friend," I said, "I can assure you that the Hmars never want to return to the "happy" way.

"Well," he grunted, "I suppose you have a right to your own opinion. As for myself, I'm still opposed to religious imperialism."

A Christian woman friend of ours ran across one of these fellows when visiting a tribe where the Wycliffe Bible Translators worked in Peru. He brought up the same old canard about giving tribal people the Bible. She handed it to him straight: "I think I know the reason you don't want these people to get the Bible. You know they will change for the better. You prefer that they stay just as they are, so you and your friends can come and study them like monkeys in cages."

In telling me about the incident, she said, "He looked embarrassed. He knew I was telling the truth."

My dear friend, the late Cameron Townsend, founder of Wycliffe, heard the "happy savage" argument hundreds of times. He had a stock answer: "My friend, I fear you've never been closer to tribal people than the movies and television. If you could talk to those who have benefited from the Bible, they would tell you immediately that they were not happy, but miserable in their old ways of life."

One of the most remarkable testimonies comes from the Aucas of Ecuador—a name which means "savages." Before missionaries gave them the Bible in their own language, these Amazonian tribal people were constantly killing one another in revenge raids, and by following a custom that called for the children of a man killed in battle to be buried alive with their father's body.

I was a student at Wheaton College in January, 1956 when news came that five young American missionaries were missing in the jungle in South America and feared dead from trying to reach the Aucas. Faculty and students at the college stayed glued to their TV sets, for some of the young martyrs and their wives had attended Wheaton.

The story made *Life* and *Time* and the front pages of newspapers all over the world. Many persons remarked that the five young men, all very talented, had been foolish to risk their lives to take the Bible to the Aucas. However, the *Portland Oregonian* editorialized after the bodies were found:

"The forefathers of most of us were European savages or barbarians. Ulfilas brought Christianity to the Goths, St. Patrick to the Irish, St. Columba to the Scots, St. Augustine to the English. Boniface brought the Gospel to Germany, Ansgar to the Scandinavians and Valadimir to the Slavs. Would Europe and America be as enlightened today if these men had not felt that strange force which still sends missionaries forth to preach the Gospel to every creature?"

After the burial of the martyrs, Elisabeth Elliot, the wife of one, and Rachel Saint, the sister of another, bravely walked into Auca territory and set up camp with this most feared group in Ecuador. The first five converts were the very men who had thrown the spears that killed the missionaries.

The book *Unstilled Voices*, by James and Marti Hefley, published 25 years after the killings, documents the Christianization of the Aucas, which followed translation of portions of the Bible into their language. The revenge raids within the group have stopped. The people are learning to read and write and to become productive citizens of Ecuador. They welcome visitors peacefully.

Thanks to the Bible, love has replaced fear and hate. The population decline, resulting from killings and disease, has been reversed. There were only about 200 when Rachel Saint and Elisabeth Elliot began living among them and translating and teaching the Bible. Without the Bible, the Aucas would have soon followed scores of other Amazonian tribal "nations" into extinction. Today there are over 1,000 Aucas living peacefully in the eastern jungles of Ecuador.

What about the influence of the Bible on the wider world? How has the Bible produced caring and concern for the less fortunate in "civilized" cultures?

No people's history has been more affected by the Bible than the Jews, who provided the cultural matrix in which the Bible was written. When these children of Abraham came into the Promised Land, after escaping Egyptian slavery, they found themselves surrounded by pagan societies practicing child sacrifice, prostitution, snake worship, and other idolatries.

God commanded Biblical Israel: "You shall not worship [the pagan] gods, nor serve them, nor do according to their deeds; but you shall utterly overthrow them, and break their sacred pillars in pieces" (Exodus 23:24 NASB). Israel was to worship one God, Jehovah, and respect human life, parenthood, the marriage bond, and private property.

The Hebrews were also given explicit directions and commands for helping the needy. Every seventh year the land was to be given "rest, . . . that the poor of thy people may eat: and what they leave the beasts of the field shall eat" (Exodus 23:11). Every 50th year—the jubilee year—liberty was given to all Israelites who might be in bondage to any of their countrymen for debts or other reasons, and ancestral possessions were returned to those who had been compelled to sell them because of poverty.

The Old Testament is replete with commands to help the needy: "Defend the poor and fatherless: do justice to the afflicted and needy." (Psalm 82:3) "If there be among you a poor man of one of thy brethren, . . . thou shalt not harden thine heart, nor shut thine hand from thy poor brother "(Deuteronomy 15:7). "Blessed is he that considereth the poor: the Lord will deliver him in time of trouble "(Proverbs 14:21). "If thine enemy be hungry, give him bread to eat; and if he be thirsty, give him water to drink" (Proverbs 25:21).

The Christian era brought the New Testament, which completed the Bible. Jesus set the example in caring for the needy. He healed the sick, exorcised demons, and fed the hungry. He told His disciples that ministering to the less fortunate was the same as ministering to Him:

" Then I, the King, shall say to those at my right, 'Come, blessed of my Father, into the Kingdom prepared for you from the founding of the world. For I was hungry and you fed me; I was thirsty and you gave me water; I was a stranger and you invited me into your homes; naked and you clothed me; sick and in prison, and you visited me.' Then these righteous ones will reply, 'Sir, when did we ever see you hungry and feed you? Or thirsty and give you anything to drink? Or a stranger, and help you? Or naked, and clothe you? When did we ever see you sick or in prison, and visit you?' And I the King, will tell them, 'When you did it to these my brothers you were doing it to me.'" (Matthew 25:34:40, Living Bible.

The disciples of Jesus proclaimed a mandate for caring. Declared the Apostle James:

"The Christian who is pure and without fault, from God the Father's point of view, is the one who takes care of orphans and widows. . . . You will be judged on whether or not you are doing what Christ wants you to. So watch what you do and what you think; for there will be no mercy to those who have shown no mercy. But if you have been merciful, then God's mercy toward you will win out over his judgment against you. Dear brothers, what's the use of saying that you have faith and are Christians if you aren't proving it by helping others? Will that kind of faith save anyone? If you have a friend who is in need of food and clothing, and you say to him, 'Well, goodbye and God bless you; stay warm and eat hearty,' and then don't give him clothes or food, what good does that do? So you see, it isn't enough just to have faith. You must also do good to prove that you have it. Faith that doesn't show itself by good works is no faith at all—it is dead and useless" (1:27, 2:12-16, Living Bible).

Because the followers of Jesus took such words from the Bible as a command for caring, they were a light in the dark uncaring world of Greek and Roman society. The Epistle to Diognetus, probably the oldest of the Christian apologies (circa A.D. 125), aptly describes the Biblical lifestyle.

"They marry as do all; they beget children; but they do not commit abortion. They have a common table but not a common bed. They are in the flesh, but they do not live after the flesh. They pass their days on earth, but they are citizens of heaven. They obey the prescribed laws, and . . . surpass the laws by their lives. They love all men, and are persecuted by all."

In contrast, the pagan Greek and Roman religions and the government of Rome permitted fathers to throw unwanted infants on garbage heaps. A common saying of the first century world was, "A man is a wolf to those he does not know." Plato and Aristotle agreed that children should be abandoned when parents could not afford to rear them, or if they did not show physical and mental promise of service to the state. The Roman philosopher Seneca candidly admitted: "Monstrous offspring we destroy; children, if weak and unnaturally formed at birth, we drown. It is not in anger, but reason, thus to separate the weak from the sound."

As Christianity spread across the Roman Empire, biblical influence on the sanctity of marriage and reverence for life increased, while polygamy, concubinage, and divorce decreased. Women rose in stature. Child abuse and infanticide declined.

Christians brought cast-off children into their homes. When the homes were full, the first orphanages were built and operated by Christian widows and deaconnesses. But there were not enough Christians to care for all the unwanted children. Relief did not come until A.D. 315 when the Emperor Constantine made Christianity the favored religion of his Empire and decreed that parents must not kill newborn children. If they could not support them, government aid would be provided.

Christians in the Roman Empire also took in thousands of the sick (even despised lepers) and homeless. Soon there were hospitals in every city with a sizable colony of Christians. Fabiola, a devout Christian, established the first charity hospital of record outside Rome in A.D. 380. The Christian scholar Jerome opened one himself at Bethlehem. The noted preacher-orator Chrysostom was responsible for several hospitals in Constantinople. It is no accident that the symbol of the medical profession today is a staff entwined by coiling serpents, pointing back to the Old Testament healing of stricken Israelites in the Sinai wilderness.

Thalasius, a Christian monk, founded a home for blind beggars on the banks of the Euphrates River—another first. Christians opened the first asylums for the insane in Spain. Christians in Italy formed the first brotherhood of nurses, with Christians in other parts of Europe following suit. Modern nursing dates to these brotherhoods. Nursing by women was initiated by Florence Nightingale, who tended British wounded and dying during the 19th-century Crimean War. The famed "lady with the lamp" was motivated by her Christian faith and the Bible.

Ministries of mercy were largely confined to monasteries during the Dark Ages when Catholic church policies effectively kept the Bible from the masses. The greatest reform and social services came after the Reformation, when the Bible was translated into many languages. Open Bibles opened hearts to minister to suffering mankind.

This was especially true in England in the century-and-a-half after the cleansing Wesleyan revivals.

John Howard, the Christian sheriff of Bedfordshire, England, took a tour of jails and found prisoners branded, brutally beaten, and some with their ears cropped. Many were in jail solely because of unpaid debt and were not to be released until the last farthing was paid. Meanwhile, their families languished in abject poverty. "O Lord," prayed Howard, "visit the prisoners and captives and manifest thy strength." John Howard launched a crusade to make prisons more humane.

Brave, compassionate Elizabeth Fry ministered to women prisoners. Appalled to find women and babies jammed into a dungeon in London's Newgate Prison like wild animals, she organized a band of Quaker "angels" who taught the prisoners the Bible and the three R's, gave them decent clothing and edible food, and pressured legislators to enact reforms.

British newspaper publisher Robert Raikes became concerned about the hordes of child waifs who scavenged and slept in the streets of England's cities. In 1780 he paid a Mrs. Meredith, living in Sooty Alley in Gloucester, to teach children the Bible on Sunday in her kitchen. The children flocked there to study the sacred Word along with reading and writing. "Sunday schools" spread to other cities.

Raikes is credited with founding the modern Sunday school movement, although the first Sunday school of record was initiated a few years earlier by Ludwig Hocker, a German Baptist in Ephrata, Pennsylvania.

Inspired by the Bible, Anthony Ashley Cooper, the titled Englishman known as Lord Shaftesbury (1801-85), set about to reform child labor laws in Britain. Cooper told his fellow members of Parliament that children as young as seven were working from before dawn until late at night in factories and given only a cot and skimpy meals. He called for legislation to shorten the "normal" 12-14 hour day for mothers, so they could spend more time with their families. He introduced laws to provide for humane care of the insane. He promoted the building of model tenements.

When some objected that government would be interfering with business, Cooper retorted that Parliament should be more concerned with the "guardians of morality" (mothers) and "citizens of tomorrow" (children) than rich industrialists. Quoting Luke 2:52—"And Jesus increased in wisdom and stature, and in favor with God and man," Cooper presented his principle of "symmetrical" growth. A Christian society, he declared, "has a moral obligation to provide for the spiritual, physical, and social needs of the less fortunate."

William Booth (1829-1912) stands in the ranks of John Howard, Elizabeth Fry, Robert Raikes, and Anthony Earl Cooper. Following Biblical commands, Booth and his wife Catherine held open-air evangelistic meetings and tried to help the poor in the squalid East End section of London. They organized converts into a missionary and social service band that played instruments, preached the gospel, and helped those in physical need. So came the Salvation Army.

The Booth family gave leadership to the Army of caring for over half a century. Bramwell Booth, succeeded his father, William as general of this organization. Another son, Ballington, commanded the Salvation Army in Australia and in the United States before stepping aside to found the Volunteers of America. A daughter, Evangeline, led the Army in Canada and the United States and was general of the international organization from 1934-39. The Salvation Army still marches by the Bible in helping the homeless, hungry, poor, and prisoners—those whom Jesus called "the least of these" (Matthew 25:40).

The Young Men's Christian Association began in England, a few years before the Booths established the Salvation Army, as a Bible-based ministry of prayer and Bible study fellowship for young Christian shopworkers in London. Its counterpart, the Young Women's Christian Association, was established for the same purpose. The YMCA is now by far the larger of the two. It accepts women as equal members and has become the leading physical fitness center in almost every Western city and in many Eastern cities as well. Unfortunately, the spiritual concern of the founders is now played down, although many Y's still ask members to sign a written statement, pledging themselves "to cooperate with others in developing Christian personality and building a Christian society."

A parallel movement for Jews, energized in part by the success of the YMCA and YWCA, resulted in the Young Men's and Young Women's Hebrew Associations. These organizations have since merged under the name Jewish Community Centers.

It is sad that so many secular historians are blind to the influence of the Bible and Christian faith in inspiring movements which developed into the great caring organizations of today. Without the Bible these would probably not exist anywhere on earth.

This biblical mandate to care was taken up by European missionaries at their far-flung posts. Where non-Christian religions permitted barbaric customs and ignored the plight of the sick and homeless, biblical faith brought social reforms, hospitals, leprosariums, and other compassionate outreaches.

In chapter three I told about the great William Carey, the missionary-Bible translator to India. Carey also crusaded against two barbaric practices among the Hindus.

The first called for sick babies, who were thought bewitched, to be left outside to die. Carey persuaded authorities that this was murder. Fearing arrest, many parents stopped the practice and, to their surprise, some babies got well. Carey, as I noted earlier, also campaigned against Sati, which demanded that Hindu widows be burned alive on the funeral pyre of their dead husbands. After many years, he was finally able to put a stop to this practice.

Biblical mercy continues to be extended to the ends of the earth by Christian church bodies and relief organizations. All major Christian denominations minister to the poor, the sick, the homeless, and the hungry. The Mennonites are loved around the world for their relief work and the young people they send to minister to needy people. Southern Baptists, United Methodists, and other major denominations have hospitals and programs for feeding the hungry in many countries. The Lutheran Relief Service, the Catholic Relief Service, and Church World Service (which channels funds from several "mainline" American denominations) serve the less fortunate in a variety of ways.

World Vision, founded by my beloved friend, the late Bob Pierce, cares for hundreds of thousands of orphans and refugees and responds to disaster calls all over the globe. At the time of this writing, World Vision and several other Christian agencies are helping earthquake victims in Soviet Armenia. Who could have imagined just five years ago that Christian relief ministries would be welcomed by the Soviet Union which defines itself as an atheistic nation?

The World Relief Commission of the National Association of Evangelicals sponsors, in cooperation with missionaries, scores of relief projects around the world. In Bangladesh, the poorest nation on earth, for example, WRC has an agricultural collective that provides survival jobs for Muslim widows. These castoffs from Muslim society have nowhere else to turn, for the Muslim government and religion provides no aid to widows.

Medical Assistance Programs, established by my good friend Ray Knighton, provides millions of dollars of emergency medical aid to needy peoples around the world. Compassion lives up to its name by providing for needy children in poverty-stricken lands. So does the Christian Children's Fund. Food for the Hungry, begun by Larry Ward, who served many years previous with World Vision, is saving multitudes from starvation. There is also Oxfam of England; Mother Theresa's loving care for the dying and Mark Buntain's hospital in Calcutta; Samaritan's Purse, founded also by Dr. Bob Pierce and now headed by Billy Graham's son Franklin; and the TEAR Fund of Britain. Many children's homes are also sponsored by Bible believing church bodies, such as those funded by state Baptist conventions in the United States.

There are many other lesser known outreaches to the needy. Bethel Bible Village in Chattanooga, TN, for example, provides for children while their parents are in prison. Bethel is directed by genial Ike Keay, who as a child was placed in an orphans' home after his father committed suicide.

Ike grew up to become a fine young man and took an office job with Standard Oil. Shortly before his 21st birthday he went to Jack Wyrtzen's "Word of Life" Bible Camp, which is still held each year on an island in Schroon Lake, New York. Ike became a Christian the first day he was there.

Ike enrolled in Moody Bible Institute in Chicago to prepare for full-time Christian service. Here he met the girl who became his wife, and they became house parents at the Evangelical Children's Home in St. Louis, Missouri.

In 1964 Ike was hired as director of Bethel, which was then sheltering prisoners' children in an old house on Signal Mountain near Chattanooga. Bethel had been started in 1945 after prison evangelist F. L. Hipp found six little boys living in an old car under a large oak tree and eating roots to survive. Their father was in jail, their mother in a mental institution. Hipp moved them to the old house and spent his last $25 to buy groceries.

Ike convinced Bethel's board members that smaller cottages with live-in house parents would be better than dormitories. A fund-raising drive among churches and business people provided the resources to build five seven-bedroom brick cottages and other buildings on a

67-acre farm campus in North Chattanooga. All of the rooms were quickly filled.

Here are just three of the scores of children who have been given homes at Bethel Bible Village:

Bettie was just eight years old, when she saw her father shoot and kill a man. When her father went to prison, no one was left to provide for her. Bethel gave her a home.

Karen, age 10, was assaulted by her guardian uncle after her parents went to prison. Concerned church people brought her to Bethel.

Jerry was four when his father committed suicide. His mother became a prostitute and criminal and was arrested and sent to prison. Jerry was brought to Bethel where he became the star catcher on the softball team.

Each cottage at Bethel houses eight "children" and house parents together with their "children." The emphasis is on homeyness and togetherness. Each "family" is a unit, living together, reading the Bible together, attending church, and vacationing together. For most of the children this is the first time in their lives when they have been in a happy home with a mother and father who love each other.

Bethel receives no government aid and depends largely on the gifts of Bible-believing people for continued operation. A big boost is provided by a summer celebrity golf tournament, directed by my friend Pat Boone. Pat and an array of Christian sports and entertainment stars give time and money to help pay the salaries of house parents and keep food on the table for the children of Bethel.

When it comes to caring, no other holy book, religion, or philosophy can stand beside the influence of the Bible. If you have traveled in Africa, Asia, and Latin America, going beyond the luxurious tourist hotels, you know there is no basis for comparing any religion to Christianity in the service of caring. The minister of relief in Bangladesh told an inquiring journalist friend of mine shortly after the Bengali war of independence, in which hundreds of thousands were killed or left homeless: "Christians number only one-fourth of one percent of our population. But they are doing almost all of the relief work." In my homeland of India, Christians represent less than three percent of the population. Yet 27 percent of all the hospital beds in Hindu India are provided by Christians and 53 percent of all the nurses come from the Christian community. It is true all over the world: Bible believers are far ahead of any other group—whether a religion, political party, or a society to promote atheism—in caring.

I have already noted a couple of instances where a Christian missionary, William Carey, led the fight to stamp out the horrible evils of child murder and widow suicides in India. Missionaries and national Christian leaders have been at the helm of movements to stamp out barbaric practices in other cultures also.

Often when I point this out to Bible unbelievers, I hear the question: "What about slavery? How could you justify the support of this terrible evil in 'Christian' America and England for so many years?"

I would like to answer those questions and tell how slavery was finally eradicated by ideas from the Bible.

It is not true that the Bible helped keep slavery alive until modern times, although some did misinterpret the Bible for this purpose. Nor is it true that the Bible alone is responsible for doing away with slavery. The Bible did play the major role in eliminating slavery, but there were other influences, notably economic and political.

Slavery was taken for granted when Jesus lived in Palestine, then occupied by the Roman Empire. Neither Jesus nor any of His apostles, in the Bible, ever called for violent revolution to overthrow slavery. Even if they had, what chance would a few Christians have had against the Roman army? The Bible did light a time bomb against this monstrous evil by setting forth principles that undermined the foundation of its existence. Jesus declared in the synagogue at Nazareth: "The Spirit of the Lord is upon me, because he hath anointed me to preach the gospel to the poor; he hath sent me to heal the brokenhearted, to preach deliverance to the captives, and recovery of sight to the blind, to set at liberty them that are bruised" (Luke 4:18). The Apostle Paul proclaimed: "There is neither Jew nor Greek, there is neither bond nor free, there is neither male nor female: for you are all one in Christ Jesus" (Galatians 3:28).

These passages and others undermine not only slavery, but cruel oppressive caste systems, and mistreatment of women as well. Scripture also commands masters to be kind and protective of slaves and slaves to be more faithful to their masters. The apostle Paul even asked a Christian brother named Philemon to receive back his runaway slave Onesimus "no longer as a slave, but more than a slave, a beloved brother" (Philemon:16 NASB)!

Slaves and ex-slaves rose to leadership in early Christian communities. By A.D. 140 an ex-slave was the spiritual leader of the Christians in Rome. The cynic Lucian observed: "The Legislator of the Christians has persuaded them that they are all brothers."

The drive to outlaw slavery throughout the world resulted primarily from the Protestant Reformation and the accompanying translation and circulation of Scriptures in the world's great languages. In 1789 William Wilberforce, a leading churchman and political leader in England, introduced a bill in Parliament to end that nation's slave trade. When the bill finally became law in 1807, Wilberforce pushed for the outlawing of slavery itself.

"Read the Bible," Wilberforce repeatedly advised friend and foe. "Through all my perplexities and distresses I never read any other book."

French rationalists led the battle against slavery in the French colonies. They attacked the evil practice on philosophical grounds, maintaining that all men have equal rights. Equal rights and human dignity are rooted in the biblical concept that man is created in the image of God.

The first antislavery society was established by Quaker Christians in England. The American counterpart was instituted in 1833 at Philadelphia and also led by Quakers.

From colonial times, slavery was opposed by almost all American church leaders. The Massachusetts legislature condemned the evil in 1641. The most influential evangelist of the first half of the 19th century, Charles Finney, crusaded for laws that would grant equal rights for blacks and women with white males.

Then in 1833 a Presbyterian minister, the Rev. James Smylie, began proclaiming biblical "proof" texts, interpreting them out of context, in an effort to claim that slavery was divinely instituted. His ideas seem weird today, but it wasn't the first time the Bible was twisted and misused for the wrong ends.

Many clergymen in the Southern United States passed on Smylie's interpretations to their congregations. Some were mistakenly persuaded that Smylie was right. Many probably acted under pressure from plantation owners and other church members who feared that the Southern cotton economy would collapse if the slaves became free.

Abolitionism captured the consciences of church leaders in the North. National denominations split. But public opinion in the North was not really aroused until the publication of *Uncle Tom's Cabin*, a book inspired by the Bible.

Author Harriet Beecher Stowe was the daughter of a minister, sister of a minister, married to a minister, and the mother of ministers. The crucial scene for her story about the misfortunes of the black slave Uncle Tom came to her while taking communion in church. "The Lord Himself wrote [*Uncle Tom's Cabin*]," she later said. "I was but an instrument in His hands."

Uncle Tom's Cabin sold over five million copies, an unbelievable sale for a book during the mid-nineteenth century. Many historians say Mrs. Stowe's book was the major catalyst in convincing millions of Americans, including some in the South, that the slaves in America must be emancipated.

It took the terrible Civil War and the lives of hundreds of thousands of young Americans, most of them white men, to do it in the United States.

Slavery is now gone in the Western world, thanks largely to people who took the Bible teaching of equality seriously. Racial discrimination continues strong in many areas of the world, particularly under the terrible evil of apartheid in South Africa, but even there the strongest opponents are Christians. In America the "back" of discrimination has been broken by the Civil Rights movement. No matter what you may hear about the plight of blacks in America, please keep these things in mind: discrimination is now against the law. The Bible does not support this evil. The crusade for Civil Rights was led by Bible-quoting black ministers. There would not have been a Civil Rights movement without the black churches and the Bible.

Volumes could be written about what the Bible's mandate for caring has accomplished. It was best summed up by Thomas Huxley, an agnostic, who said, " The Bible has always been the Magna Carta of the poor and oppressed."

Chapter 8

"The Book That Builds Civilized Culture"

Our children were home for the Christmas holidays. "Good morning, Mary, did you sleep well?" I greeted my lovely 22-year-old daughter. I turned to our second son who was already at the table. "John, after breakfast, will you give us a special showing of the documentary film you recently made in India?" I called to our firstborn, who was in the living room, pouring over a mathematics journal, "Paul, come and join us for breakfast."

We gave Biblical names to our children because of what the Bible means to us. In this we are not unusual. Millions of other parents—in every nation to which the Bible has gone—name their children after honored Bible personages. Think of all the English "Johns," the German "Johanns," and the Spanish "Juans."

On this snowy December morning I look at the calendar and see again the influence of the Bible. Even Communist nations date the years from the birth of Christ: A.D., meaning Anno Domini—the year of our Lord.

I look out the window and see neighbor children boarding a yellow school bus for the last day before their Christmas break. I see more influence of the Bible, for universal, free public education is a result of the Protestant Reformation, which swept across Europe, bringing education in its wake, as the Bible was translated into the vernaculars of the people.

Recently I drove to O'Hare Airport and took a jet to Washington without asking a government agency for permission to travel outside of my home area. If Mawii and I so choose, we could move from Illinois to California without asking the permission of any government bureaucrat. Freedom is a biblical concept and usually available only in nations founded on precepts of Holy Scripture.

Almost all the good things of life that we take for granted bear the stamp of the Bible's influence—marriage, family, names, calendar, institutions of caring, social agencies, education, benefits from science, uplifting books, magnificent works of art and music, freedom, justice, equal rights, the work ethic, the virtues of self-reliance and self-discipline, and on and on. Sir Francis Bacon sagely declared: "There never was found, in any age of the world, either religion or law that did so highly exalt the public good as the Bible.

Let us look first at the Bible's influence on education. The fount of education is in the home. Research shows that the teaching and example of parents is actually more crucial for learning than the school a child attends. That's why I'm not surprised to learn that Wheaton College has a larger ratio of students going on to earn doctorates than any other college in Illinois. Almost all of the students at Wheaton and other good Christian schools come from Christian homes.

Mawii and I have tried to bring up our three children by the Bible. We're truly proud of all three. Mary, our young career woman, is a recent graduate of Wheaton College. John, also a graduate of Wheaton, is an award-winning film producer. Paul is now completing his Ph.D. in mathematics at the University of Illinois. When we look at our children and their success in life, we thank God again for the Bible.

The Old Testament commanded Jewish fathers to "diligently" teach their children divinely revealed precepts on worship, family, and social relations, skills in agriculture, and hygiene—"when you sit in your house and when you walk by the way and when you lie down and when you rise up" (Deuteronomy 6:7 NASB).

The Jewish emphasis on family education helps explain why the Jews have given the world, in ratio to population, more great scientists than any other group. Let me illustrate: From 1901-39 only 14 Americans became Nobel Prize winners in science while the Germans received 35 such awards. But from 1943-55 (no Nobels were given from 1940-42) the count reversed. Americans won 29 Nobels and the Germans only 5.

This turnabout came largely because of the brain drain of Jews fleeing from Nazi Germany to the United States just before World War II.

It is not by chance that many of the world's greatest musicians, playwrights, novelists, newspaper publishers and columnists, and financiers have also been Jews. Ann Landers and Abigail Van Buren are twin Jewish sisters. Adolph Ochs, founder of The New York Times, was Jewish. So was Joseph Pulitzer, founder of the St. Louis Post Dispatch, the Columbia University School of Journalism, and the prizes for excellence in writing and photography that bear his name.

The one sad note to the above is that many American Jews have departed from their heritage and are no longer committed to Biblical absolutes in morality. Over half of the producers and directors for motion picture studios in Hollywood, for example, are Jewish. Some have played a major role in the loss of values in the American entertainment world.

Now let us look at education beyond the home. What part has the Bible played in the development of public education?

The Jews established an early elementary school system after the Babylonian exile. Schools were developed as adjuncts to synagogues, with each community of 120 or more Jewish males expected to organize a ruling council and levy taxes for education. Attendance was compulsory for boys and optional for girls. The first five books of the Bible and the three R's were taught. This system continued long after the Jews were driven from Palestine by the Romans late in the first century.

Christian schools were opened in church buildings after A.D. 313 when Christianity became a legal religion in the Roman Empire. Schools to train monks, priests, and other religious workers continued in monasteries during the Dark Ages.

A big advance came when the powerful European monarch Charlemagne (742-814) invited Alcuin, a devout Christian from York, England, to direct an educational program. Under Alcuin's guidance elementary schools were set up for children in local communities. So began the first movement toward general public education. Some of these schools grew into theological seminaries; one seminary developed into the University of Paris.

The Protestant Reformation brought a burst of Bible translations, but what good was a Bible in your own language if you couldn't read it? The people cried for schools. In 1528, in the German province of Saxony, Luther helped begin the first system of compulsory, universal education. Similar educational systems, under the auspices of Reformation groups, sprang up across Europe, except in England where private Protestant schools flourished.

Reception of the Bible always whets a desire for education. Schools almost always follow.

Scholars of the Middle Ages and the Reformation period held the Bible in first importance. The greatest minds of the time were devout Bible students, including the founders of modern science.

The Greeks and Romans believed in a plurality of deities who fought among themselves in a disorganized universe. The prevailing view was that everything beyond the moon was of a different nature than that of earth. The Greek philosophers suggested that you sit in an armchair and meditate on how certain principles work and all knowledge would ultimately be yours. Not surprisingly, the Greeks thought they knew most of what there is to know. Some moderns still feel the same way!

The Bible brought a unified, interconnected view of the universe with the one supreme God at the center and over all. Man's knowledge is infinitesimal, according to Scripture: "When I consider thy heavens, the work of thy fingers, the moon and the stars, which thou hast ordained; what is man, that thou art mindful of him." (Psalm 8:3, 4.) "Behold, God is great, and we know him not, neither can the number of his years be searched out . For he maketh small the drops of water: they pour down rain according to the vapour thereof: Which the clouds do drop and distil upon man abundantly .... Can any understand the spreadings of the clouds, or the noise of his tabernacle?" (Job 36:26-29).

I chuckle when I read those verses from Job. Modern meteorologists with all their gauges and computerized instruments still cannot control the weather.

All of the great Christian thinkers who laid the foundations for modern science were humbled by the majesty and consistency of the creation. Not one was an atheist. They believed that God had disclosed Himself in two great books, the Bible and Nature. It was the duty of God's servants to study and apply both to life.

The four great shapers of modern astronomy and space science—Nicholas Copernicus (1473-1543), Johannes Kepler (1571-1630), Galileo Galilei (1564-1642), and Sir Isaac Newton (1642-1727)—were all reverent believers in divine creation and the divine inspiration of the Bible. They did not believe, as was commonly thought, that comets foretold death, pestilence, famine, invasion, or war.

For centuries Aristotle's theory of astronomy had been accepted as dogma by the hierarchy of the Catholic Church. The Greek philosopher thought that the heavens were made of clear crystal spheres that touch each other like gears and carry the stars and planets. Earth is a motionless globe, he said, positioned at the center of the universe, with everything revolving around it.

A minority of scholars—who kept their voices down—accepted the view of Ptolemy, a Greek astronomer in Alexandria, Egypt during the second century A.D. Ptolemy surmised that the earth and other planets revolved around the sun. One of the problems of Ptolemy's theory was that every once in a while some of the planets stopped in their forward motion and made a backward loop. Ptolemy explained this retrograde looping motion by drawing a combination of smaller circles moving around larger circles. To make his calculations match the actual motions of the planets, he had to use more than 70 circles.

Nicholas Copernicus, the first of the four great shapers of modern space science, became exasperated at the number of circles required by Ptolemy's calculations. Copernicus hypothesized that the earth spun around on an axis while revolving around the sun. This idea was so ridiculed by fellow scholars that Copernicus feared to make it publicly known. Said he: "I do not want to be hissed off the stage. What I know, the public does not approve, and what it approves, I know to be error." He did not send his ideas to a printer until near the end of his life. As he lay dying a friend put his book *The Revolutions of the Spheres* in his hands. An hour later he was dead.

Copernicus is lauded today as a great hero of secular science. What often goes unmentioned is that he was the canon of a cathedral in East Prussia and a lover of the Bible. Despite his disagreement with Aristotelian church prelates, Copernicus never left the Church.

Kepler and Galileo lived about a century after Copernicus and were born only seven years apart. They lived in a time of great religious ferment. Kepler was always a devout Lutheran, Galileo always a faithful Catholic, despite condemnation of his scientific beliefs by a papal inquisition.

Kepler first planned to be a minister. He learned the original languages of the Bible because he wanted to understand Scripture better. Kepler's research into Biblical history showed that Christ had been born five years earlier than previously thought. He read in Josephus about an eclipse of the moon that had occurred during the year of Herod's death. By calculating the date of the eclipse against the Biblical record of the death of King Herod, Kepler established the date of Christ's birth.

Kepler believed that a perfect God had made a perfect universe, although he was frustrated by Copernicus' system of circular motions. After many years of calculations, Kepler showed that the planets moved, not in circles, but ellipses. His famous "Three Laws" of planetary motion accurately describe the revolutions of the planets around the sun.

Kepler believed nothing had been created by God without a plan. There had to be a pattern. One of his favorite Bible verses was Psalm 19:1: "The heavens declare the glory of God; and the firmament showeth his handiwork."

After completing a successful mathematical calculation, Kepler was prone to burst into prayer. When he discovered his Third Law of planetary motions (showing that the ratio of the cube of the average distance of the planet from the sun to the square of the time the planet needs to complete one revolution around the sun is the same for all the planets), he wrote:

"Great is God our Lord, great is His power and there is no end to His wisdom. Praise Him, you heavens, glorify Him, sun and moon and you planets. For out of Him, through Him, and in Him are all things . . . . We know, oh, so little. To Him be the praise, the honor, and the glory from eternity to eternity."

"So much pain and suffering in this world is caused by blind superstition," Kepler said. He sought to establish laws for the heavens so people would no longer see comets, for example, as portents of disaster. He longed for the day when people would "no longer accept nonsense when they see how order and reason govern the world."

Persecution and conflict touched Kepler's life many times. His father disappeared in the confusion of war. His mother was arrested and tried as a witch. Kepler himself once had to leave the town where he was then living before sundown or face execution because of his biblical beliefs. When Archduke Ferdinand demanded that he renounce his faith, he said, "It is sweet to suffer loss and insult for my faith and Christ's honor."

The Italian astronomer Galileo, who corresponded with Kepler, called Kepler a great friend of science. Galileo found experimentally that bodies do not fall with velocities proportional to their weights, a conclusion received with hostility because it contradicted the accepted teaching of Aristotle. In 1609 he constructed the first astronomical telescope, which he used to discover the four largest satellites of Jupiter and the stellar compositon of the Milky Way. Amazed at what he saw thru his telescope, he said, "Being infinitely amazed thereat, so do I give infinite thanks to God who has pleased to make me the first observer of marvelous things unrevealed to bygone ages."

In 1632 Galileo published his *Dialogue Concerning The Two Chief World Systems,* a work which marked a turning point in scientific and philosophical thought. In 1633 he was brought before a council of inquisition in Rome and made to renounce all his beliefs and writings supporting the idea that the earth is not the center of the solar system. According to a legend, Galileo said what the council wanted to hear, then whispered to himself, "Nevertheless, the earth still turns."

Sir Isaac Newton, born the year Galileo died, is still considered by many to be the greatest scientist of all time. His many accomplishments include discovery of the law of universal gravitation and invention of the first reflecting telescope. The respect of his peers is shown by the fact that he served as President of the British "Royal Society" of scholars from 1703 until his death in 1727. Einstein said his own scientific accomplishments would have been impossible without Newton's discoveries. The knowledge Newton developed, Einstein declared, is "even today still guiding our thinking in physics." Newton, however, believed his greatest work was done in theology. The great English scientist was a devout Christian and held the Bible to be the supreme authority.

The five greatest British physical scientists of the nineteenth century (Davy, Maxwell, Faraday, Joule, and Kelvin) were also devout Bible-believing Christians.

Sir Humphrey Davy (1778-1829)—the chemist who isolated sodium, potassium, barium, boron, calcium, and magnesium—said the object of science was not only to apply the different substances in nature to the advantage, benefit, and comfort of man, but likewise to set forth that wonderful and magnificent history of wisdom and intelligence which is written in legible characters both in the heavens and on earth.

James Clerk Maxwell (1831-1879) was the first professor of experimental physics at Cambridge. His theory of the electromagnetic field and discoveries in electricity and magnetism are still used today. Able to quote much of the Bible from memory, Maxwell dedicated his scientific work as a service to God. He gave this prayer: "Teach us to study the works of Thy hands that we may subdue the earth to our use, and strengthen our reason for Thy service."

Michael Faraday (1791-1867), an elder in his church and a regular Sunday preacher, passionately believed that the Creator must have made the universe an interconnected, unified whole, with everything within linked together in some way. So he worked tirelessly to find the connection between magnetism and electricity. Again and again he brought wires close to magnets without any sign of an interacting electric current. Then during a short work break he suddenly grasped the secret of electromagnetic induction upon which so much of technology hangs today. He discovered that moving a magnet through a coil of copper wire caused an electric current to flow in the wire. The electric motor and electric generator were developed by applying this principle.

James Prescott Joule (1824-1907) was the first to determine the relationship between heat energy and mechanical energy and was also the discoverer of the first law of thermodynamics.

Joule said: "The study of nature and her laws . . . is essentially a holy undertaking." Having learned from the Bible how to know and obey God, Joule declared, the believer must next seek to know His work.

William Thomson Kelvin (1824-1907) built on Joule's work in thermodynamics. He was the first to succeed in deflecting cathode rays by an electric force. Among many other things, he also discovered the electron, for which he received the 1906 Nobel prize in physics. Kelvin's biography reveals that he frequently talked with other scientists about the Bible and his Christian faith.

These founders of modern science believed that the biblical and natural revelations of God were complementary. They saw no conflict between science and theology. They did their scientific work as a service to God. They believed that science was a way of teaching school children the wonders of creation, indeed they thought that the more a student knew about science, the less he was likely to become an atheist.

Thomas Edison (1847-1931), perhaps the greatest inventor of the 19th century, believed that "the existence of an intelligent Creator, a personal God, can, to my mind, almost be proved from chemistry." While trying to find material from which electric light filaments could be made, Edison said: "Somewhere in God Almighty's workshop is a dense woody growth, with fibers almost geometrically parallel and with practically no pith, from which we can make the filament the world needs."

One evening, Edison sat idly toying with a mixture of tar and lampblack. He noticed that when rolled out, the composite looked like wire. He twisted a small strand, inserted it into a bulb, and drew out the air. Then he turned on the current and the bulb glowed, but only for a brief time. A short while later, he managed to place a filament of carbonized thread into a bulb. The bulb burned for two days. The electric light was born.

It is a fact that the founders of modern science held the Bible to be superior to all other books. Without their discoveries the great advances of science and technology which benefit mankind today would not be possible. Why were these discoveries made almost entirely in the West and not in the East where non-biblical religions prevail? I submit it was largely because of the availability of the Bible and the effects of the Protestant Reformation.

Indeed, the modern missionary movement which was propelled by biblical commands, brought revolutionary, culture-changing education to countries which had long languished in poverty and spiritual darkness. The model was set by William Carey, of whom I spoke earlier. When Carey arrived in India he found no grammar or dictionary in any language. He prepared his own books and translated the Bible into the four major languages of the country and guided others in the translation of the Bible into 32 more Asiatic languages. Carey also put out the first newspaper ever printed in an Asian language and supervised the setting up of 126 mission schools and a college.

The present leaders of India, where only one person in about 40 is even a nominal Christian, must admit that the nation's climb up the ladder of literacy and education is largely due to the Bible. Leaders of Africa also know that over 85 percent of all the schools on this vast continent were opened by Christian missionaries.

The Bible has served to bring tribal groups into the mainstream of national culture. Members of the Wycliffe Bible Translators have entered some tribes where the people did not know the name of the country in which they lived. The only other nations they "knew" were their tribal neighbors, with whom they sometimes fought. With the blessing of the Bible and literacy, these tribes became responsible citizens of their respective countries.

Education continues to be a fruit of missionary enterprise. The Laubach Literacy Crusade, founded by Methodist missionary Frank Laubach, has taught over 300 million illiterates in over 100 counties to read. Members of Wycliffe Bible Translators have trained hundreds of bilingual teachers in South America, Africa, Asia, and the islands of the Pacific. These teachers are certified by their governments and teach the Bible, the three R's, carpentry, home economics, health care, and many other subjects helpful in bringing tribal peoples into the 20th century.

Advances in agriculture go hand in hand with the Bible and education. There is a marvelous example of this on the Philippine island of Mindanao. Around 30 years ago, a Filipino-Chinese Christian businessman, John Sy Cip, and an American missionary couple, Jared and Marilee Barker, founded the Philippine Evangelical Enterprise. Today this Bible-based organization sponsors two colleges, two elementary schools, youth camps, health care programs (combining medicine and nutrition), and numerous agricultural projects. Thousands of people have been helped and a whole region transformed spiritually and economically.

Where would education and health care be today without the Bible?

As to the Bible's influence on literature, I must start by stating that the Bible itself is the world's greatest literary masterpiece. The story of Joseph in Genesis is acclaimed as a model for short story writers. The Book of Job is recognized as the greatest epic poem ever penned. Said Thomas Carlyle (1795-1881), the greatest English author of his day, of Job: "There is nothing written, I think, . . . of equal literary merit." Everyone has his favorite part of the Bible. John Adams, America's second president, called the Psalms "superior to all odes, hymns, and songs." Thomas Jefferson affirmed the Beatitudes the richest selection in all literature. Daniel Webster called the Sermon on the Mount the greatest legal digest in the world.

The Bible is the one Book which has inspired countless other books. The great educator William Lyon Phelps declared: "The Bible has been a greater influence on the course of English literature than all other forces put together." Indeed, without the Bible the English language might not exist as we know it. When John Wycliffe made the first English translation of the Bible in the 14th century, Britons spoke almost 200 dialects. Often people in one village could not understand neighbors in the next. The spread of Wycliffe's translation, more than any other work, made English a common tongue. Likewise, Luther's Bible translation became the standard for establishing German as a national language.

The greatest literary masters of Western literature perused the Bible for inspiration, ideas, and plots. Some years ago a scholar listed 1,065 titles of English books of fiction, drama, and poetry not written for religious purposes. He found that 254 of the titles were quotations or adaptations from the words of Jesus in the Bible. DeFoe, Stevenson, Burns, Scott, Chaucer, Shakespeare, Browning, Milton, and Kipling are only some of the great writers whose works reveal the influence of the Bible. They knew the Bible. They incorporated Biblical ideas and quotations into their writings. Robert Burns said, for example: "Without the Bible my poetry would be woefully lacking."

Biblical themes appear in some of the greatest works of the modern era. Four examples are Albert Camus's *The Fall* (the theme of sin), Franz Kafka's *The Trial* (judgment), William Faulkner's *The Sound and the Fury* (suffering), and Graham Greene's *The Heart of the Matter* (love).

Why has the Bible been such a force in Western literature? Said Henry Van Dyke: "The fountainhead of the power of the Bible in literature lies in its nearness to the very springs and sources of human life."

The influence of the Bible is just as evident in the greatest art, music, and architecture of the West.

Since the beginning of the Christian era, the Bible has inspired great works of art. The frescoes of the Roman catacombs reveal Biblical concepts of faith and hope. When Christianity became a legal religion in the Roman Empire, Christian art blossomed in the churches and on monuments. Through the 19th century, the greatest sculptures and paintings were based on characters or incidents in the Bible. The greatest artists—Raphael, Leonardo da Vinci, Michelangelo, Rembrandt, and others—are most remembered and appreciated for their biblical masterpieces.

Who can ever forget William Holman Hunt's masterpiece (now hanging in London's St. Paul's Cathedral) "The Light of the World," which depicts the thorn-crowned Savior knocking on a fast-closed door? Or Dante Gabriel Rossetti's "The Annunciation" and "The Beloved?" Or Michelangelo's Biblical panorama on the ceiling of the Sistine Chapel in St. Peter's Church of Rome? Or Raphael's "The Crucifixion" and "The Deliverance of St. Peter?" Or Rembrandt's "The Sacrifice of Abraham?" And these are just a few.

With architecture, the story is much the same. The Notre Dame Cathedral in Paris, Westminister Abbey and St. Paul's in London, St Peter's in Rome, the National Cathedral in Washington, and the Crystal Cathedral in California are among the great structures that portray man's aspirations and worship of the God of the Bible.

What shall we say of the Bible's influence on music? The creators of the greatest oratorios, anthems, symphonies, hymns, and other classics were inspired by the Bible. Bach's "Jesus Joy of Man's Desiring," Mendelssohn'a "Elijah," Handel's "Messiah," Brahms's "Requiem," Beethoven's "Mount of Olives," and Haydn's "Creation" are some of the best known works inspired by the Bible. After hearing his magnificent work, Haydn said, "Not I, but a power from above created that." Bach often wrote I.N.J. for the Latin words meaning "In the Name of Jesus" on his manuscripts.

The Bible's influence on music continues, not only in classical works, but in hymns, spirituals, country gospel, contemporary gospel, and musicals. From ex-slave trader John Newton's much loved "Amazing Grace" to the black spiritual, "Swing Low Sweet Chariot," to Ron

Huff's stirring praise arrangement "Alleluia!" Bible-based music keeps hearts ringing today.

What of the Bible's influence in government, law, and political freedom? Here also the Bible has proved to be a powerful force. Indeed the Book of God has been such a power that I doubt if civilized government, as exemplified in the American Constitution, would even exist today without the Bible.

The Jews, guided by God's promises and the commands in The Torah (the books of Moses), advanced from a disorganized mob of newly freed slaves to become, under David and Solomon, the most glorious nation on earth.

The Bible was first outlawed in the Roman Empire, then exalted and taken as a basis for reforms by Emperor Constantine. Without these reforms, the Empire might have fallen a century earlier than it did.

The Dark Ages descended when barbarians invaded and church leaders withdrew into their monasteries. Social needs went neglected, and the public good was disdained by churchmen who were more concerned about preserving their earthly power than with giving the Bible to the masses.

The influence of the Bible was not dead. Under Charlemagne (742-814), the Bible began emerging again as an influence in public life. Biblical principles of jurisprudence were written into his *Capitularies*, sparking a move toward democratic government.

A half-century later Alfred the Great, the Christian King of the West Saxons and a student of the Bible, saved the future country of England from the barbaric Danes and introduced a legal code based on the Ten Commandments and other portions of Scripture.

Three centuries beyond Alfred, in the year 1215, the barons of England forced King John to sign the momentous Magna Carta, which placed the king under law. A leading proponent for this revolutionary action was Henry DeBracton, a Christian judge, who developed the foundations of the legal system of present Western democracies. DeBracton used as his rationale the biblical doctrine of redemption, noting that God could have crushed Satan, but chose to satisfy justice by sending Christ to die for man's sin. Justice, Judge DeBracton said, must take precedence over power—a revolutionary idea straight from the Bible.

Judge DeBracton's thesis, according to philosopher-theologian Dr. Francis Schaeffer, became the basis for English Common Law. The Reformation, noted Schaeffer, stripped away religious "encrustations" and positioned authority in Scripture alone rather than in ecclesiastical or political rulers.

Sir William Blackstone (1723-80) was the first to teach English law at a British university, as opposed to Roman law. Blackstone authored the epochal *Commentaries on the Laws of England*, which until recent times was required reading in all Western law schools. Blackstone saw only two foundations for law, nature, and revelation. By revelation he meant "the divine law found only in the holy scripture." The Bible, Blackstone said, has "always been regarded as part of the Common Law of England."

Thanks to the Bible, England became the most advanced civilized nation in the world. The three greatest periods of British history coincide with the times when the Bible was most highly recognized by the government and citizens of that nation.

—During the reign of Alfred the Great England rose from barbarism, division, and ignorance into a united, civilized nation.

—During the reign of Queen Elizabeth (the first English monarch to promote circulation of the Bible; King James merely authorized a translation) England became a world power for the first time.

—During the reign of Queen Victoria, when the sun never set on an English possession, the British Empire, under England, reached its zenith. Asked by a foreign prince the secret of her country's greatness, Victoria replied, "The Bible, my lord."

France never rivaled England in greatness, although French rationalists, who rejected the Bible as divinely inspired, had some noble ideas. The bloody French revolution (1789-99) showed that rationalism, which elevated the wisdom of man above the authority of the Bible, could not provide the strong undergirding that England had received from the Bible. England was spared such an upheaval, probably because of the biblical revival and social reforms resulting from the preaching of John Wesley.

The French agnostic Renan said in 1866: "If rationalism wishes to govern the world without regard to the religious needs of the soul, the experience of the French Revolution is there to teach us the consequences of such a blunder." Historians Will and Ariel Durant quoted this statement from Renan in their *Lessons of History* and added: "There is no significant example in history . . . of a society successfully maintaining moral life without regard to the aid of religion."

European rationalism, which flourished during the 18th century Enlightenment, brought in the so-called Age of Reason. The left wing of the Enlightenment called for overthrow of governments to accomplish social reforms. This became the seedbed for the growth of Communist philosophies during the 19th century, which in turn led to the bloody Marxist-Leninist revolutions of the next century. History shows that when the Bible is rejected as authoritative and man enthrones himself as God, social decay and destruction are sure to follow.

After World War I, the Bible had more beneficent influence in Africa than in Europe. This was a time when the European colonial powers were bending to the spirit of nationalism in distant colonies. The Bible played an important role in the forming and shaping of many of these new nations.

Ironically, it was Bible translation, mission schools, and the preaching of European missionaries that helped pave the way for the establishment of many new nations. Johann Krapf, the great German Lutheran missionary to East Africa, refuted the idea that Africans could not progress without European dominion by saying satirically: "Do not think that because East Africans are 'profitable in nothing to God and the world' they ought to be brought under the dominion of some European power, in the hope that they may bestir themselves more actively and eagerly for what is worldly and, in consequence, become eventually more awake to what is spiritual and eternal."

The great majority of Africa's nationalistic firebrands were trained in mission schools. Julius Nyerere, for example, attended mission schools and was the first of his countrymen to graduate from a British university. When he led Tanzania to independence, the new nation was already one-fourth nominally Christian.

The Bible also contributed greatly to the independence of Asian countries. The great Mahatma (meaning "Great Soul") Gandhi was leading his nonviolent crusade for Indian freedom when I was attending a mission high school. Before his death at the hands of an assassin, Gandhi declared that his ideas came from the life of Jesus and the writings of Thoreau. Though Gandhi did not accept the divinity of Christ, he said, "The Bible gives me great comfort and boundless joy."

Often I am asked, "What about Russia? If the Bible is so great, why did Communism take hold in such a religious nation?" Religious, yes, but the Russian Czars who headed the state church allowed corruption to permeate their church much as Roman Catholic popes did before the Protestant Reformation. They also did not promote the translation and circulation of the Bible. When Lenin came to power by force and trickery in 1917, the Russian masses were largely ignorant of the Bible, and evangelicals who proclaimed the Bible were being persecuted by the state church. Now, 80 years later, Mikhail Gorbachev, the head of the Soviet Union, is admitting that the Communist system is threatened by bureaucratic corruption and an unproductive economy and must be renewed. As part of that renewal he is pushing his government to allow more Bibles into the country.

Why is England so weak today, if the Bible is so powerful? It is true that once-mighty England is now a second-rate power and plagued by rising crime, family breakdowns, and social unrest. This is primarily because many of her leaders have turned away from the Bible and because some influential clergymen in the Church of England have rejected the miraculous elements of Scripture. A larger percentage of the people of the Soviet Union are said to attend weekly worship and read the Bible than in England where hundreds of once thriving churches are now boarded up as relics of history.

Other European countries are also in spiritual decline.. In the Scandinavian country of Sweden, where Lutheranism is the state church, as few as one percent of the population attend church on an average Sunday. Marriages have also declined substantially with many couples simply setting up housekeeping without the blessing of Christian clergy.

The *World Christian Encyclopedia* estimates that Westerners are ceasing to be practicing Christians at the rate of 7,600 a day, while Africa is gaining 4,000 Christians each day through conversion from other religions and a high birth rate. In West Germany the birth rate has actually fallen below the death rate. In 1900 two-thirds of all Christians lived in Europe and Russia; by the year 2,000, if current trends continue, three-fifths will live in Africa, Asia, and Latin America. The influence of the Bible is shifting away from the Western world.

Without the Bible, Western society would not have grown and developed as it has during the past 400 years. Most Western leaders—particularly intellectuals and artists—now seem blind to this. Psalm 14:1 applies to them: "The fool hath said in his heart, there is no God. They are corrupt, they have done abominable works. . . . "

The winds of secularism—denial of divine authority, departure from Biblical moral standards, and the rapid diffusion of depraved and dissolute life-styles—are blowing at hurricane force in Western films, television, art, literature, and public education. The glory of God as revealed in the Bible is departing from the West, as Francis Schaeffer and Malcolm Muggeridge have well noted in their writings. Barring the return of Christ, nuclear holocaust, or totalitarian conquest, the West could within the next century fall back into paganism and barbarism. But the Bible will not be left without a witness. God's banner will be lifted in other nations that choose to obey Him and follow the precepts of His eternal Word.

The Western nations—principally the United States, England, Canada, Australia, Germany, Norway, and Sweden—have, by sending missionaries and financial aid, been the leading force for world Christianization during the past 200 years. But the flow of missionaries from the West is fast being reversed, as theological liberalism, secularism, materialism, and form without spiritual reality replaces the spiritual fervor of the past.

The Bible is essential to the building of civilized culture. Why else would the acclaimed social critic E.D. Hirsch begin his recently published *Dictionary of Cultural Literacy* with 24 pages of biblical references. Says Hirsch, known for his previous bestseller *Cultural Literacy:* "The Bible is a central book in our culture . . . . Far from being illegal or undesirable, teaching about the Bible is not only consistent with our Constitution, it is essential to our literacy."

More than this, I must add, the Bible is essential to the maintaining of all civilized, humane culture.

Chapter 9

"The Book That Made America Great"

The greatest nation in the world today is still the United States of America. But when I was a boy in the jungle I did not even know there was an America. I thought the only white people in the world were the British. Then near the end of World War II, a young white soldier walked into our village and told us he was from America. I thought perhaps he might be from some island off the coast of England.

Later, when I was attending Carey Baptist Church while a college student in Calcutta, I saw Americans almost every week. They wore fine, white muslin short-sleeved shirts without ties. They would slap me on the shoulder and say, "Hi, how're you doing?" I thought America must be a very rich and friendly country. I wanted so much to go there.

One day I came back to my room and was handed a package from America. I opened it with great excitement. Inside was a beautiful leather-bound reference Bible with the inscription, "From a friend in America who loves the Lord and the people of India." Never had I seen such a fine copy of the Scriptures. I rubbed my palm across the cover. I examined the fine hand-sewn binding. I held the Book out before me just to admire it again. I felt more certain than ever that Americans were rich. I read that Bible all the way through within a month. I looked up everything I could find in reference books about America. I thought if I could go to America, it would almost be like going to heaven.

One day my pastor told me, "The American evangelist Bob Pierce is coming to speak at our church next Saturday night. Bring all the youth you can find to hear him."

What a preacher! Bob Pierce made each of us feel we could do something for God that would make a difference. I wrote in my Bible, "Little is much when God is in it."

In the goodness of God, Dr. Bob Pierce and Watkin Roberts, the Mr. Youngman who brought the Bible to my people, arranged for me to come to America. Soon after I got here, a train ticket and a note came from Dr. Pierce. "Use this to get acquainted with our country," he said.

Never had I dreamed I would take such a trip. I set out by train from Chicago. In Philadelphia I stood in the very room where the Declaration of Independence and the American Constitution were adopted. I saw the Liberty Bell and the verse from the Bible engraved on it: "Proclaim liberty throughout all the land unto all the inhabitants thereof" (Leviticus 25:10). I felt I was standing on holy ground.

What wonders awaited in Washington! I strolled through the Library of Congress. I gazed up at the big letters across the Supreme Court that proclaim EQUAL JUSTICE TO ALL. I walked the halls of the majestic Capitol where the senators and representatives pass. I was even allowed to take a tour of the White House. No one stopped me. I could hardly believe this was possible.

I had read so much about the Great Emancipator, who kept a Bible on his desk, and who said, "All things desirable to men are contained in the Bible." I wanted to see the Lincoln Memorial. I stood reverently before the gigantic sculpture of this noble president. I read again his famous Gettysburg Address: " . . . Resolve that these dead shall not have died in vain—that this nation, under God, shall have a new birth of freedom—and that this government of the people, by the people, and for the people, shall not perish from the earth."

In New York City I took the ferry to the Statue of Liberty. I saw such beautiful words inscribed on the pedestal:

. . . Give me your tired, your poor,
Your huddled masses yearning to breathe free,
The wretched refuse of your teeming shore.
Send these, the homeless, tempest-tossed to me,
I lift my lamp beside the golden door!

Back in Manhattan, I rode the elevator to the top of the Empire State Building and stared breathless at the great city below. I took a west bound train and whizzed past bustling cities, sleepy towns, and fields of golden grain, then crossed the splendid Rockies into the sun-baked desert. By the time I got to Los Angeles, I had to stop and reflect on all the wonders I had seen. America was so big and wonderful!

Thirty-four years have passed since my discovery of America. Never a day goes by that I do not thank God for this beloved country and its greatness.

What made America such a great nation? Was it her courageous pioneers and architects of freedom? Her vast natural resources? Her genius for technology, science, and agriculture that enables, for example, one farm worker to grow enough food for 52 people? Her diversity of immigrant-citizens? Her military might? Her colleges and universities that attract thousands of foreign students? Her democracy and freedom? Her opportunity for economic success? Her helping hands of goodwill to the less fortunate? These, I suggest, are only manifestations of the real greatness of America—only branches on the mighty national tree that has given so much to the world. To find the source of America's strength and power you must dig into the foundations of its institutions. You must locate the tap root from which it grows.

The tap root of America is the Holy Bible. All the historians and records I have consulted say that America was founded and developed as a Biblical, Christian oriented nation. America, I believe, is the world's greatest nation because of the place and influence of the Bible in her formative years. The Bible is the foundation stone—"the rock on which our Republic rests," according to President Andrew Jackson—on which was built the greatest citadel of freedom and prosperity in the history of the world.

America, in some ways, may not appear so now. You would certainly not think so by watching television and looking at secular magazines. But America's history cannot be changed.

The documents of the colonies of early America shout the primacy of the Bible and Christianity. Maryland's charter declared that its settlers were driven by a "pious zeal for extending the Christian religion." Delaware's charter called for "the further propagation of the Holy Gospel." Connecticut's constitution bound its citizens "to preserve the liberty and purity of the Gospel of the Lord Jesus Christ."

In 1892 the Supreme Court made an exhaustive study of the relationship of biblical principles to the government, laws, and culture of the United States. The court noted that the state constitutions echoed the voice of the citizenry that biblical laws and ideas were part of the common law. The court went on to say: "If we pass beyond these matters to a view of life as expressed by its laws, its business, its customs, and its society, we find everywhere a clear recognition of the same truth. Among other matters note the following: The form of oath universally prevailing, concluding with an appeal to the Almighty; the custom of opening sessions of all deliberative bodies and most conventions with prayers; the prefatory words of all wills, 'In the name of God, amen'; the laws respecting the observance of the Sabbath; with the general cessation of all secular business, and the closing of courts, legislatures, and other similar public assemblies on that day; the churches and church organizations which abound in every city, town, and hamlet; the multitude of charitable organizations existing everywhere under Christian auspices; the gigantic missionary associations, with general support, and aiming to establish Christian missions in every quarter of the globe. These, and many other matters which might be noticed, add a volume of unofficial declarations to the mass of organic utterances that this is a Christian nation."

That opinion from the Supreme Court is taken verbatim from the case Church of the Holy Trinity v. United States. 143 U.S. 226.

In 1931 Justice George Sutherland reviewed the 1892 Supreme Court decision in reference to another case and asserted that Americans are a "Christian people." In 1952, Justice William O. Douglas, never known for traditional Christian beliefs, declared in Zorach v. Clauson: "We are a religious people and our institutions presuppose a Supreme Being." Yale University's Dr. Sidney Ahlstrom, in his award winning *A Religious History of the American People* (Yale University Press, 1973), says that America from the first European settlements had a "religiously oriented sense of mission."

One of the most important books ever printed is *The Bible in America* by P. Marion Simms, Ph.D. It was published in 1936 by the Wilson-Erickson Company of New York. Dr. Simms made an exhaustive study of the records of the various European nationalities that settled in America. He consulted with historians at the University of Chicago, Yale, Harvard, Princeton, and many other distinguished institutions. He paged through the files of the Bible societies, the leading Christian denominations, and the earliest missionary agencies. He looked at the Bible's influence on American law, government, and education. He concluded: "No nation in all history was ever founded by a people so dominated by the Bible as America."

Many of America's greatest scholars acknowledge the Bible's overarching influence. Dr. Robert Bellah, a sociologist at the University of

California in Berkeley, chides secularists for seeking to "eradicate from public life" traces of religious belief. America's religious and biblical heritage cannot be denied, he says.

That is obvious to anyone who looks at the old maps and notes American towns bearing such Biblical names as Salem, Bethlehem, Antioch, and Macedonia. Some of these towns have disappeared, but the names are still on the old documents. In south central Georgia, for example, you will find on old maps Lebanon and Plains of Dura, named for the Babylonian plain where Daniel refused to bow down to Nebuchadnezzar's giant golden image. When the railroad came through a few miles away, people from Plains of Dura and Lebanon relocated around the train stop. The new town became known as simply Plains. It is famous today as the home of President Jimmy Carter. Only tombstones remain to indicate the location of the old towns with Bible names.

So great was the influence of the Bible during the American Revolution that a motion was made in the Continental Congress to make Hebrew the official language of the new nation. The motion failed, but for many years the study of Hebrew, as well as Greek, was required in many colleges and academies. Annual commencement addresses at Harvard were given in Hebrew until 1817.

The Bible was studied in every school in early America, from first grade through university. Yet a galling trade restriction, which benefited the printers of England, forbade the printing of Bibles in the American colonies. All Bibles came from the old countries, as Europeans immigrated to America, bringing translations in their native languages.

Norse explorers may have brought the first Bible to America around A.D. 900. If so, they would have brought the Latin Vulgate translation. Greenland was discovered around 876 and bishops were appointed by the Roman Catholic Pope in 1112 for Greenland and Vinland (thought to be New England). This was almost 400 years before Columbus.

Columbus—despite his moral failings—passionately believed that God intended him to make great discoveries in order to spread Christianity. He prayed several times daily and attended Catholic mass whenever possible. He probably carried several Spanish Bibles on his first voyage. Catholic missionaries accompanied him on his second voyage and would certainly have had Spanish Gospels translated from the Latin Vulgate in 1490.

The first Protestants to arrive in America stepped ashore near present Beaufort, South Carolina, in 1562. A second group arrived two years later. These French and German Huguenots came fleeing persecution and hoping to set up a free Christian state in the New World. The French likely brought a translation of the Bible by Olivetian, a relative of John Calvin. The Germans probably carried Luther's German translation in their baggage. The Huguenot colonies did not survive. Many of the settlers died from starvation and disease. The rest returned to Europe.

The chaplain who accompanied pirate-explorer Sir Francis Drake (the son of a minister) probably brought the first English translation of the Bible to America. On the history-setting trip around the world (the first for an Englishman), the Drake expedition sailed into San Francisco Bay in 1579 to take on supplies. The chaplain probably used the Bishop's Bible, then the favorite in England, for worship services.

The first authentic record of Scripture in America places one or more Bibles in 1585 in present North Carolina, which was then included in the colony of Virginia. Captain John Smith asserts that the colony had a Bible; likely it was the Bishop's Bible. The historian Bancroft says that Thomas Hariot, a brilliant mathematician and devout Christian in the colony, "displayed and explained the Bible" in every Indian village he entered.

This early Virginia colony also failed. The first permanent English settlement, as every American schoolchild should know, was established in 1607. Jamestown was named for King James I, who authorized the translation of the Bible that bears his name. Here the first Protestant church in America was organized.

The Jamestown congregation read from the Bishop's Bible or the Geneva Bible, translated under the direction of Pastor William Whittingham. The Geneva version was the first to employ verse numbers and fill-in words (printed in italics) to make a literal translation easier to read. It was popularly known as the Breeches Bible, because Genesis 3:7 was rendered, ". . . they sewed fig leaves together and made themselves breeches."

Dutch traders came ashore two years after Jamestown, probably carrying the Dutch translation of Luther's German Bible. Danes brought a translation in their language to New Denmark (northeastern Canada) in 1619. Swedish and Finnish colonists brought Bibles in their respective languages in 1638.

The famous Pilgrims landed at Plymouth Rock in 1620, over 700 years after the Norsemen set foot in the New World. The Pilgrims had the Geneva Bible, as did the Puritans who arrived in 1629.

The Indians obviously could not understand the English and French Bibles, even when read to them. One day John Eliot, a missionary preacher, asked an old brave to pray. The Indian replied, "How can God understand me if He does not speak our tongue?" Eliot set out to prepare a translation in the language of the Massachusetts Indians.

A herculean task lay before Eliot. First, he had to analyze the exotic, tongue-tripping language, then prepare a grammar and dictionary. He spent endless hours searching for Indian terms to describe concepts foreign to Indian ways of life. The Massachusetts Indians had no words for God, temple, father, heaven, and many other biblical terms. Eliot pressed on tirelessly. In 1663, after many trials and bureaucratic delays, he was given an exemption from the law forbidding the printing of Bibles in America. His translation into the difficult Massachusetts language was the first Bible printed in America.

Eighty years later a German Bible was printed illegally in the colonies. There is no clear record of an English version being published in America before 1782. Printed by Robert Aitken, this was the first and only Bible ever recommended for publication by an act of Congress.

Aitken's Bible was merely a copy of the King James. The first distinctly American Bible in English was translated by Charles Thomson and published in four volumes in 1808. A renowned scholar, Thomson had been the first secretary of the United States Congress and the one designated to notify George Washington of his election to the presidency.

The freedom won by the American Revolution was now producing a tidal wave of Bible printing and distribution in America. By 1816 more than 100 Bible societies were distributing Bibles. That year several of the societies merged to form the American Bible Society (ABS). John Jay, the first chief justice of the Supreme Court, was elected the first ABS president.

In 1827 the ABS began providing Scriptures for foreign missionaries. Two years later the society launched a campaign to supply every family in the country with a Bible. Never in the history of the world had such a crusade been undertaken in one nation. The society printed Bibles in every major immigrant tongue. In 1846 the ABS began putting free Bibles into hotels. This mission was later taken up by the Gideons.

The King James version continued to be the most popular. Not until the 1870s did a team of British and American scholars attempt a major revision of the Bible in English. The new Anglo-American New Testament created so much excitement that the *Chicago Tribune*, the *Chicago Times*, and several other newspapers printed the entire new translation in a single edition.

Since the day the first European colonists unpacked a Bible on American soil, the Bible has increased in distribution and popularity. Many new Bible distribution agencies, besides the American Bible Society, have emerged, including the New York Bible Society, the Gideons, and the World Home Bible League. The Bible societies not only distribute copies and portions of Scripture throughout America and other nations, they also publish translations in minority languages for Wycliffe and other missionary translators.

Gideons International was formed in 1899 by two Christian businessmen in a hotel room in Janesville, Wisconsin. In 1908, the association began placing Bibles in hotel rooms. Since then, the Gideons have become active in more than 75 countries and have distributed over 12 million Bibles and 100 million New Testaments to hotels, motels, hospitals, and prisons, and to public nurses, military personnel, and students. For many, many people, a Gideon Bible or Testament is the first Bible they ever read.

Near the beginning of World War II, a layman visited a Christian businessman who lay seriously ill in a hospital. The layman prayed that God would heal William Chapman and call him into Christian service.

Chapman partially recovered and took a trip to Mississippi to regain his strength in a warmer climate. One night he and his wife stopped at a motel in the city of Biloxi. Picking up the Gideon Bible in their room, he said, "Betty, I wonder how many homes in America are without a Bible." Then he remembered the layman's prayer that he might be called into Christian service. That night Chapman vowed that if he lived he would put a Bible in every American home. Thus came the great World Home Bible League.

Allied victory in World War II brought a new spurt in Bible publishing., Soldiers were returning from distant lands telling of miracles wrought by the Bible. One was a young naval officer named John F. Kennedy. The future president recalled that as his PT boat was sinking off a Pacific island, Christian natives came running to help him ashore, singing, "Jesus Loves Me."

Another soldier told of rebuking a South Sea native who came proudly showing off his Bible. "We've outgrown that sort of thing," the American said.

The former cannibal patted his stomach and grinned back. "Good thing for you that we haven't. If it wasn't for this Book, you'd be in here."

Hundreds of these American servicemen, who saw firsthand what the Bible had done among primitive people and fellow soldiers, became missionaries.

Dawson Trotman founded the Navigators in World War II to win sailors to Christ and disciple them in the Christian life by a Scripture memorization program. Trotman became a close friend of Cameron Townsend. One result was that many Navigators joined the Wycliffe Bible Translators and married single women members of the Bible translating organization. A popular saying sprang up among single women called to missions: "Join Wycliffe and get a Navigator." Trotman also became closely associated with Billy Graham and helped the rising young evangelist develop a Bible follow-up program for his converts. Twenty-five years after World War II, three liberal theologians—Thomas J.J. Altizer, Paul van Buren, and William Hamilton—made headlines by proclaiming that the God of the Bible is dead. Now hardly anyone can remember their names, but almost everyone knows and respects the name of Billy Graham.

Look at these sales figures for new Bible translations from 1950-80: Revised Standard Version, 50 million copies; Living Bible, 26 million; Today's English Version, 12 million; New American Standard Version, 14 million. This doesn't include the King James Version, which continues to be the best seller of all Bibles in America. Neither God, nor the Bible He inspired, is dead.

There is no question that more Bibles have been printed and circulated in America than in any other country in the history of the world. But what difference has the Bible made in American history? How has the Bible molded the spirit and ideas of "America the Beautiful?"

First, the Bible made America's founders believe that God had a great destiny for them. They were convinced that God was about to do something special in history. They were excited about being a part of God's great plan for America.

Looking back from this century we can see the seeming hand of Providence at the time of the first settlements. The discoveries of Columbus and other explorers were stirring Europe. Multitudes were looking beyond the Old World with new hope.

Second, Europe was pulsating with revival fires fed by new Bible translations and printings.

Third, many Bible-believing Christians were suffering terrible religious persecution and looking for refuge.

Fourth, new political ideas were in the air. "Radical" scholars and politicians were saying that government should be for the people and by the consent of the people—a concept based upon man's creation in the image of God.

The time was right for the building of a great nation.

Thomas Carlyle dates the beginning of the "soul" of America to the landing of the Pilgrims in 1620. This little band of brave English Christians believed in democracy with responsibility. By their Mayflower Compact, they were one for all and all for one: "We are knit together in a body in a most strict and sacred bond and covenant of the Lord, of the violation whereof we make great conscience, and by virtue whereof we do hold ourselves strictly tied to all care of each other's good, and of the whole by every one, and so mutually."

This sounds a lot like the preamble to the American Constitution which came over 160 years later.

Heart and soul, the Pilgrims believed they were part of a larger destiny. Governor Bradford wrote after they had put down stakes on the rocky Massachusetts shore: "Thus out of small beginnings greater things have been produced by His hand that made all things of nothing, and gives being to things that are; and as one small candle may light a thousand, so the light here kindled hath shone unto many, yea in some sort to our whole nation; let the glorious name of Jehovah have all the praise."

The warm-hearted Pilgrims were more "low church" than the Puritans who began arriving nine years later. But the Puritans soon outnumbered the little band of Pilgrims and absorbed the smaller group. The Puritans saw themselves as the "New Israel," called to build an Old Testament society in New England.

Dissenters were not tolerated. Banished from Massachusetts in 1635, Roger Williams set up a colony in Rhode Island that guaranteed "soul liberty" to all. Williams founded the first Baptist church in America at Providence in 1639. His principle of church government is considered a model for democracy.

Thomas Hooker and three dissenting congregations fled Massachusetts in 1635 and established "an orderly and decent government according to God" in Connecticut. Hooker's "Fundamental Orders of Connecticut" became the prototype for future democratic constitutions.

William Penn was the third member of the great American triumvirate of democracy's forerunners. Penn's "Frame of Government" for the colony of Pennsylvania guaranteed every free man a vote and religious freedom.

Penn said good men were the basis of good laws. "Though good laws do well, good men do better, for good laws may [lack] good men, and be abolished or evaded by ill men; but good men never [lack] good laws nor suffer ill ones."

Good men, Penn declared, would be obedient Christians. "Liberty without obedience," he stated, "is confusion," while "obedience without liberty is slavery." Penn was the first to call for a union of all the colonies and the first to propose a United States of America.

After Williams, Hooker, and Penn passed from the scene, the colonies sunk into low morality. Only about one in 20 persons professed Christianity. Drunkenness and sexual misconduct abounded. Crafty Europeans plied Indians with whiskey to dupe the red men out of their lands. Slave ships disgorged thousands of tribal captives from Africa.

The light of the Bible flickered, then flamed again as the Great Awakening brought cleansing and new moral purity that provided a moral base for the coming Revolution.

From the Bible came the revolutionary new idea of liberty. Four centuries before the American Revolution John Wycliffe declared: "The Bible is for the government of the people by the people for the people." Daniel Webster said after the Revolution: "It is not to be doubted, that to the free and universal reading of the Bible in that age, men were much indebted for right views of civil liberty."

Signing the Declaration of Independence in 1776 took more than ordinary courage. Thomas Jefferson, the principal author, and John Witherspoon, a Presbyterian minister, called on the "protection of Divine Providence" to secure the "certain unalienable rights" with which "all men are created equal" and "endowed by their Creator." The Declaration is a Bible-based document.

Biblical truths gave the outnumbered Americans courage to fight in the Revolutionary War. A Congregationalist announced in a newspaper: "Brethren, we are in a good cause; if God be for us, we need not fear what man can do."

By the winter of 1777 the American cause looked bleak. Many of George Washington's officers were threatening mutiny. If the troops did not freeze to death, it was feared they would starve. Washington dropped to his knees in prayer, and from that time morale and strength picked up. The American soldiers survived the terrible winter and emerged in the spring with stamina for victory. Washington would later say, "It is impossible to rightly govern . . . without God and the Bible."

The leaders of the new nation met in Philadelphia to write a Constitution. But they couldn't agree on many points, and it looked as if the body might dissolve in wrangling. At the darkest moment venerable Benjamin Franklin, 83, stood and asked that "prayers imploring the assistance of heaven, and its blessings on our deliberations, be held in this assembly every morning before we proceed to business."

Not all of the elected delegates to the Constitutional Convention were orthodox Christians who believed in the divine inspiration of the Bible. Jefferson, for one, did not accept the supernatural parts, yet he said, "The studious perusal of the Sacred Volume will make better citizens, better fathers, and better husbands."

The Christian sabbath was recognized in the expression "Sundays excepted." If a bill passed by Congress was not returned signed or vetoed by the president within ten days, "Sundays excepted," it would become law.

The First Amendment did not separate government from God. It only says that "Congress shall make no law respecting an establishment of religion, or prohibiting the free exercise thereof." At the time several states, following patterns of European nations, still had "official" churches, while others did not. The architects of the Constitution wanted only to prohibit Congress from favoring one denomination over another.

America's founders could hardly have been more clear. Yet there are people today who mistakenly believe that it is unconstitutional to have prayer before an official meeting. Some would erase "In God We Trust" from coins and currency and dismiss all chaplains from the military services. Such extremists have pressured courts in some localities to remove all religious symbols and traditions from Christmas. Recently, for example, a court ruled that "Silent Night" could not be played as Christmas music at O'Hare Airport in Chicago. The ablest lawyers and legislators I know tell me the basic laws of the states of the American federal government are based upon the Ten Commandments and English common law.

No one is above the law. Senator Sam Ervin, former chairman of the Senate Watergate Committee, said: "Every man must stand equal before the law no matter how high or how low his place in society. And if any man goes out and violates the law, he must be punished like every other man."

The influence of the Bible is amply evident in American literature, music, and art, especially before 1920. I do not know of a single American poet, novelist, or essayist, writing prior to 1920, whose work does not to some extent reflect the influence of the Bible. The gloomy Edgar Allen Poe, to cite only one example, is not my favorite writer. Yet Dr. William Mentzel Forrest, a distinguished professor of literature at the University of Virginia, analyzed Poe's works and found hundreds of biblical quotations and allusions. Said Dr. Forrest: "There is no mystery about [Poe's] familiarity with Scripture. He absorbed it from his environment; he met it in literature he critically examined; he was taught it in childhood and youth; he studied it in mature years.

America's first books were religious books. Biblical themes permeated most popular novels into the early 20th century. Religious novels ranked among the top best sellers for generations. *Uncle Tom's Cabin, In His Steps,* and *Ben Hur,* all religious novels of the 19th century, are still considered classics.

In a previous chapter, I cited the influence of *Uncle Tom's Cabin* in the fight to overthrow slavery. Charles Sheldon's *In His Steps* is the story of a small band of Christians who covenanted to follow as closely as possible in the steps of Christ. Their lives were forever changed.

The novel by Sheldon—a Congregational minister—was first printed in serial form in a Christian magazine. He failed to copyright the story, and it was thus thrown into the public domain. Few of the companies who published the serial as a book paid the author royalties. Sheldon was not bitter. The lack of a copyright, he believed, made more publishers willing to print and promote the book. This was reward enough for him. The novel still sells well today, almost a century after it was first published.

Interestingly, a modern novel, *In His Steps Today,* follows the same story line, except the characters are 20th century people in a Chicago suburb. Author Marti Hefley read Sheldon's book at 16 and waited 20 years for someone to write an up-to-date version. When no one came forward, she penned her story. The theme of biblical discipleship is timeless.

Ben Hur is better known as a film epic than as a novel. The movie is recent; the book was written by General Lew Wallace in the last century.

Wallace began his research into the life of Christ with "no convictions about God or Christ. I neither believed nor disbelieved," he said. The noted agnostic and popular lecturer Robert Ingersoll challenged Wallace to make up his mind. Wallace later wrote: "Before I was through with my book, I had become a believer."

Christian oriented books have made a dramatic comeback in recent years. You would not know this by the *New York Times'* and *Time* magazine's bestseller lists. A typical non-fiction work classified as a bestseller has sold from 60,000 to 120,000 copies; fiction works can make the list with fewer sales. Christian books rarely appear on these lists, even though each year some sell far more copies than many of the so-called best sellers. The reason for the non-appearance of Christian bestsellers is that the lists in *The New York Times* and *Time* are compiled from sales in bookstores which carry few Christian books, not from representative Christian bookstores that are members of the Christian Booksellers Association.

Most American music before the "swinging" 1920s was permeated by Bible themes and expressions. I find it interesting that almost all of the older country music stars in Nashville began their careers singing hymns and gospel songs in churches. Folk music expresses the deepest beliefs of a people.

Christian music has also made a comeback in recent years. Contemporary gospel and other Christian music now make up a large portion of record sales in the U.S. This is in large part owing to the playing and performing of Christian music over the hundreds of Christian radio and television stations which now dot the country.

The Bible's influence on American education before World War II was of a magnitude that is hardly believable to those who attended the more secularized schools of the last thirty years.

For over 200 years, after the landing of the Pilgrims, classroom education in America tended to be Bible-centered and under the sponsorship of Christian denominations and associations. The first public school system in America was established in New York in 1633 by the Dutch Reformed Church and financed by tax revenues. Not until 1842 did the city of New York take over the Protestant Public School Society.

Quakers set up the public school system in Philadelphia. Puritans provided education for all children in New England. The preamble to the Puritan school law of 1647 purposed to thwart the "old Deluder [Satan] that learning may not be buried in ye grave. . . . "

Pupils learned the alphabet from the famous New England Primer by catechetical verse, beginning, "In Adam's fall/we sinned all." They memorized Bible facts, verses, prayers, and the Apostle's Creed and learned Bible-based moral lessons from this primer. Similar texts followed. One researcher surveyed schoolbooks up to 1776 and found that 92 percent of the subject matter was permeated by biblical ideas.

For at least a hundred years after the Revolution the texts continued much the same. The best known schoolbook of the early 19th century was Noah Webster's *Blue-backed Speller*. It began with this prayer: "No man may put off the law of God. My joy is in His law all the day. O may I not go in the way of sin. Let me not go in the way of ill men."

The "American Schoolmaster," as Webster was popularly known, is most remembered for his dictionaries, which were later highly edited. Few Americans know that this evangelical choirmaster of a Congregational church encapsulated biblical ideas in definitions for his original dictionary. For example:

"Hope: A well founded Scriptural hope is, in our religion, the source of ineffable happiness."

"Love: The Christian loves his Bible. If our hearts are right, we love God above all things."

The McGuffey Readers, written by a Presbyterian minister, were even more popular than Webster's *Blue-backed Speller*. Total sales reached 122 million copies and are now undergoing a revival of interest. *The Readers'* moral teachings are based on the Bible.

When public school systems began coming under wider community control, no one really became alarmed, according to historian Timothy L. Smith. An evangelical consensus of faith and ethics had come to so dominate the national culture that a majority of Protestants were now willing to entrust the state with the task of educating children, confident that education would be religious still."

This expectation was too high. Secular thought gradually enveloped public education. Several factors were involved. America became more pluralistic in population. Darwin's dogma of evolution captured the minds of many intellectuals. German higher criticism swept the theological moorings from under some denominations. But the major molder of secular education was John Dewey, who was born the year (1859) that Darwin's *Origin of Species* was published. Dewey convinced many educators that the goal of education should be to help students adjust to change and change to adjust. Truth, Dewey held, is not fixed, but always in process and changing. The Bible, he said, is merely a reflection of cultural change in past societies. Religion is a product of culture, invented by man to ward off evil influences and to gratify his appetites.

Dewey's ideas developed into the dogma of "progressive" education which dominates American public school curriculum and teaching today.

As for higher education, America's oldest colleges and universities were established by Bible-based denominations, primarily to train ministers. Look at this list of schools and their founders: Harvard, 1636, by New England Puritans; William and Mary, 1693, by Anglicans; Yale, 1701, by Congregationalists; Princeton, 1746, by Presbyterians; Columbia, 1754, by Anglicans; Brown, 1765, by Baptists; Rutgers, 1766, by Dutch Reformed churches; Dartmouth, 1770, by Congregationalists.

The last five of these were direct fruits of the Great Awakening. Another school, Dartmouth, was founded to train missionaries to the Indians. Dartmouth's official seal proclaims *Vox Clamantis in Deserto* ("the voice of one crying in the wilderness," Matthew 3:3). And virtually all the elite women's colleges in the East (including Vassar, Wellesley, Radcliffe, Smith, and Mount Holyoke) were established to train women for missionary service.

Many more colleges and universities were established after the Revolution by Bible-believing Christian denominations and organizations. Only a minority remain true to the intent of their founders. One is Wheaton College, founded in 1860. A leading abolitionist, Jonathan Blanchard, was Wheaton's first president. Both Mawii and I received Bible-centered training at this fine college. All three of our children are graduates.

The Bible further made America into the most caring nation of the world. No matter what you've seen in the movies, America's real founders did not first fall on their knees and then on the aborigines. The Pilgrim fathers invited the red men to their Thanksgiving feasts, nursed sick Indians, provided jobs, and taught the American natives the Bible. Some Americans did treat Indians badly, violating their women and cheating tribes of their ancestral lands. It is unfortunate that we often hear only this side of the story from some modern novelists and film makers who are only parading their ignorance.

Much also has been made of the cruelty of whites in driving the educated and Christianized Cherokees off their lands in Georgia and Tennessee and forcing them to march along the infamous Trail of Tears to a reservation in Oklahoma. Hundreds collapsed in hunger and exhaustion and were left to die along the way. All this is true. But we don't hear so much about the dear Christian missionaries who fought the Cherokee removal and then walked the Trail of Tears with their brothers and sisters, offering consolation from the Bible.

Americans still give more money to charity than any other nation in the world. Many of this nation's charitable institutions have become secularized to the extent that some have almost lost their original identity. Organizations such as the United Way, the YMCA, and Goodwill flowed from great outbursts of caring that followed national revivals. In response to the biblical mandate to care, Americans of the first half of the 19th century produced a league of societies to promote social welfare, fight slavery, help the poor, overcome drunkenness, combat injustice, and strengthen morality. They carried such names as the American Tract Society, the American Female Moral Reform

Society, the Association for the Relief of Respectable Aged, the Fund for Pious Uses, the Philadelphia Society for the Encouragement of Faithful Domestics, and the Connecticut Society for the Reformation of Morals.

Many Americans also do not know that some of their greatest healing institutions were founded by Bible-believing Christians in obedience to Christ's command to heal the sick. Massachusetts General Hospital, Boston City Hospital, Philadelphia Hospital, and Bellevue Hospital of New York City are just four of many that were established by Bible believers.

There is not space to list all the caring institutions in America founded upon the Bible. Many societies lasted only a few years. Some are still in existence, as for example, the American Tract Society and the American Bible Society. Some evolved into broader outreaches. The Fund for Pious Uses was a precursor of modern pension plans and Social Security. The original Fund was a depository for the pensions of retired Presbyterian ministers and their widows. Now known as the Presbyterian Ministers' Fund, it insures thousands of ministers and religious workers.

Many, many Biblical arms of caring go relatively unheralded today. The Evangelical Child Welfare Assocation serves scores of ministries that provide loving care for needy and abused children. Many ministries to pregnant, unwed girls operate out of local churches, such as the one at First Baptist Church, Euless, Texas. The national organization Birthright helps young women avoid the tragedy of abortion. Bethany Christian Services, the nation's largest adoption agency, provides permanent homes for hundreds of children each year. Bethany's philosophy of adoption, according to Sheryl Johnson, a director and social worker, "is molded after the biblical concept of adoption into God's family. The Scriptures are clear," she says, "that God sent His Son to redeem those under law that we might receive adoption as sons."

One of the most notable Bible-based rescue missions is Four State Christian Missions in Hagerstown, Maryland. A quarter century ago Jimmy and Ellen Resh opened a rescue mission for down-and-outers in an old house behind the city jail. They lived upstairs in a dingy apartment with five small children. From this small beginning has come rescue missions in Hagerstown and seven nearby towns. The Hagerstown mission rehabilitates alcoholics, provides jobs for the unemployed, sponsors summer camps in the country for poor children, operates a chain of thrift stores, and serves as a relief agency for the whole area. Any burned-out family can come to the mission and get furniture and a new start. The mission's motto is: "If you haven't a friend in the world, you have one here." Four States Christian Missions, like most Biblical ministries of its types, receives no federal aid or tax money.

Bible-inspired caring in America has gone far beyond the many private institutions and organizations that serve the needy at home and as missionary ministries on every continent. Even greater caring has been expressed in vast outpourings of giving and personal service.

On April 24, 1915, an estimated 600,000 Armenian Christians were brutally murdered by sword-wielding Muslims in Turkey. Generous Americans gave over $100 million to the Near East Relief Fund for the survivors. The Bible prepared America for such generosity.

In 1921 Americans provided millions in relief to stave off mass starvation in Communist Russia. During World War II America gave billions of dollars worth of "lend-lease" supplies to the Soviet Union, China, and Great Britain. After the war America sent $13 billion in food, machinery, and other products to both former allies and enemies in Europe and Asia. America also took in hundreds of thousands of war refugees after World War II. More recently, American Christian relief agencies provided medicines and other aid to victims of the terrible 1988 earthquake in Soviet Armenia.

Following the end of American's involvement in the Vietnam War, America received more thousands of refugees. At the same time Americans gave millions of dollars in food and medicine to stave off starvation among refugees in suffering Southeast Asia.

My country of India has received hundreds of millions of dollars of free aid from the United States. Whenever I hear one of my fellow citizens criticizing America, I stop to remind him of all that America has given away. The Bible, more than anything else, made America a caring nation.

You would expect me to say something about the churches in America and their great missionary programs. Sixty percent of Americans belong to around 350,000 churches. They give billions every year for Christian causes at home and abroad. Southern Baptists alone give well over $100 million to foreign missions every year.

I have not mentioned the material prosperity of America. A few nations now have a higher per capita income than the United States. But more people are prospering in America than anywhere else. This prosperity, I believe, is the fruit of her Bible heritage.

Yes, America has problems. Not because of the Bible, but because the nation has drifted into secularism. The secularization of the public schools and the blatant bias of the entertainment industry and the secular mass media against Biblical Christianity have, among other things, produced a generation that knows not the Bible.

Prayer and Bible reading in public school classes and assemblies have been ruled unconstitutional. School curriculum has been bowdlerized of moral values which guided generations past. A particular disaster in public education has been the so-called values education which teaches that every person is his own moral authority. Children have been denied the knowledge of their nation's religious heritage by secular zealots.

Immorality is flaunted on TV. Child pornography has become a billion-dollar enterprise. Millions of Americans are addicted to alcohol, cocaine, and other dangerous drugs. Over a million unborn babies are murdered each year in abortion clinics. Guess who is leading the fight for renewal and moral change? Again, it is organizations which operate on Biblical ideals, such as James Dobson's Focus on the Family, National Right to Life, Concerned Women of America, Teen Challenge, The National Coalition Against Pornography, The National Federation for Decency, and Mel and Norma Gabler's Educational Research Analysts.

The Gablers have been particularly effective in getting better curriculum into public schools. Their crusade for the restoration of America's religious heritage in curriculum is now being taken up by liberal groups who have suddenly discovered this lack. At a recent meeting in Chicago, several scholars said the great sin of omission in America's history texts is the dearth of material presenting the nation's religious heritage. The Gablers were saying this for 20 years, when they were being branded as "right wing kooks."

America has strayed far from its Judeo-Christian Biblical foundations. Yet in thousands of ways every day the influence of the Bible upon this great country is still being felt. God bless America. May she return to her biblical heritage and her source of true greatness.

Chapter 10

"The Book That Builds the Church"

A long time ago, when I was just nine years of age, I was sitting in a little bamboo church in the Hmar village of Phulpui, listening to my father preach. I had been thinking about becoming a Christian. "Ro," my father had said to me, "it says right here in God's Book that He will forgive you and accept you into His family if you will believe and take Jesus as your Savior."

Now Father was extending an evangelistic invitation. "If you truly believe and want to follow Jesus, you will not be ashamed to say so publicly," he declared.

I hesitated, looking around to see if anyone was watching, then I walked down the aisle between the rough benches. "My father, I want to give my name to Jesus. I believe, and I have asked Jesus to forgive me."

Father looked me straight in the eye. "Has He, my son?"

"Yes, my Father. If it is written in His Book that He will forgive those who ask Him, I know God would not lie."

"It is written in His Book," Father assured me.

Since that day when I set out to follow the God of the Bible, I have spoken and worshiped in some of the greatest churches in the world. I have seen thousands accept the Bible promises on forgiveness and salvation. I have noticed that churches grow where God's Book is available and proclaimed, and that churches do not grow where the Bible is not proclaimed.

The church that is composed of all true believers is a mighty oak that has grown from a little acorn. Sometimes when I get discouraged I take an imaginary trip back through nineteen-and-a-half centuries to that crowded upper room in Jerusalem where a small band of believers were praying. The last few weeks had been momentous beyond description. Their Messiah had been arrested, tried, and crucified. Three days later He rose from the dead. For 40 more days He was on earth, giving His disciples personal instructions for carrying on His work. Then after telling them to wait in prayer for the coming of the Holy Spirit, He promised: " . . . You shall receive power when the Holy Spirit has come upon you; and you shall be My witnesses both in Jerusalem, and in all Judea and Samaria, and even to the remotest part of the earth" (Acts 1:8 NASB). The next thing they knew He was gone, ascended into heaven.

Jesus departed, leaving only 120 believers in that upper room. How many are there now, believing, worshiping, and serving Him on this great planet?

To get this and other information for the *World Christian Encyclopedia* (published in 1982), Dr. David B. Barrett, an evangelical Anglican missionary, spent 14 years, traveling to 212 countries and consulting with 500 local experts. His tally came to 1,433,000,000 in all nations. These, however, are professing Christians. We have no way of knowing how many are true believers.

From 120 to 1,433,000,000 is a staggering increase of almost 12,000,000 percent.

But we can't congratulate ourselves—yet. This is still less than one third of the world's population. And the percentage of professing Christians to world population has actually been dropping since 1980 and at present rates will continue declining until we find more fruitful methods of proclaiming God's Word more effectively to more people.

Here are the figures (in millions) from the *World Christian Encyclopedia*, with the projection for the year 2000 if the recent trend continues:

	1900	1980	2000
World population	1,620	4,374	6,260
Number of professing Christians	558	1,433	2,020
% of Christians to world population	29.03%	30.52%	30.99%

Three large non-Christian belief systems have been increasing faster than Christianity and are expected to continue to outgrow the Church.

Hindus advanced from 12.5 percent of world population in 1900 to 13.3 percent in 1980. By the year 2000 Hindus are expected to comprise 13.7 percent (859 million) of world population.

Muslims have been growing even faster—from 12.4 percent of world population in 1900 to 16.5 percent in 1980. At present growth rates Muslims will rise to 19.2 percent (1,201 million) by A.D. 2000.

The fastest growing belief system in this century is classified "non-religious and atheists." Starting with only two-tenths of one percent of the world's inhabitants in 1900, unbelievers bounded to 20.8 percent by 1980 and are expected to compose 21.3 percent (1,334,000) of mankind by the year 2000.

Christianity is losing ground fastest in the "Christian" West. Westerners are dropping out of the church at a rate of 7,600 per day, while Africa is reaping 4,000 Christians per day by conversion from other religions and gaining three times that many through the birth rate. Dr. Barrett notes that in 1900 two-thirds of the world's Christians lived in Europe and Russia. If present predictions hold, by the dawn of the next century, three-fifths of the church will reside in Africa, Asia, and Latin America.

The biggest Christian losses in the West are in Europe, where Islam and atheism are making rapid gains. The major reason is that many Christian institutions in Europe have ceased to proclaim the Bible as the inspired, infallible Word of God.

Roman Catholics are still increasing in number. Eastern Orthodox and "mainline" Protestants (Anglican, Episcopalians, Methodists, Presbyterians, American Lutherans, the United Church of Christ, the American Baptist Churches USA, and a few others) have been losing ground. Many denominational leaders and congregations in these denominations have drifted from Biblical foundations.

Indigenous evangelical churches in the Third World, which fervently preach and teach the Bible as the Word of God, are growing fastest. Some individual congregations have tens of thousands of members. The Church of Jotabeche in Chile, for example, has 60,000 members and 18 pastors. Each week 15,000 members meet for prayer and street evangelism; 15,000 gather in homes for Bible study; 15,000 assemble in small prayer meetings; and 15,000 attend the church worship service in the building which will only hold that many.

The latest reports and research merely confirm what I've observed among my own Hmar people and wherever I've traveled throughout the world: Where the Bible is freely circulated in the language of the people and taught as inspired by God, the church goes forward. Where the seed of God's Word is faithfully and prayerfully sown and cultivated, the church grows. Many receive the good seed of the Word joyfully, allow it to take root, and bear much fruit (see Mark 4:1-20).

Every evangelical leader and authority on church growth agrees that this is true. When Simon Ibraiham, general secretary of the Evangelical Church of West Africa, received his first copy of the Bible in the Hausa language, he said, "It is important to remember that you cannot evangelize without the Scriptures . . . in the language of the people."

Morris Watkins, a Lutheran missionary leader, says, "We know of no permanent indigenous church that did not have the Scriptures in its own language, and at least one leader who was able to read those Scriptures or who had committed to memory a large amount of Scripture.

Dr. Sherwood Wirt, longtime editor of Billy Graham's *Decision* magazine, told me in an interview: "During my sixteen years as editor I wrote more editorials about the authority of the Bible than about any other subject. One reason was that I knew a lot of Christians were struggling with this question. Another was that for years I struggled with it; and not until I had been an ordained minister for eleven years did the Lord give me peace about my relationship to His Word. I ceased being a non-Bible person and joined the Bible people. I stopped being an authority on Scripture because I learned that Scripture was in fact an authority on me. I think of the Bible not as a relic, or an artifact, or a record of a historical movement. It is a rapier of steel, to be seized and used to pierce men's consciences and to ward off the enemy. God never intended His Word to be bound in morocco and placed on a shelf. He did not send it to the world for the convenience of clergymen or the edification of scholars. He did not send it to keep kings in power. He wrote the Bible for you and me, and He sees to it that the message is trustworthy."

Dr. Billy Graham has preached to more people than any person who ever lived. His power is in the Bible. His most characteristic way of prefacing a statement about truth and morality is, "The Bible says . . ." His biographer, John Pollock, reports Dr. Graham telling a meeting of 2,400 British ministers: "There is authority when this Book is quoted. And the more Scripture I quote the greater number of people come and respond to the invitation; I found that out night after night. The Word of God, even though the hearer doesn't understand all about it, somehow becomes a hammer and a sword that hurts and cuts and convicts and washes and cleanses. . . . "

All the great evangelists and pastors I have ever read or heard were men of the Bible. The Bible has been the Book that built the church from the first century until today. Declares A.M. Chirgwin in his excellent study, *The Bible in World Evangelism*: " . . . The weapon that is more needed than any other [in world evangelism] is at hand . . . . It is the weapon par excellence of the Church's warfare which, if well wielded, may have a large part in winning the world for Christ. It is the Bible."

Return with me to Jerusalem in the first century. As the 120 disciples of Christ waited in prayer, a multitude of devout Jews speaking eighteen languages arrived to celebrate the Feast of Pentecost.

Suddenly there was a roar like a violent, rushing wind that filled the whole house. Everybody was startled. Dancing tongues of fire lighted on the disciples as they proclaimed the Good News that Jesus died and rose from the dead.

The foreign visitors were amazed at this miracle: "'How is it that we each hear them in our own language to which we were born? . . . What does this mean?' Others, mocking, said, 'They are full of sweet wine'" (Acts 2:8,12,13 NASB).

Peter, the spokesman for the 120, stood to explain: "These men are not drunk, as you suppose, for it is only the third hour [nine a.m.] of the day; but this is what was spoken of through the prophet Joel . . . . " (Acts 2:15,16, NASB). Peter proclaimed the Bible (see vv. 17-36), setting the precedent for the growth of the church from the sowing of the seed of the Word.

That very day 3,000 souls were added to the church (v. 41). The next verse reads: "And they were continually devoting themselves to the apostles' teaching and to fellowship, to the breaking of bread and to prayer." They first gave attention to the apostles' teaching—the oral Word of God, for the New Testament was not yet written down. What was the result? "The Lord was adding to their number day by day those who were being saved" (v. 47, NASB).

One afternoon, a few days later, Peter and John were entering the temple for prayer when a lame beggar asked them for money. "Look at us!" Peter commanded (Acts 3:4, NASB). The beggar lifted his eyes expecting a coin. "I do not possess silver and gold, but what I do have I give to you: In the name of Jesus Christ the Nazarene—walk!" Peter seized the beggar by the right hand and pulled him up. The beggar felt strength return to his withered limbs and began "walking and leaping and praising God" (Acts 3:4-9, NASB).

People came running from everywhere, giving Peter another opportunity to proclaim God's Word: "But the things which God announced beforehand by the mouth of all the prophets, that His Christ should suffer, He has thus fulfilled" (vs. 18, NASB). Peter then referred them to Deuteronomy 1:15,18, where Moses predicted: "The Lord God shall raise up for you a prophet like me from your brethren; to Him you shall give heed in everything He says to you" (Acts 3:22, NASB).

This time 5,000 were converted (Acts 4:4). What marvelous church growth. Eight thousand new believers within a few days, plus the additions mentioned in Acts 2:47.

So it goes throughout the thrilling saga of the early church as recorded in Acts. When persecution came, forcing the new believers to scatter, what happened? They went "everywhere preaching the Word" (8:4). The Bible is the Book that builds the church.

It cannot be said often enough: As goes the Bible, so grows the church. During the early centuries the church grew rapidly in the Middle East. When the Bible became unavailable, a powerful Islamic tide almost wiped out Christianity in that region. Many great church sanctuaries were converted to mosques. Churches that survived were forbidden to evangelize. This situation persists in many Middle Eastern countries today.

How did it happen? Historians cite a number of factors: When persecution stopped, the church became more comfortable, centralized, bureaucratic, political, and indifferent to the missionary mandate. Doctrinal quarrels and power struggles among church leaders chilled the spirit of love. Pagan "mystery" cults led many uninstructed Christians astray. The Roman Empire weakened and divided, bringing political uncertainty. But the main reason for the church's losses in the cradle of its birth was this: The church leadership failed to have the Bible translated and distributed in the indigenous languages.

This tragedy continued until the Reformation. In Europe where the militant Muslims were turned back, Bible reading had been confined to monasteries and bishops' palaces. The Reformation broke down the doors and freed the Word of God for translation, printing, and distribution.

Still it was not until William Carey founded the modern missionary movement—almost 200 years later—that the church regained its passion for world missions.

Where does the church stand in missions today? Can the missionary force now in service evangelize the world? Around 65,000 trained, career, full-time evangelical missionaries serve outside their home countries today. Fifty-six percent of these, according to P. J. Johnstone's handbook *Operation World*, are from the United States, which provides 90 percent of all funds for world missions. Some 10 to 15 thousand missionaries are supported from outside North America and Britain.

By adding the 16,000 Campus Crusade for Christ staff members, we arrive at a total of around 80,000 missionaries. At least one-fourth of these 80,000 will be home on furlough at any given time, some for as long as a year. This leaves 60,000 active on fields of service. To these let us add an estimated 15,000 short-term workers who go to assist the career missionaries. This brings the number back up to 75,000 missionaries who are assigned to five billion people—an average of one missionary for every 66,667 persons in the world.

But at least half of these 75,000 are not engaged in direct Bible ministry. They are doing very good work as teachers, doctors, nurses, agriculturists, etc., but they are not giving full-time to personal evangelism, preaching, broadcasting, and Bible and literature distribution. This brings us to one missionary evangelist for every 133,334 persons.

However, through no fault of their own, the missionaries are not evenly distributed. The People's Republic of China, with slightly over one-fifth of the world's population, does not admit career missionaries from other nations. Nor does the Soviet Union and most other Communist countries. My country, India, which has almost 800 million people, will not accept missionaries involved in direct church-related evangelism. Indonesia, population 180 million, is one of a number of predominantly Muslim countries which places severe restrictions on missionary residencies. Visa restrictions by Indonesia may force nearly two thirds of the resident missionaries to leave this year.

This gloomy pattern is expected to broaden until by the year 2000, 100 countries out of 250 are expected to deny visas to foreign missionaries from the West.

Furthermore, there are "pockets" of "hidden peoples" which until recent years have been almost entirely overlooked by mission strategists. Dr. Ralph Winter, general director of the Center for World Mission, and World Vision have identified 16,750 groups of "hidden peoples" who have no churches and are not being reached. These are not small groups of a few hundred people. Some number in the millions.

Dr. Winter estimates that 95 percent of all career evangelical missionaries are working among three categories of people: existing churches, newly founded churches, and in cultures where the gospel has already penetrated. Only one of every 171 full-time Christian workers is presently trying to reach the hidden peoples.

Dr. Keith Parks, President of the Southern Baptist Foreign Mission Board, recently convened a meeting of mission leaders to ask: "How can we enhance what each other is doing and reach the world." From that meeting came a call on the whole Christian world to join in a period of fasting and prayer for world evangelization. Afterwards, Dr. Parks announced that his agency would "try to take on at least 400" of the hidden people groups.

What results are our missionaries getting in the countries where they are working? How many nationals are they training in Bible evangelism? How many people are coming to Christ as a direct or indirect result of foreign missionary work? This is difficult to determine since some missionary agencies report "decisions for Christ," while others record only convert baptisms.

The Southern Baptist Foreign Mission Board is the largest sending agency of any denomination. At the end of 1987 Southern Baptists reported having 3,839 missionaries serving on 112 foreign fields. The SBC reported 14,727,770 members in 37,286 churches at home, giving $165,233,000 to foreign missions. This averages out to $11.22 in annual giving per member for ministry abroad.

The SBC's foreign mission agency reports that related churches baptized 203,824 persons during 1987. This is over twice the number of convert baptisms reported just seven years before. By dividing the number of baptisms into the total expenditure by the SBC for foreign missions, we find that $810.67 was required, on average, for each convert, not including expenditures by national churches.

Methodist, Presbyterian, and Lutheran foreign mission agencies probably incur more in average expenditures for each convert. Some smaller denominations, notably the Christian and Missionary Alliance, do much better on the average. This, of course, does not take into consideration the many worthy non-evangelistic ministries which missionaries perform.

The Southern Baptists are goal oriented. They expect to have 5,000 missionaries on the field by the year 2000. I pray that this worthy goal will be met. Even so, 5,000 Southern Baptist missionaries cannot by themselves evangelize the world.

Let's look at the Interdenominational Foreign Missions Association (IFMA) to which the so-called "mainline" denominations do not belong. Allen Finley and Lorry Lutz, in *Mission—A World Family*

Affair, noted that in 1978 the IFMA, with 49 member agencies, reported a total career missionary force of 10,662 missionaries (including those serving in home offices). By 1980 the IFMA missionary force had grown to 10,679, a net gain of only 17 persons in two years.

The Evangelical Foreign Missions association (EFMA), with 81 member organizations and 7,632 career missionaries, actually declined in personnel by two-tenths of one percent over the same period.

What of the great mainline denominations? Except for Southern Baptists, the record of those affiliated with the National Council of Churches (NCC) is dismal. In 1957, 42 percent of American missionaries were related to the NCC. This is now down to five percent.

What of the great missionary-supporting churches? Dr. Harold Ockenga served the famous Park Street Congregational Church of Boston for 40 years before retirement. While he was pastor, that church helped support 142 missionaries at a cost of $250,000 a year. In 1959, Park Street church gave $786,000 to support 88 missionaries. The church now gives around $500,000 per year to support 40 to 50 missionaries. (Several other large evangelical churches have similar missionary programs.) Many of Park Street's missionaries must also secure additional support from other churches and individuals, for it presently costs an average of more than $30,000 a year to keep a missionary family on the field. Inflation will keep that figure escalating in the years ahead.

God forbid that anyone should think I am trying to "put down" foreign missions. I support the foreign missionaries of my own church. I thank God for every person won to Christ on the various mission fields. My point is simply that the world cannot be evangelized by career missionaries alone.

It would take 4,000 missionaries at least a thousand years to speak just once to every person in India about Christ, even if the population stopped growing at the present rate of over a million persons each month! We simply cannot reach India and the world by depending on missionaries alone.

This thesis is not unique with me. Missionary leaders have been saying for years that we must develop more strategies for reaching the unreached.

What about electronic media? Isn't everybody now within the "sound" of the gospel by television, radio, or cassette player cassette? And if this isn't so, won't it be true in just a few years?

The electronic media has brought us almost to the age of Buck Rogers. Theoretically it is possible to send Christian programs by satellite into every home on earth. We have the technology. Yet this is not likely to be a reality for many years, if ever.

Satellite dishes are available in almost all countries, but radio and TV receivers are limited. There is an average of two radios in every American home and one TV set for every two Americans. But broadcast sets are not so abundant in some of the most populous countries. Bangladesh has only six radios for every 1,000 persons. Ethiopia has only seven. India does better with 33 radios per thousand population.

However, most of the broadcasting sets are concentrated in pockets of affluence. Once I was in New Delhi, and the head of the government broadcast service asked me to give a 15-minute goodwill broadcast for the Mizo tribal people of northeast India. I asked him, "Out of 100,000 Mizos, how many do you think will have radios?" He said, "Oh, maybe about 200." Then I remembered hearing a Christian broadcaster say that he was "blanketing" that whole area with the gospel.

A second reason the world cannot be reached by Christian broadcast media within the next few years is that gospel programs are available in so few languages. I would guess that 90 percent or more of all religious broadcasting in the world is in English. Some of these broadcasts in other languages—particularly the missionary outreaches of the Far East Broadcasting Company, Trans World Radio, and HCJB in Quito, Ecuador—are very effective.

This does not take into consideration the excellent Bible-on-cassette ministries provided by some missionaries to isolated tribes. It is a simple and beautiful idea. A Christian in a tribal village is given an inexpensive tape player and several cassettes in the local language. He calls together his neighbors to hear the Bible messages. Worthy as they are, the cassette ministries cannot possibly fill the language gap in broadcasting.

A third reason is that religious broadcasting tends—by economic necessity—to go where the donors are. Listener gifts in Kenya, for example, cannot finance a Christian radio station. Support must come from outside the country. Many governments will not allow foreigners to operate a radio or TV station in their countries.

But there is hardly anywhere in the United States where you cannot pick up a Christian radio station when driving. Each of the large metro areas has a number of Christian stations from which to choose, along with Christian programs on secular stations. There are sufficient donors to support these Christian stations and the programs on other broadcast outlets.

I am certainly not opposed to Christian radio stations and programs. I am blessed by listening, especially when I am on the road in my car.

I am only saying that the world is not going to be won by electronic media alone. Beware of any broadcaster who tells you that. And I have not mentioned cultural problems in communication and the impermanence of a broadcast message.

What about missionary literature? Well, I know of no organization doing more than Bruce Wilkinson's "Walk Thru the Bible Ministries" and Dale Kietzman's "Every Home for Christ" (EHC), the new name for World Literature Crusade. Bruce Wilkinson first presented his idea "to take people on a walk thru the Bible step by step" as a thesis for his studies at Dallas Theological Seminary. The idea developed into *Daily Walk*, a publication that takes the reader through the Bible in a year while offering scriptural insight and application for each day. To date, more than 40 million of the devotional guides have been published.

Every Home for Christ is entering its 42nd year and is distributing good Christian reading material in at least 60 countries. During one year EHC distributed over a million pieces of Bible-based literature and received many cards recording a spiritual decision of some sort.

Other groups are also getting the gospel message out with literature and achieving wonderful results. Thank God for missionary literature. We're just waking up to the fact that Communists are providing most of the reading material for many persons whom Christians have taught to read. In India 70 percent of all literature reportedly comes from Marxists.

But allow me to make this comment. A tract or booklet represents some particular interpretation and application of Scripture. There is even subjectivity in the verses chosen for a Scripture tract. The finest literature cannot replace the pure Word of God.

The Bible is the best missionary tool for evangelizing the world and for building the church. "The Word of God is living and active and sharper than any two-edged sword, and piercing as far as the division of soul and spirit, of both joints and marrow, and able to judge the thoughts and intentions of the heart." God promises, "So shall My Word be which goes forth from My mouth; it shall not return to me empty, without accomplishing what I desire, and without succeeding in the matter for which I sent it" (Hebrews 4:12; Isaiah 55:11, NASB).

The Bible is more than a tool. It is the best of all missionaries. One day, over a quarter century ago, while reflecting on this great truth, I felt a sudden surge of inspiration. I wrote: "I have seen hundreds of missionaries both at home and abroad, but I want to tell you of the missionary I love most. He has deeply influenced my heart and greatly enriched my life. He is the missionary after my heart, and God's heart too. Given a chance, he would conquer the world within our generation. Surprisingly, this missionary idol of mine is the frailest of all missionaries I have met. He looks thin, ill clad, despised. He can hardly stand upright and spends most of his days leaning upon others. He cannot walk a block unless transportation is provided for him. He sits speechless most of the time, though he loves to talk to someone. He loves to be handled like a little child, but he is so frail that a child can mistreat him or a drunken man can trample him under his feet. I have seen this amazing missionary at work. Fifty years ago he was sent to India to evangelize a sin-degraded headhunting mountain people. When he arrived in the village, the chief examined his credentials and issued him a permit to stay. Before long, everyone was impressed with his message, and night after night people came to see him. He was so humble that everyone loved him. His long-suffering and gentleness especially impressed the people. He was calm even when the children handled him roughly. Before long, five men, including the chief, announced their willingness to accept his message. Since that day, the missionary has multiplied his witness a thousand times. He has learned many new languages while traveling much of the time. He has had the joy of seeing over 200 indigenous churches established and has had a part in winning thousands of souls to Christ. I have known him for the past 25 years, and the more I work with him, the more I love and appreciate Mr. Written Word."

For many years I wondered how many copies of Mr. Written Word had been distributed since Gutenberg built his press with movable type and printed the first Gutenberg Bible. My curiosity led me to make a fresh study of Christian history.

I found that the Old Testament was available in both Hebrew and Greek before the coming of Christ. The 27 New Testament books were all written in the first century. For the next 1,360 years, all Bibles had to be copied by hand. Almost all of the complete Bibles were in the possession of scholars, monks, and high church officials. Few Christians ever so much as saw a complete Bible. That, I concluded, was the major reason why the established church became so corrupt.

Almost certainly more Bibles came off the presses during the 50 years after Gutenberg than were hand-copied and distributed during the past 14 centuries. Since Gutenberg's marvelous invention, millions upon millions of Bibles and Testaments have been sold or given away. Thousands of church groups and organizations distributed printed Bibles. To my dismay, I found that many kept no records. Some have long since ceased to exist.

The American Bible Society is the world's biggest publisher and distributor of Bibles. The ABS works within the global network of the United Bible Society. The ABS reported that 624,053,932 Scriptures were distributed worldwide in 1987. This represented an increase of 4.0 percent over 1986. Of this total, 116,155,119 copies were distributed in the United States.

Most of these "Scriptures" were portions. A breakdown of distribution in a previous year shows that only two percent of the Scriptures distributed by the Bible Society were complete Bibles, and only four percent were New Testaments.

One of the major highlights in Bible distribution in 1987 was the completion of the Amity Printing Press in the People's Republic of China. The first order of 100,000 Chinese Bibles were off the press.

In 1987 the United Bible Societies and the Baptist World Alliance sent 100,000 Russian-language Bibles for the celebration of the 1,000th anniversary of the coming of Christianity to the Soviet Union. In December, 1988 the Soviet Union granted a permit to the All-Union Council of Evangelical Christians and Baptists in the USSR to import an additional 100,000 Bibles.

The figures for the Bible societies do not include the distributions of Living Bibles International (LBI) and other non-affiliated organizations. Living Bibles, under the direction of Lars Dunberg, has published for missionary outreach over 20 million New Testaments in more than 35 languages, plus several hundred thousand complete Bibles in a number of languages. LBI is presently working in over 100 languages.

Wycliffe Bible Translators (WBT) continues to be the great leader in Bible translation. In August 1988, Wycliffe reported these figures:

- Almost 6,000 languages are spoken in the world.
- Some or all of the Bible is in print in 1,747 languages.
- Wycliffe members are at work in 840 additional languages.
- There is a definite need for translators in 843 more languages.
- There is a possible need for translators in 2,483 languages.

After adding up all the figures available on Bible translation and distribution, I concluded that around 2,500,000,000 Bibles and New Testaments have been printed since the Gutenberg Bible was published in A.D. 1451. I say "around," because the exact tally can be known only by God.

Praise God for the efforts of the Bible societies and translation agencies. It is hard for American Christians who have always had the Bible to understand the hunger of people who have never held in their hands this greatest of all books. In Malawi recently, Scripture distributors going to camps for Mozambician refugees were greeted with a stampede. People were crying, "Give me a Bible!" The police had to be called to restore order.

What the Bible societies and translators do is absolutely essential to the growth of the kingdom and the church of God. But many gaps remain in Bible distribution and they become wider every year.

Here is another startling fact that should jar every Christian: Eighty-five percent of all Bibles printed today are in English for the nine percent of the world's people who read English. Eighty percent of the world's people have never owned a Bible while Americans have an average of four in every household.

As the Wycliffe figures show, many languages are still without any portion of Scripture. Still, if every spoken language had a translation of the Bible, there would remain hundreds of millions of people who have not received the Word of God, even though it could be printed in their language.

The biggest block is distribution.

William Carey's translation in Hindi has been available in India for 160 years. Yet only one-and-a-half million copies have ever been printed and distributed. Today there are over 375 million Hindi speakers in my country.

The saintly Henry Martyn (whose motto was, "Let me burn out for God!") translated the New Testament into the Persian language in 1811. He lived only one year after completing his great translation. Since Martyn's death, only 300,000 copies of the Bible are known to have been distributed in Iran. Only 300,000 in the last 170 years. What if 100 million Bibles had been made available to Iranians during just the past century? Iran might not have been taken over by radical Muslims. The terrible war between Iran and Iraq, which only recently ended, might not have occurred.

Bibles are sadly lacking even in Europe. Greater Europe Mission did a survey in Paris and found 79 percent of the women did not own a complete Bible. Bibles can be bought in bookstores in Western Europe, but they are expensive. There is an even greater shortage of Bibles in Eastern Europe and the Soviet Union where Communist governments still hold down the circulation of God's Word. The executive secretary of the Bible society in Poland declared, "Instead of thousands of Bibles, we need millions." The problem in Poland is the shortage of paper.

For years I labored and prayed over the need for wider Bible distribution. I was especially concerned about the well-to-do and the leaders of countries such as my native India, who influence the masses as foreign missionaries can never do. I rarely saw a Bible when visiting government and business leaders. Many admitted to me they had never read a single verse. From talking to missionaries and national pastors, I learned that most Christian missionary work was among poor people. Some national Christians actually told me, "If the rich people want Bibles, they can go to Christian bookstores." But I observed that Hindus and Muslims almost never go into Christian bookstores, apparently because of fear they will be identified as Christians.

Finally, the Lord gave me a plan. When I shared it with Dr. Richard Halverson, who is now chaplain of the United States Senate, he said, "Ro, the idea is so simple, only God could have thought of it."

I would like to share this idea in the closing chapter. Perhaps it will be a way in which you can participate. Or perhaps you will be challenged to find another effective method of making the greatest Book ever written available to more people.

Chapter 11

"The Book Which the Whole World Must Read"

When I completed the translation of the Hmar New Testament, I rented a tiny office in Wheaton, Illinois. There, Partnership Mission was born.

"A missionary—Watkin Roberts—brought the gospel to our tribe," I told the 114 friends on our first mailing list. "But then he had to go away, leaving the first Hmar believers to evangelize their own people, build their own churches, educate their own children.

"Thanks to Mr. Roberts and the Bible most members of our tribe are now Christians. We have hundreds of young people willing to go as missionaries themselves to other tribes. But we are poor and unable to train and send all of them.

"Remember, a national does not need passage money, expensive equipment, or language training. He speaks the language and is acquainted with the customs of the people. He cannot be expelled, for he is not a foreigner.

"So we ask for your financial partnership in our program of nationals training and telling nationals."

My, how God blessed Partnership Mission. Just ten years later, in 1969, we could report 400 national missionaries, 135 churches, 65 village schools, a high school, and a hospital. But this was just one small corner of India.

One day I took a pencil and estimated that it would take evangelical Christianity 1,249 years to reach all of India's people. "We cannot expect to live 1,249 years," I told my dear wife, Mawii.

I did a little more research and found that world population was growing by more than 190,000 per day—more than a million and a quarter a week. By the end of that year there would be 67 million more people on earth.

The Holy Spirit kept nudging my mind with the Great Commission of our Lord: "Go ye therefore, and teach all nations . . . " (Matthew 28:19). I also kept thinking of Matthew 24:14: "And this gospel of the kingdom shall be preached in all the world for a witness unto all nations; and then shall the end come." Was our Lord's return being delayed by the simple fact that the Gospel of Christ had not yet been proclaimed to all nations?"

I looked at the world and saw Communism spreading. A story about a postman in northeast China haunted me. It was said that he blazed a trail through an almost impenetrable forest to deliver mail to Communist production teams, stopping to carve the words, "Long live Chairman Mao!" on trees as he walked.

"Dear Lord, " I prayed, "show me how to blaze new trails and get your Word out to the world."

Through spring and into the summer of 1970, I prayed and meditated. I thought of how the church had grown in my tribe, Hmars winning Hmars, then moving out to witness in adjoining tribes. How could we break through to the rest of India? What would be the best strategy?

Suddenly it seemed clear that India could only be evangelized by national leaders, teachers, lawyers, doctors, and government officials. But these were the very ones not being reached. It was known everywhere in India that Christianity had made its greatest inroads among the lowest castes. How often had I heard the upper class refer to these converts as "rice Christians."

The burden lingered. One warm autumn afternoon I was reflecting again on how the Word of God had come to our people. God had told one little British woman to send Watkin Roberts five pounds, which the missionary had used to print the Gospel of John in the language of a tribe that adjoined the Hmars. The dear woman, who could not go to the mission field herself, gave the missionary money to buy seed—the Word of God. The missionary sowed that seed, and some of it fell among my people. It sprang up and bore much fruit. My family was part of that fruit.

"Lord, Your Word is the seed. But how do I spread it? How do I get it to the leaders?"

As I continued to pray, the telephone company jingle, "Let your fingers do the walking," broke my concentration. I couldn't stop thinking of it.

My eyes caught two telephone directories on my desk. It was as if a voice shouted, "Here are the names and addresses of every person in New Delhi and Calcutta, the best educated, most influential people, the very ones you want to reach!

"Thank You, Lord! Thank You! You've given me the idea. We can let our fingers do the walking. We can mail the New Testament to every person in the telephone directories of India. They won't reject it as foreign propaganda because it will be coming from one of their own.

"Maybe we can do it for the whole world. Somewhere there must be directories for every country in the world. We can print Your Word in bright paperbacks to get reader interest. Books with colorful pictures.

"But why me, Lord? I'm only a little tribesman." The answer came back, "Because I chose you to be my messenger. Now go and obey."

I shared the idea with Mawii, who was busy preparing our current newsletter. "Ro, it's wonderful," she declared.

A few days later, Dr. Ken Taylor, the man who did The Living Bible paraphrase, dropped by. He wanted my opinion of the copy for a Living New Testament intended for Asian distribution. I liked the title, *The Greatest is Love*. But the cover showing a white man with a dark child on his back bothered me. "Asians won't like it," I told Ken. "They know whites don't go around carrying blacks on their back."

"Well, what would you suggest?" he asked.

The Lord gave me the answer. "Use the Taj Mahal, Ken. The Indian ruler Shah Jahan had this beautiful marble monument built in memory of his wife. It took 20,000 workmen 21 years to build it. The Taj is an Asian symbol of love."

Ken liked the idea. A couple of weeks later we were looking at the artist's version of the new cover. "It's beautiful, Ken," I said. "Asians will see the Taj and want to look inside the book."

Then I shared the idea the Lord had given me of sending New Testaments to the leaders of India through the mail. "Could we use this same edition with the Taj cover?" I asked.

"Of course."

"Could we put the Gospel of John first instead of Matthew? That way our readers will immediately begin with the heart of the Bible's message."

"Yes, if you think it best, Ro."

With Ken's permission, I talked to his distributors for the Asian Living New Testament. They readily agreed to have the New Testaments for our test mailing printed at cost.

I began gathering information on the world telephone and postal systems. I learned that there were 275 million listings of names and addresses in the directories for the various nations.

We already had the directories for Calcutta and New Delhi. We needed them for other cities in India and the rest of the world. I called the telephone company and was referred to Steve Allen, an executive with International Telephone and Telegraph in New York.

Mr. Allen was fascinated with what we wanted to do. "Getting the directories will be no problem," he assured. "Except for the Soviet Union. We know the Russians publish directories for about 16 million subscribers, but they won't let us have them. When you get some," he laughed, "will you make copies for us?"

The telephone directories would tell us where to send Bibles. They would be delivered by "missionaries" from the post office. I thought of the line, "Neither rain nor snow nor heat nor gloom of night stays these couriers from the swift completion of their appointed rounds." When I looked it up, I found it had been written by the Greek historian Herodotus about the Persian postal messengers of 500 B.C. Now God was going to use modern messengers of the mail to deliver his Word.

But could we mail Bibles to any post office in the world where there were telephones? Would there be special restrictions and a variety of rates to the various countries?

I found that a universal postal agreement had been in operation since July 1, 1875. This brought the signatory countries into a single postal territory for the exchange of mail at uniform postage rates.

I immediately wrote the Universal Postal Union in Berne, Switzerland about our plan. "Can I really mail packages from one post office to all other post offices in the world for the same amount of postage?" I asked.

Back came the answer. "Yes. It is the same for over 830,000 post offices." The Swiss official went on to explain that under the international agreement a package had to be delivered in the recipient country or returned to the sender with an explanation for why it could not be given to the addressee.

I called a meeting of our Partnership Mission board and explained the plan.

"Am I reading you right, Ro?" one board member said. "You propose to mail a copy of the Living New Testament to everybody in India whose name and address is in the telephone directory. Then to Pakistan and Nepal and Thailand and on until you mail to the whole world? How much will this cost?'

Well, at present rates, for printing and postage, we estimate it can be done for around a dollar each. The cost will likely go up before we are finished."

"And how many listings do you estimate there are in all the telephone directories?"

"Right now about 275 million. There will be more by the time we are done." I could almost hear computers clicking in my board members' brains. "You're talking of 275 million dollars, at least," one noted.

"At least."

"And how much was our income for Partnership Mission last month?"

"I think it was about $25,000." The board members talked some more. We prayed about it. Then they voted to begin. Later we changed our name to Bibles For The World.

We gave a print order for 50,000 copies and appealed to local churches for volunteers to come in and begin typing labels, beginning with the Calcutta directory. People began responding.

I was so excited I could hardly eat or sleep. I envisioned a Buddhist mailman delivering the Word of God to another Buddhist, a Hindu handing the Book of the one true God to another Hindu, a Muslim taking the Bible to another Muslim, even a Communist delivering the Scriptures to a fellow Communist. What a great open door!

I thought of how, as a youngster, Sadhu Sundar Singh was given a copy of the New Testament. The message troubled him so much that he tore up the book and threw away the pieces. Later he had second thoughts, retrieved the pages, and put the book back together. Within a few hours he had received Christ as his Lord and Savior. Singh became India's greatest evangelist, traveling the world to win others to the Lord.

All the time I kept talking up the idea to whoever would listen. I took a stack of copies to a Christian Businessmen's Committee meeting. Holding up a New Testament with the beautiful color picture of the Taj Mahal on the cover, I said, "If you'll buy one like this for ten dollars I'll send nine more to India." I "sold" over thirty copies that way.

On Sunday I shared the need with a small country church in Carlock, Illinois, where I was speaking. We had five minutes of silent prayer, asking God to provide. The church gave liberally. The money came in.

The first shipment came from the printer. A swarm of volunteers helped address, package, and lick the mailing labels. Our most faithful worker was wheelchair-bound Carl Schingothe. "Maybe I can't walk," he laughed, "but I can serve the Lord by letting my fingers do the walking."

Each "love gift" of the New Testament contained a brief personal testimony from me and an invitation: "If you have any question or problem concerning Jesus Christ or on how you may have peace and everlasting life through Him, please write me." A return-address envelope was enclosed.

We opened an office in New Delhi and waited prayerfully for the first replies. What a thrill to receive a cablegram from our New Delhi representative: HUNDREDS OF LETTERS ARRIVING DAILY. FORWARDING SELECTIONS ON TO YOU.

Many of the letters told of spiritual hunger.

"I finished the book sent by you."

"I was so moved by its eternal appeal that I couldn't restrain myself from writing a few lines to you."

" It is really the wisest book ever any human being read. "

"I do not find words within me to express my gratitude for *The Greatest Is Love*. Beliefs on concept of religion may differ from person to person—but the fact remains that without truth peace can't be achieved. Your book will help me find the way. . . . "

"I acknowledge *The Greatest Is Love* you sent me recently. . . . It is really good and marvelous. I want to read more literature. I am much interested to spread my knowledge in the Bible and also want to know the life of a Christian."

"I have a religious bent of mind and have been reading several books on Hindu religion. . . . Although I started my school career in a Christian mission school and had read the Bible as a textbook, I could never develop the taste and admiration for the holy Christ as I have done from the text provided by you. I have hardly finished two chapters so far but could not restrain my desire of thanking you for the valuable gift which is almost a God-sent present to me at the opportune time."

Our first 50,000 mailing brought 20,000 letters with many writers requesting additional copies for friends. Many others wrote saying they had seen a copy of *The Greatest Is Love* at a friend's house and would like a copy of their own. These requests had not been expected, but our board voted to send them as long as funds permitted.

Our bank balance was dipping low when a Christian foundation offered to match every dollar given by others up to $250,000. The matching gifts were provided.

By Christmas, 1972, we were past the 300,000 mark for India with almost a million yet to mail. Still the letters kept coming, thousands and thousands. Never in my wildest dreams had I expected such an outpouring.

We began making plans to mail to other countries: 6,200 to Nepal; 162,000 to Burma; 62,000 to Sri Lanka; 165 to tiny Bhutan; and 250 to Sikkim.

A pastor in Ohio asked if his family could take Sikkim with its 250 telephone listings as their Christmas present to the Lord. His children were willing to give up some presents so that the leaders of Sikkim might have God's Word. We mailed them the books and labels. The parents typed the addresses, and the four children helped pack and apply the labels and stamps. Then after delivering the Bibles to the post office, they knelt and prayed that the Lord would use their love gift.

After mailing almost a half million to India, Mawii and I could wait no longer to return home and see firsthand how the mailing was being received. It was more than I had anticipated. I saw *The Greatest Is Love* almost everywhere I went—in the hotel lobby, the post office, and even the bank where I went to exchange some money.

I took a flight to Calcutta and as I walked down the aisle of the big Boeing jet, I saw a familiar face engrossed in one of the books. There was a vacant seat beside him, and I asked if I could sit down. "Certainly," he said.

"Oh, by the way, what book are you reading?"

He looked at the cover and said, "It's called *The Greatest Is Love*."

"How did you get that book?"

"It came by mail quite a few weeks ago, but I never had the time to read it. I told my wife to tuck it in my briefcase, and I would read it on my next trip."

"Do you know who sent it?"

He flipped back the first two pages and saw the pencil drawing of my face. "You are the one?"

"Yes, I happen to be the one, and I'm glad you are reading it."

He told me he had once been the Indian ambassador to Washington and after that a cabinet member. Now he was the chief justice of the Supreme Court of India. Of course, I already knew that.

"Do you know," he continued, "that while I was an ambassador in America I had a secret longing to read the Bible through at least once while I was out of the country? But I never owned one. I would see one once in a while in a hotel room, but I didn't think I should take it away. I could have bought one in a Christian bookstore, but I didn't feel I should go there. When this book came, I saw it as the fulfillment of my desire, so I asked my wife to save it for a time when I could read it."

Then he said, "If I have any questions or problems, could I get in touch with you?"

"Of course," I assured him. "I would be honored to hear from you. My address is in the front of your Bible."

Because of the excitement created by the arrival of two truckloads of Bibles just prior to my own arrival in New Delhi, I was swamped by reporters requesting interviews. My good friend Mr. V.V. Purie, a leading Indian businessman, arranged a press conference for me at the Intercontinental Hotel and invited the newspapers and broadcast stations to send representatives. A large number of curious reporters came to meet the former tribesman whose organization had been mailing Bibles all over India.

After everyone else had asked questions, the reporter for the *Hindustan Standard,* one of the largest newspapers in India, asked very courteously, "Do I have my information right, Sir, that you hope to mail a Bible to every telephone subscriber in the world, and there are now over 300 million people in the world's phone books?"

"Yes, that is correct. When we started there were only 275 million. The total now is around 300 million."

"And you have phone books from all these countries?"

"Either we have them, or we can get them."

"Will you then be mailing to Russia?"

"Yes," I finally said, "but right now the door isn't open so we can't mail there."

The reporter for the *Indian Express* popped up. "Mr. Pudaite, do you know about the cultural agreement signed between India and Russia just two years ago? It provides for each country to send books to the other. Since you are an Indian and the Bible is your cultural book, why not send Bibles under that agreement?"

"Well, I didn't know about that agreement," I said in surprise.

"Go to the Soviet Embassy," the reporter proposed. "Show them your book. Ask if they will let you mail under the agreement. If they say 'no' call another press conference and tell us."

I called the embassy and asked for an appointment. "Yes, I'll be glad to see you tomorrow at ten," the cultural attache said.

When I walked in the next morning, they received me like royalty. I had hardly given my name to the secretary when the attache, a huge bear of a man, came rushing from his office, arms extended, shouting, "Russie, Hindi, bhai! bhai!" ("Russians and Indians are brothers!")

I didn't know what to do except hold out my short arms and say, "Yes—Hindi, Russie, bhai, bhai!" He was so big I couldn't get my arms halfway around him.

"Come into my office, my friend, and tell me what you need," he said, leading the way.

I had hardly begun, when he interrupted. "Yes, yes, I know the whole story. One of our reporters was at your press conference."

"Then we can mail Bibles into Russia?"

"Of course. But you must help me by please accepting certain conditions."

"What do you wish?"

"Number one, you will please print from a Bible that has already been published inside the Soviet Union so the customs will not stop it. Number two, you will please print in India. And number three, you will please mail from India."

"That will be no problem," I assured him. "How many may we mail?"

"Ten thousand a month. If you mail more, we might have difficulties."

I left, eager to find an Indian printer. But first there was an engagement to keep. I had rented the well-known Sapru House auditorium and placed ads in New Delhi's two biggest newspapers, inviting those who had received *The Greatest Is Love* in the mail to come at seven the following evening and "hear the life story of the man who sent you this book."

As the time drew near for the meeting, I paced up and down in our hotel room. "What if no one shows up?" I told Mawii. "What if we didn't do enough?"

I needn't have been concerned. Ninety minutes before the meeting was to start, the auditorium manager called excitedly. "Please come now," he urged. "The building is already packed and we're turning people away."

We hurried over. Because my voice was beginning to tire, I asked Mawii to give her witness first. Then the Lord restored my voice, and I spoke for 40 or 50 minutes telling what God had done through the Bible in our tribe. Finally—and huskily—I said, "I cannot talk any longer. If any one of you wishes to speak with us about believing in Jesus Christ, then please come to the front and we will try to help you."

No one moved for a second or two; then it was like a wall that started forward. At least half the audience wanted to come. "My friends," I said, "so many are wanting to come it is impossible to see you all. Could you please call our office and make appointments? Here is our telephone number."

The phone never stopped ringing the next day.

Before leaving New Delhi for a nostalgic visit to Hmar country, I met again with Mr. Purie who owns and operates one of the largest printing presses in Asia. I told him about the Russian opportunity and said, "If you can help us get a Russian Bible and the telephone directories, I'll give you the printing orders."

"How many telephone subscribers are there in Russia?" he asked.

"Sixteen million," I replied, quoting the figure given to me by Steve Allen, the telephone company executive in New York. "But right now we can only send ten thousand a month."

Mr. Purie smiled. "That will be sufficient to send a man to Moscow."

The Hindu printer sent his Hindu associate to a Communist country for the cause of the Bible. He returned with the Moscow telephone directory, which the man at IT&T had been unable to get. Within a short time we were mailing Bibles inside the Soviet Union to those telephone subscribers whose addresses were in the directory.

The years hurried by. The mailings continued. We built a new headquarters and enlarged our staff. We experimented with new covers and titles. We printed in new languages. The New Testaments went out. The letters came back—thousands and thousands.

A professor in Pakistan found one of the New Testaments in his college library and wrote: "I am a Muslim believing in all the prophets from Adam to Muhammed . . . . Please send me the Holy Book in English or Urdu and also books on Christianity."

A man from Malaysia wrote: "I was filled with great joy when I saw your book . . . . I am slowly stepping into the world of Christianity."

From Bermuda, the wife of the managing director of an internationally known insurance company said that her husband had found *The Greatest Is Love* on his desk. Thinking it a novel meant for her, he took it home. She wrote: "It certainly was intended for me, as I was, at the time, a nonbeliever. Soon, however, I became fascinated by the greatest love story of all time. I now write, as a growing Christian, confident in the strength of my Lord and Savior Jesus Christ, and today during my prayer time, He reminded me that I should write to thank you. I do so sincerely for the important part you played in bringing me before the throne of grace."

God supplied the money needed to print and mail millions of Bibles. We received a few large gifts, but most donations were from ten to one hundred dollars.

Christian celebrities helped us with big rallies. Pat and Shirley Boone, two of our most loyal and devoted friends, headlined a meeting at Auburn University in Alabama that was attended by the governor, lieutenant governor, a future governor, and Miss Alabama, with my old friend Bob Pierce, president of World Vision, as a special guest. Alabamans sent Bibles to Bangladesh.

Our dear brother Doug Oldham sang for a Bibles For the World rally in the Pickard Auditorium of little Neenah, Wisconsin. Some of the overflow watched on closed circuit TV. Others had to be turned away. The people of Neenah provided Bibles for every telephone subscriber in Afghanistan. We didn't know then that Afghanistan would soon be invaded by the Soviet army.

Even with postage rates rising, the Bibles kept going out and the letters kept coming. One of our Hmar evangelists wrote that an entire Burmese family had become Christians through reading one of the New Testaments we mailed. A gentleman from Hong Kong said, "My house has never seen a Bible before today. From now on I will thank God for this New Testament in Chinese that you have kindly and freely mailed me."

A young man told our representative in Taiwan that he had been depressed about life and was on his way to throw himself in front of a train when he saw a Bibles For The World Chinese New Testament lying on a seat in a bus. He picked up the book and began to read. He confessed his sins to God and dropped his plan for suicide.

The wife of a businessman to Zimbabwe wrote that her husband was at his sports' club when he noticed a copy of the book on the manager's desk. When the manager said he had no use for it, the businessman asked if he could take it home "That was one month ago," the businessman's wife wrote. "My husband has given his life to God. I do feel this Bible had a lot to do with it as Trevor could understand what he was reading. On behalf of my children and myself we thank you for your love in sharing God with others." She added a P.S. "Will you send a copy to two friends who went to church for the first time with us last Sunday?"

One of the most thrilling stories came from our friend Ed Lacaba who told about meeting a dynamic new Christian from the Philippines at a prayer breakfast in Los Angeles. The Filipino, a wealthy real estate broker named Tony Isit, had told the group: "I am a believer in Jesus Christ because an Indian man sent me a Bible from Illinois. I got so excited about God's Word that I bought all the Bibles I could find and gave them to friends and neighbors. At my Bible studies and prayer groups, more than 500 people have accepted Jesus Christ as Savior."

When Ed contacted us, I lost no time getting in touch with this remarkable Filipino. I finally reached him by telephone in Las Vegas where he was arranging a real estate transaction for a client.

"Am I really talking to the person who made all that difference in my life?" Tony asked in amazement after I introduced myself. "Are you really the one who sent me the Bible?"

"Well," I said, "I head an organization that sends millions of Bibles overseas through the mail, so a lot of people worked together to send you that New Testament. All of us thank God it got to you safely."

My new Filipino friend then told me about reading the book. "I came to where it said, 'Except a man be born again, he cannot see the kingdom of God' (John 3:3). That statement went round and round in my mind for a long time, and then I just prayed, 'Lord Jesus, I can't solve it for myself. Come into my heart and take over my life.' That is the way it happened to me."

Tony became a one-man Bibles-for-the-Philippines operation. He gave Bibles to thousands of people.

We didn't print the story of the Russian mailing in our newsletter for a long time. When we did mention it, people began immediately asking, "Are your Bibles really getting into Russia? Are you sure they aren't being intercepted at the post offices and confiscated before they can reach the people?"

We wanted to be very cautious in following up, because the Bibles were continuing to go out at the rate of 10,000 a month. But on a trip into Russia for Bibles For the World, Dr. Cliff Robinson found evidence in a most unusual way.

Cliff and his party were in a city some 2,000 miles south of Moscow. Their official interpreter had helped them find Christian leaders and churches and worked tirelessly in their behalf. One day Cliff said to her, "We do so appreciate your good work and would like to reward you with a small bonus."

"Oh, no, I wouldn't think of it. This has been a totally new experience for me. I was never in a Christian church before, and I have learned many new things."

"But isn't there something I can do for you or get for you—just as a friend?" Cliff persisted.

She repeated Cliff's words "as a friend" aloud. Then she said, "You are 'Bibles For The World'—right? Do you print anything besides the Bible?"

When Cliff said we did not, she asked, "But what about the *Evangelische*?"

Cliff didn't understand so he asked her what the book was about.

"Oh, it is all about Jesus Christ and what He taught. I especially liked His statement that we are not to judge lest we also be judged. And He said if you are slapped on one side of the face to turn the other side also. If we did that, there certainly would be no war. There must be two to fight." As Cliff listened, she told him other bits and pieces from the Sermon on the Mount.

"Tell me about this *Evangelische*," Cliff said excitedly. "Was there a picture of the Cathedral in the Kremlin on the cover?"

"I don't know," she told Cliff, "since I've never been to Moscow. But there was a building with yellow towers—it could have been a church."

Cliff could hardly believe his ears. She was talking about the very book Bibles For the World had been sending into Russia for several months. But how could she have gotten the book so far from Moscow? All of our mailings up to this time had been in the Moscow area. Cliff asked her to tell him more.

"A friend from Moscow visited here recently," she explained, "and showed me the book she had received through the mail. I found it exciting and asked if she would lend it to me. I had it all to myself for two days before giving it back."

"Do you mean," Cliff said, "that what you told me about Jesus was what you learned from reading the New Testament for just two days?" he asked her in amazement.

"Yes," she replied, "I was very sad when my friend took back her book and returned to Moscow—but you said you wanted to do something for me as a friend. Do you think you could get me a copy of the New Testament for my own?"

Cliff and his wife Betty had already given their personal Bibles away. That night when he told the story to their group, one of the members, Phyllis Weaver, offered her leather bound Testament in English. When Cliff presented this "*Evangelische*" to the interpreter, she burst into tears and sobbed, "Thank you! Thank you!"

Cliff passed the thrilling story along to us. We immediately sent this young woman a Russian New Testament through our New Delhi office.

A few months after this unusual experience, Cliff met three Russian evangelical leaders at the Washington airport and escorted them to the National Prayer Breakfast. At the prayer breakfast one of the group, Dr. Ilia Orlov, a medical doctor and dentist as well as an ordained minister, praised Bibles For The World before the large audience, which included President Carter, many U.S. senators and representatives, Chief Justice Warren Burger, foreign ambassadors, and numerous other dignitaries. Dr. Ilia Orlov said further: "The Word of God is needed all over the world, but especially do the people of my country love the Bible. I know that God's Word will not return unto Him void, but always accomplishes the divine purpose. We are so thankful for the vision of Bibles For The World, for it is sowing the seed of the Word all over the world. Many thousands of my compatriots are receiving Bibles today because of these beautiful Christian brothers and their ambitious program to send the Bible to everybody listed in the telephone books of the world. We know that God's Word is not bound, and it cannot be!"

By the end of 1988 we had mailed ten million New Testaments to persons listed in the world telephone directories. Six hundred and fifty thousand of those went into the Soviet Union.

The New Testaments come in packs of 12. We provide these with mailing materials and address labels to families at no cost. We are looking for a million families who will each take one pack and mail the books at their local post office. We will send a 12-pack to any family who writes us and promises to pay the postage for each copy of God's Word sent.

At the same time, we believe God is going to provide the funds to pay for the production costs for printing and packaging these Bibles.

Our goal for the next decade is one billion Bibles, for that is the number of telephone listings which are expected to be available by A.D. 2,000. This many New Testaments, put end to end, will reach from earth to the moon. It is not an impossible dream.

Mailing Bibles to the millions of people whose addresses are listed in the world's telephone directories is God's calling for us. There are many other worthy ways to evangelize the world, including preaching, teaching, Sunday school, home witness, television, radio, cassette players, campus ministries, prison outreaches, relief programs, neighborhood and office Bible studies, and personal witness of missionaries and national believers. The method is not important so long as the Word of God is given to every person in his own language.

We must harness every appropriate method of modern technology for distributing God's Word, which is sharper than any two-edged sword, more powerful than any nuclear bomb, and more penetrating than any laser beam.

My prayer is that every Bible-believing Christian the world over will be captured by the dream of giving every person on God's earth the Bible in his own language. No denomination, Bible agency, church, or special ministry group can do it all. Every one of us must do his part in speeding God's eternal Word to the masses yet in darkness.

I am one of many Christians alarmed at the vast and terrifying world arms buildup. The nations have been stockpiling weapons and building armies at a cost of over 500 billion dollars a year. There are already enough bombs to destroy the world ten thousand times over.

At this moment there is a lessening of tensions. The diplomats are more cordial to one another. The Russian leader, Mikhail Gorbachev, is calling for more openness in his country.

I would like to challenge Mr. Gorbachev, President George Bush, and the other world leaders to consider the Bible as the best means for leading the world into peace and good will.

This true story from World War II, told by war correspondent Clarence Hall, shows what the Bible can do.

Mr. Hall was accompanying Allied soldiers advancing from one island to another during the closing months of the Pacific War. On one assault, he followed American soldiers across Little Shimmabuke Island near Okinawa. As the advance patrol moved up to a village, two little old men suddenly stepped out, bowed low, and began to speak. An interpreter explained to the Americans that these were village elders welcoming them as fellow Christians.

The flabbergasted servicemen called up their chaplain. He and an escort toured the village and were astounded at the spotlessly clean homes and streets. The friendly natives looked incredibly healthy and showed evidence of prosperity and great intelligence. The Americans had seen other villages in the South Pacific, villages of indescribable poverty. The village of Shimmabuke shone among them like a diamond on a dungheap.

The headman, Shosei Kina, took the amazement of the Americans for disappointment. "Sirs, we are sorry if we seem like such a backward people. We have tried our best to follow the Bible and live like Jesus. Perhaps if you will show us how...."

"How did you get the Bible?" the astounded chaplain interrupted.

The headman recalled that 30 years before an American missionary had stopped briefly on the island, just long enough to make a couple of converts, the old men who had welcomed the soldiers, leave them a

Japanese Bible, and go on his way. They hadn't seen another missionary since.

One day the war correspondent and a tough old Army sergeant were strolling around the village. Compared to what he had seen on other islands, the grizzled sergeant just couldn't believe his eyes. "I can't figure it, fellow—this kind of people coming out of only a Bible and a couple of old guys who want to live like Jesus." Pausing, the soldier then delivered what Clarence Hall called "an infinitely penetrating observation." "Maybe," the sergeant said, "maybe we've been using the wrong kind of weapons to make the world over."

Surely, when so many billions are being spent for weapons of destruction—surely when Christians in America alone can spend four billion dollars for brick and mortar in building churches during one year—surely when we have at our disposal the means to speed the Word of God to the ends of the earth—surely we can rededicate our lives and accept the challenge given by David to Solomon: "Be strong and courageous and get to work . . . . " (1 Chronicles 28:20, The Living Bible). Surely we can give this Book of books, the greatest of all books ever written, to the whole world.

That is my prayer, my dream, my hope, my commitment, my life.

I know what this Book can do. It is the Book which the whole world must read.

A PERSONAL WORD FROM THE AUTHOR

Dr. Howard Kelly, one of America's greatest surgeons, said, "The Bible appeals to me strongly as a physician, because it is such excellent medicine; it has never failed to cure a single patient if only he took his prescription honestly. In the realm of spiritual therapeutics, it is just what we long to find for all our bodily ailments, a universal remedy."

Whatever my need, I have always found Dr. Kelly's advice to be true."

Here are some examples of how I apply God's Word to my life.
- When I find myself in sudden difficulty or sorrow, I seek assurance from Hebrews 12:5-11.
- When discouragement creeps over me and I feel that I have been a failure, I hold tight to my heart Isaiah 41:13.
- When I am filled with foreboding about the future, I meditate long and deep on Psalm 23.
- When I am encompassed by a dark cloud of oppression, I take as my shield Psalm 91.
- When I grow weary from a heavy load of responsibilities, I look to Matthew 11:28-30 for the lifting of my burdens.
- When my faith seems to be failing and my prayers choke in my throat, I reach for the tonic found in John 5:13-15 and Romans 10:17.
- When the taste of a bitter spirit lingers in my mouth and I want to lash back at someone who has wronged me, I take a good draught of 1 Corinthians 13 and Psalm 34:12,13.
- When guilt darkens my soul and leadens my spirit, I cast myself upon the promises of Isaiah 55:7 and I John 1:9.
- When my memory fails in remembrance of my blessings, I feast my eyes on Psalm 103.

The Bible is all this and more to me. It shows me the way I must go. It gives me manna for the journey. It is the bank in which my balance is always sufficient for the need at hand. It tells me of the sufficiency of God, who lovingly leads me past pitfalls and snares and up to the smooth highway where I walk with my God in joy and delight.

When you finish reading this book, I believe you will agree with me that the Bible is truly the "greatest Book ever written."

But if you have a deep personal need, I urge you to stop right now and apply the Bible remedy to that concern. If you cannot find the solution in Holy Scripture for which your heart cries, please write me and allow me the opportunity to share a passage from God's Word which will help meet your need of this moment.

Write Rochunga Pudaite, P.O. Box, 805, Wheaton, IL, 60187.

A Word About Sources

Substantial portions of this book appeared in a previous book by me, titled *My Billion Bible Dream* (Thomas Nelson Publishers, 1982). Dr. James C. Hefley was my co-author for both *My Billion Bible Dream* and *The Greatest Book Ever Written*. Dr. Hefley and his wife, Marti, have conducted numerous interviews with me and understand me as well as any Americans I know. Mrs. Hefley, with some editorial assistance from Dr. Hefley, wrote my biography, *God's Tribesman*.

We present this book with the awareness that no book has ever had more "reviews" and "commentaries" written about it than the Bible. Thousands upon thousands of such books are housed in libraries today. In our work on this book and the previous edition of *My Billion Bible Dream*, we consulted and made reference to scores of books and articles relating to the Bible, including a number that were written by the Hefleys. Some are listed in the bibliography which might be helpful reference to those who wish to learn more about the greatness of the Bible. We also received invaluable help from a number of Bible ministries. Prominent among them were the Wycliffe Bible Translators, the American Bible Society, and the organization which I serve as president, Bibles For the World. We thank these friends and kindred spirits and all others who gave assistance.

BIBLIOGRAPHY

Anderson, J. N. D., *Christianity and Comparative Religion*, Downers Grove, IL: Inter-Varsity Press, 1970.

Archer, Lettie Gertrude, *In His Image*, Allhambra, CA: Privately Printed, 1972.

Archer, Gleason L., *Eycyclopedia of Bible Difficulties*, Grand Rapids: Zondervan Publishing House, 1982.

Bhagavad Gita, Translated by Eknath Easwaran, Blue Mountain Center of Meditation: Nilgiri Press, 1985.

Blaiklock, E.M., *The Archaeology of the New Testament*, Grand Rapids: Zondervan Publishing House, 1970.

Bloom, Allan, *The Closing of the American Mind*, New York: Simon & Schuster, 1987.

Browne, Lewis, *This Believing World*, New York: The Macmillan Company, 1933.

Browne, Lewis, *The World's Great Scriptures*, New York: The Macmillan Company, 1946.

Bucaille, Maurice, *The Bible, the Qur' an and Science*, Delhi, India: Taj Company, 1986.

Cairns, Earle E., *Christianity Through the Centuries*, Grand Rapids: Zondervan Publishing House, Revised and enlarged edition, 1981.

Chirgwin, A.M., *The Bible in World Evangelism*, New York: Friendship Press, 1954.

Clark, Robert E.D., *Christian Belief and Science*, Philadelphia: Muhlenberg Press, 1960.

Colson, Charles W., *Born Again*, Old Tappan, NJ: Fleming H. Revell, 1976.

Conner, W.T., *Christian Doctrine*, Nashville: Broadman Press, 1937.

Copeland, E. Luther, *Christianity and World Religions*, Nashville: Convention Press, 1963.

Cruden, Alexander, *Cruden's Unabridged Concordance*, Grand Rapids: Baker Book House, Revised edition, 1954.

Dana, H. E., *Searching the Scriptures*, Kansas City: Central Seminary Press, 1946.

Davis, S.D., *The Westminister Dictionary of the Bible*, Philadelphia: Westminister Press, 1944.

DeMoss Ted and Tamasy, Robert, *The Gospel and the Briefcase*, Wheaton, IL.: Tyndale House, 1984.

Engel, James F. and Norton, Wilbert, *What's Gone Wrong With the Harvest*, Grand Rapids: Zondervan Publishing House, 1975.

England, Don, *Faith and Evidence,* Delight, AR: Gospel Light Publishing Co., 1983.

Fickett, Harold L. Jr., *A Layman's Guide to Baptist Beliefs,* Grand Rapids: Zondervan Publishing House, 1965.

Freedom and Faith, Edited by Lynn R. Buzzard, Westchester, IL: Crossway Publishers, 1982.

Gabler, Mel and Norma, *What Are They Teaching Our Children?* Wheaton, IL: Victor Books, 1986.

Gaussen, L., *The Inspiration of the Holy Scriptures,* Chicago: Moody Press, 1949.

Goodspeed, E.J., *The Story of the Bible,* Chicago: University of Chicago Press, 1936.

Halley, H.H., *Halley's Bible Handbook,* Grand Rapids: Zondervan Publishing House, Revised edition, 1962.

Harris, Stephen R., *My Anchor Held,* Old Tappan, NJ: Fleming H. Revell, 1970.

Hefley James C., *Adventurers With God,* Grand Rapids: Zondervan Publishing House, 1967.

Hefley, James C., *America: One Nation Under God,* Wheaton, IL: Victor Books, 1975.

Hefley, James C., *Businessmen Who Believe,* Elgin, IL.: David C. Cook Publishing Co., 1964.

Hefley, James C., *The Cross and the Scalpel,* Waco, TX: Word Books, 1971.

Hefley, James C., *Heroes of the Faith,* Chicago: Moody Press, 1963.

Hefley, James C., *How Great Christians Met Christ,* Chicago: Moody Press, 1973.

Hefley, James C., *How Sweet the Sound,* Wheaton, IL: Tyndale House, 1981.

Hefley, James C., *Lift-off!,* Grand Rapids: Zondervan Publishing House, 1970.

Hefley, James C., *The New Jews,* Wheaton, IL: Tyndale House, 1971.

Hefley, James C., *Scientists Who Believe,* Elgin, IL: David C. Cook Publishing Company, 1963.

Hefley, James C., *Textbooks on Trial,* Wheaton, IL: Victor Books, 1974.

Hefley, James C., *What's So Great About the Bible?,* Elgin, IL: David C. Cook Publishing Company, 1969.

Hefley, James C., *The Youth Nappers,* Wheaton, IL: Tyndale House, 1977.

Hefley, James C. and Beekman, John, *Searchlight on Bible Words*, Grand Rapids: Zondervan Publishing House, 1972.

Hefley, James and Marti, *Arabs, Christians, Jews*, Plainfield, NJ: Logos International, 1978.

Hefley, James and Marti, *Christ in Bangladesh*, New York: Harper & Row, 1973.

Hefley, James and Marti, *The Church That Produced a President*, New York: Wyden Books, 1977.

Hefley, James and Marti, *Dawn Over Amazonia*, Waco, TX: Word Books, 1972.

Hefley, James and Marti, *God's Tribesman*, Philadelphia: A. J. Holman Company, 1974.

Hefley, James and Marti, *The Liberated Palestinian*, Wheaton, IL: Victor Books, 1975.

Hefley, James and Marti, *Uncle Cam*, Waco, TX.: Word Books, 1974.

Hefley, James and Marti, *Unstilled Voices*, Chappaqua, NY: Christian Herald Books, 1981.

Hefley, James and Marti, *Where in the World Are the Jews Today?* Wheaton, IL: Victor Books, 1974.

Hefley, James C. and Plowman, Edward E., *Washington: Christian in the Corridors of Power*, Wheaton, IL: Tyndale House, 1975.

Hefley, Marti, *In His Steps Today*, Chicago: Moody Press, 1976.

Holy Quran, English Translation by Mohammed Marmaduke Pickthall, Karachi, Pakistan: Quran Council of Pakistan, 1974.

Hume, Robert H., *The World's Living Religions*, New York: Charles Scribner's Sons,1959.

Hunt, Gladys, *The Christian Way of Death*, Grand Rapids: Zondervan, 1971.

Jackson, Jeremy C., *No Other Foundation*, Westchester, IL: Cornerstone Books, 1980.

Kenyon, F.G., *Our Bible and the Ancient Manuscripts*, New York: Harper & Row, 1940.

Kelso, James L., *An Archaeologist Follows the Apostle Paul*, Waco, TX: Word Books, 1970.

Kelso, James L., *An Archaeologist Looks at the Gospel*, Waco, TX: Word Books, 1969.

Kyokai, Bukkyo Dendo, *The Teaching of Buddha*, Tokyo: Kenkyusha Printing Co., 1966.

LaSor, William Sanford, *Men Who Knew God*, Glendale, CA: Gospel Light Publications, 1970.

Lindsell, Harold, *The New Paganism*, San Francisco: Harper & Row, 1987.

Lindskogg, Kathryn Ann, *C.S. Lewis: Mere Christian*, Glendale, CA.: Gospel Light Publications, 1973.

Lockyer, Herbert, *The Man Who Changed the World*, Two Volumes, Grand Rapids: Zondervan Publishing House, 1966.

McDowell, Josh, *Evidence That Demands a Verdict*, San Bernardino, CA.: Campus Crusade for Christ, 1972.

McDowell, Josh and Stewart, Don, *Understanding the Cults*, San Bernardino, CA: Here's Life Publishers, 1982.

Nave, O.J., *Nave's Topical Bible*, Chicago: Moody Press, 1896.

Packer, J.I., *Fundamentalism and the Word of God*, Grand Rapids: Wm. B. Eerdmans Publishing Co., 1958.

Pfeiffer, C.F., and Harrison, E.F., *Wycliffe Bible Commentary*, Chicago: Moody Press, 1962.

Phillips, Harold L., *Translators and Translations*, Anderson, IN.: The Warner Press, 1958.

Pollock, John, *Billy Graham*, Grand Rapids: Zondervan Publishing House, 1967.

Pollock, John, *Moody*, Grand Rapids: Zondervan Publishing House, 1963.

Practical Christianity, Compiled and Edited by LaVonne Neff, Ron Beers, Bruce Barton, Linda Taylor, Dave Veerman, and Jim Galvin, Wheaton, IL: Tyndale House, 1987.

Pudaite, Rochunga, *The Education of the Hmar People*, Navana Printing Works: Calcutta, India.

Pudaite, Rochunga, *The Dime That Lasted Forever*, Wheaton, IL.: Tyndale House Publishers, 1985.

Price, I.M. *The Ancestry of Our English Bible: An Account of Manuscripts, Texts, and Versions of the Bible*, ed. W.A. Irwin and Allen Wikgren, New York: Harper & Row, 1949.

Robb, Edmund W. and Robb, Julia, *The Betrayal of the Church*, Westchester, IL: Crossway Books, 1987.

Ryrie, Charles C., *Neo-orthodoxy: What It Is and What It Does*, Chicago: Moody Press, 1956.

Schaeffer, Francis A., *A Christian Manifesto*, Westchester, IL: Crossway Books, 1981.

Schaeffer, Francis A., *The Complete Works of Francis A. Schaeffer: A Christian World View*, Volume 2, Westchester, IL.: Crossway Books, 1982.

Schlossberg, Herbert, *Idols for Destruction*, Nashville: Thomas Nelson Publishers, 1983.

Scientific Creationism, Edited by Henry M. Morris, San Diego: Creation-Life Publishers, 1974.

Seamands, John T., *Tell It Well*, Kansas City: Beacon Hill Press, 1981.

Sheldon, Charles M., *In His Steps*, Fleming H. Revell, Old Tappan, NJ: Spire Edition, 1963.

Shorrosh, Anis A., *Islam Revealed*, Nashville: Thomas Nelson Publishers, 1988.

Souther, A., *The Text and Canon of the New Testament*, New York: Charles Scribner's Sons, 1913.

Sumrall, Lester, *Where Was God When Religions Began?* Nashville: Thomas Nelson, 1980.

The Sword Book of Treasures, Compiled by John R. Rice, Wheaton, IL: Sword of the Lord Publishers, 1946.

Tenney, M.C., Zondervan *Pictorial Bible Dictionary*, Grand Rapids: Zondervan Publishing House, 1963.

Terrien, S., *Golden Bible Atlas*, New York: Golden Press, 1957.

Tesh, S.E., *How We Got Our Bible*, Cincinnati: Standard Publishing Company, 1951.

Tiner, John Hudson, *Johannes Kepler: Giant of Faith and Science*, Milford, MI: Mott Media, 1977.

Why I Am Still a Christian, Compiled and Edited by E. M. Blaiklock, Grand Rapids: Zondervan Publishing House, 1971.

Wiester, John L., *The Genesis Connection*, Nashville: Thomas Nelson Publishers, 1983.

The Word . . . Inspired . . . Infallible . . . Inerrant, Nashville: The Gideons International, n.d.

Wright, G.E., and Filson, F.V., *Westminister Historical Atlas to the Bible,* Philadelphia: Westminister Press, Revised edition, 1956.

Zinsser, William, *A Family of Readers*, New York: Book-of-the-Month Club, 1986.

Index

A

Abraham . . . . 11 - 12, 21, 101
Adam 12, 174
Adams, John 122
Adams, John Quincy 12
Afghanistan 8, 65
Africa 50, 108, 121, 127
Africa, East 126
Africa, North 49
Africa, West 152
Ahlstrom, Dr. Sidney 132
Aijal 2
Aitken, Robert 135
Alabama, Mobile 88
Alcuin 115
Alexander The Great 18
Alexandrenko, Captain Nikolai . . . . 86 - 87
Alexandrinus, Codex 36
Alfred the Great . . . . .124 - 125
All-Union Council of Evangelical Christians 161
Allahabad College 74
Allen, Steve 168
Altizer, Thomas J.J. 137
Ambrose 49
Ambrose, Bishop (of Milan) 48
America . . . . 7, 15, 59, 62, 64, 66, 71, 97, 100, 130 - 131, 146, 172, 179
America, Latin 127
American Baptist Mission 36
American Bible Society 97, 136, 145, 161
American Board of Commissioners..... 35
American Female Moral Reform Society 144
American Revolution 135
American Tract Society . . . . .144 - 145
American Vietnam POW's 58
Amity Printing Press 161
Anabaptists 52
Analects, The 66
Andropov 55
Antioch 133
Apoocrypha, The 14
Aristotle 103, 116
Arkansas, Ozarks 38
Asia 1, 36, 108, 127
Assam 1
Assn. for the Relief of the Respectable Aged 145
Athanasius 15
Augustine, St. Aurelius 18, 49, 89, 100

Augustulua, Romulus 49
Augustus, Caesar 43
Australia 39, 105, 128
Avesta, The 67

B

Babylon 18, 21, 65
Babylonia 115, 133
Bach 123
Bacon, Sir Francis 114
Baer, Phillip 39
Bancroft 134
Bangladesh 8, 106, 108, 158
Baptist Sunday School Board 13
Baptist World Alliance 161
Baptists in the USSR 161
Barker, Jared 121
Barker, Marilee 121
Barnhouse, Dr. Donald Grey 96
Barrett, Dr. David B. 150
Baruch 42
Beethoven 123
Belgium 31
Bellah, Dr. Robert 132
Bermuda 174
Bernardone, Francis 90
Bethany Christian Services 145
Bethel 107
Bethel Bible Village . . . . 107 - 108
Bethlehem 103, 133
Bible, Aitkens 135
Bible, Bishops 134
Bible, Breeches 134
Bible, Geneva 134
Bible, Gideon 136
Bible, Gutenberg 161
Bible, Japanese 180
Bible, King James Version 137
Bible, Living 137
Bible, Luther's German 134
Bible, New American Standard Version 137
Bible, Pueblo 58
Bible, Revised Standard Version 137
Bible, Today's English Version 137
Bibles For The World . . . . 7, 93, 169, 176 - 178
Bilozi 136
Birthright 145
Blackstone, Sir William 125

Boardman, Sarah 36
Boghaykoy 22
Bohemia (Czechoslovakia) 30
Boone, Pat 62, 108, 175
Boone, Shirley 175
Boorstin, Daniel J. 82
Booth, Ballington 105
Booth, Bramwell 105
Booth, Catherine 105
Booth, Evangeline 105
Booth, William 105
Bradford, Governor 138
Brahm 123
Brahma . . . . 68 - 69, 72
Breshnev 55
Britain 43, 50, 104
British 2
British and Foreign Bible Society 7
Brown College 35
Browning 122
Buddhism 65, 68, 70,74
Buddhist 169
Bulganin 55
Buntain, Mark 107
Burger, Chief Justice Warren 178
Burma . . . . 35 - 36
Burns, Robert 122
Bush, George 179
Byblos 13
Byzantium 49

C

Caesar . . . . 44, 46 - 47
Caesar, Julius . . . . 42 - 43
Calcutta 34
California, Hollywood 59
Caligula 43
Calvin 33
Calvin, John 134
Calvin, William Thomson 120
Cambridge 31
Campbell, Dr. Ross 57
Campus Crusade for Christ 97, 155
Campus Life 97
Camus, Albert 122
Canaan 19
Canada . . . . 96 - 97, 128
Capernaum 23

Cardinal Hugo 29
Carey Baptist Church 35, 129
Carey, William . . . . 33 - 35, 38, 106, 108, 121, 154, 162
Carlyle, Thomas 122
Caro, Robert 82
Carroll, B.H. 16
Carter, President Jimmy 133, 178
Cash, Johnny . . . . .95 - 96
Castle Church 33
Cathedral, Crystal 123
Cathedral, National 123
Cathedral, St. Paul's 123
Cathedral, St. Peters 62, 123
Cathedral, The Notre Dame 123
Catholic Relief Service 106
Center for World Mission, The 155
Chaldees, Ur of the 11, 21
Champollion, Jean Francois 21
Chapman, William 136
Charlemagne 115, 124
Charles V, Emperor 52
Charlesworth, Dr. James H. 23
Chaucer 122
Chawnga 2, 4, 7
Chen, Wilson 91
Chernenko 55
Chicago 87
China 1, 9, 57, 68, 76, 146, 155
China Inland Mission 38
Chirgwin, A.M. 153
Christian and Missionary Alliance 156
Christian Businessmen's Committee 93, 169
Christian Children's Fund 107
Christian Medical Society 96
Chrysostom 103
Church of Jotabeche, The 151
Church of Rome, St. Peters 123
Church of the Holy Sepulchre 23
Church World Service 106
Cicero 28
Claudius 43
Clemens, Domitilla 45
Clemens, Flavius 45
Clement 16
Codex Sinaiticus 37, 54
Coe, Doug 94
Coleridge, Samuel Taylor 97
Colson, Charles 93, 97
Columba, St. 100
Columbia University School of Journalism 115

Columbus 133, 137
Concerned Women of America 147
Confucianism . . . . 65, 68, 72 - 74
Confucius 66, 76
Constantine . . . . 48 - 49
Constantine, Emperor 103, 124
Constantinople 103
Cooper, Anthony Ashley (Lord Shaftesbury) 104
Cooper, Anthony Earl 105
Copernicus, Nicholas . . . . .116 - 117
Cops for Christ 97
Council of Constance 30
Cross, Way of the 12
Cyrus 67
CySip, John 121

D

da Vinci, Leonardo 123
Darwin, Charles 54, 143
David, King 12, 15, 49, 90
Davy, Sir Humphrey 119
Dead Sea Scrolls 28
DeBracton, Henry 124
DeFoe 122
Delaware 131
DeMoss, Ted 93
Dewey, John 143
Diocletian 48
Diocletian, Caesar 47
Diognetus, The Epistle to 102
Divine Light Mission 62
Dobson, Dr. James 147
Domitia 46
Domitian . . . . 45 - 46
Douglas, Justice William O. 132
Drake, Sir Francis 134
Drexel University 20
Dunberg, Lars 161
Dura, Plains of 133
Durant, Ariel 125
Durant, Will 125

E

Eames, Jacob 35
Eastman, Bob 39

Ebla Tablets 23
Ebla, Syria 23
Ecuador . . . . 1, 84, 100 - 101
Edison, Thomas 120
Educational Research Analysts 147
Edward III, King . . . . 29 - 30
Egypt 13, 18
Egypt, Alexandria 13, 117
Einstein, Albert 119
Eliot, John . . . . 134 - 135
Elizabeth, Queen 125
Elizabeth, Queen (of England) 53
Elliot, Elisabeth . . . . 100 - 101
England . . . . 31, 50, 105, 110, 116, 125, 127 - 128, 133
England, Bedfordshire 104
England, London 62, 105
England, York 115
Ephesus 46
Epiphanes, Antiochus 42
Ervin, Senator Sam 140
Ethiopia 158
Europe 62, 100
Eusebius 28, 48
Evangelical Child Welfare Assn., The 145
Evangelical Children's Home 107
Evangelical Christian Church 56
Evangelical Foreign Missions Association, The 157

F

Fabiola 103
Fadiman, Clifton 82
Far East Broadcasting Company 158
Faraday, Michael 119
Farrar, Dean 44
Faulkner, William 122
Fellowship Foundation 96
Fellowship of Airline Personnel 97
Fellowship of Christian Athletes 96
Fellowship of Christians in the Arts 97
Ferdinand, Archduke 118
Finklestein, Joe 20
Finley, Allen 156
Finney, Charles 110
First Baptist Church, Euless, Texas 145
Flat Earth Society 24
Florida 88
Food For The Hungry 107
Forrest, Dr. William Mentzel 140

Forsyth, Frederick 82
Fort William College 35
Four State Christian Missions . . . . .145 - 146
France 62, 125
France, Lyons 51
France, Paris 54
France, Toulouse 50
Franklin, Benjamin 52, 139
Frederick the Great 19
Frederick, Prince 33
Freerks, Sicke 52
Fry, Elizabeth 104, 105
Fuchida, Captain Mitsuo (of Japan) 54
Fund for Pious Uses, The 145

G

Gabler, Mel and Norma 147
Galilee, Sea of 12
Galilei, Galileo . . . . .116 - 119
Garden of Eden 11
Garstang, Dr. John 22
Gaul 50
Georgia, South Central 133
Germany . . . . .31 - 32, 100, 128
Germany, West 127
Gethsemane, Garden of 12
Ghana 85
Ghandi 126
Ghandi, Indira 9
Ghandi, Mahatma . . . . 12, 63 - 64, 126
Gideons . . . . .135 - 136
Glueck, Dr. Nelson 24
Golgotha 12
Goodwill 144
Gorbachev 55, 57, 126
Gorbachev, Mikhail 179
Graham, Dr. Billy 7, 11, 15, 58, 93, 107, 137, 152
Graham, Franklin 107
Great Britain 146
Greece 11
Greene, Graham 122
Gregory, Bishop (The Great) 50
Guatama, Siddartha 65, 75
Guatemala 37
Gutenberg, Johann . . . . 31 - 32, 160

H

Hackett, Alice Payne 82
Hall, Clarence . . . . 179 - 180
Halverson, Dr. Richard 163
Hamilton, William 137
Hammurabi 21
Handel 123
Hariot, Thomas 134
Harris, Esther 58
Harris, Lieutenant Commander Stephen 58
Harvard University 58
Harvey, William 24
Hashem el-Quaraysh, Muhammed ibn Abdallah... 67
Hawaii, Pearl Harbor 54
Haydn 123
Hazeltine, Ann 36
Healthy Happy Holy Organization 62
Hefley, James and Marti 100
Hefley, Marti 141
Hegel 53
Herod, King 43, 117
Herodotus 168
Hezekiah 41
Himalayas 75
Hinduism . . . . 62, 65, 68, 70, 72, 73 - 76, 151
Hipp, F.L. 107
Hipparchus 24
Hirohito, Emperor (of Japan) 54, 74
Hirsch, E.D. 128
Hitler, Adolph 54
Hittite 22
Hocker, Ludwig 104
Holman Correctional Institution 97
Holy Spirit 15
Homer 28
Hooker, Thomas 138
Howard, John . . . . 104 - 105
Huff, Ron 124
Hughes, Senator Harold 94
Hunt, William Holman 123
Huss, John 30, 51
Huxley, Thomas 111

I

Ibraiham, Simon 152
Illinois, Wheaton 92, 165

Illinois, Wilmette 64
India . . . . 1 - 2, 7 - 8, 11, 34 - 35, 62, 64 - 65, 68, 74 - 75,
India, cont'd . . . . 108 - 109, 121, 155, 157 - 160, 166, 169, 171 - 173
Indiana 56
Indonesia 155
Ingersoll, Robert 141
Injil, The 67
Inner Light Foundation 62
Integral Yoga Institute 62
Interdenomination Foreign Missions Assn. .156
InterVarsity Christian Fellowship 97
Iran 11, 162
Iraq 11, 87, 162
Isit, Tony 176
Islam . . . . 62, 67 - 68, 70, 74, 76
Islamic Council of Europe 62
Israel . . . . 17 - 19, 101
Italy 50, 103
Italy, Assisi 90

J

Jackson, President Andrew 131
Jahan, Shah 167
Jainism 68
James I, King 32, 134
James, King 125
Jamestown 134
Japan 62, 66
Jay, Justice John 135
Jefferson, Thomas 122, 139
Jehoiakim 42
Jehovah 41
Jeremiah 15, 42
Jericho 22
Jerome 103
Jerusalem 19, 32, 153
Jewell, John 59
Jewish Community Centers 105
Jews 115
John . . . . 15 - 16, 45 - 46, 153
John, King 124
John, The Apostle 14
Johnson, Sheryl 145
Johnstone, P.J. 155
Josephus 75, 117
Josiah 42
Joule, James Prescott 120
Judah 41

Judson, Adoniram ....35 - 36, 38
Judson, Ann 36

K

Kafka, Franz 122
Kamikaze 66
Keay, Ike 107
Kennedy, John F. 136
Kepler, Johannes ....116 - 118
Khoser River 18
Kietzman, Dale 159
Kina, Shosei 179
Kipling, Rudyard 122
Kirshna, Hare 62
Knighton, Ray 107
Knox 33
Koop, Dr. C. Everett 96
Koran, The ....67, 69, 72 - 73
Korea 91
Kosachevich, Luba 55
Krapf, Johann 126
Krishna Consciousness 62
Krishna, Dr. Paul ....85 - 86
Krishna, Hare 64
Krushchev 55
Kshatriyas 70
Kurds 87

L

Lacaba, Ed 175
Lacaba, Edward 92
Landers, Ann 115
Lao-Tze 66
Latin America 108
Laubach Literacy Crusade 121
Laubach, Frank 121
Lebanon 11, 133
Legters, L.L. 37
Lenin 55, 126
Letterman, David 94
Lewis, C.S. 93
Liddy, G. Gordon ....94 - 95
Lienrum ....4 - 6
Lincoln, Abraham 12
Living Bibles International 161

Livy 46
Lousma, Jack 25
Lucian 46, 109
Luther, Martin . . . . 16, 31 - 33, 50, 52, 115, 122, 134
Lutheran Relief Service, The 106
Lutz, Lorry 156
Lyttleton, George 25

M

Maccabee 42
Macedonia 133
Magi, The 67
Mahomed 64
Mainyu, Angra 69
Malaysia 174
Malenkov 55
Malik, Dr. Charles 97
Manasseh . . . . 41 - 42
Manipur . . . . 1 - 2, 9, 76
Mao Tse Tung 65, 166
Marsh, James 39
Martyn, Henry 162
Marx, Karl 55, 83
Marxism 85, 90
Marxist 159
Mary, Queen (of England) . . . . 52 - 53
Maryland 131
Massachusetts Indians 135
Mawii 7
Maxwell, James Clerk 119
Mazda, Ahura 67, 69
McClaine, Shirley 62
McDowell, Josh 25
Medical Assistance Program 107
Mediterranean Sea 11, 13, 17
Mendelssohn 123
Mennonites 52, 106
Meredith, Mrs. 104
Mesapotamia 12
Methodist Publishing House 13
Mexico 85
Michaelangelo 123
Mikado 66
Milton 122
Milvian Bridge, Battle of 48
Mindanao 121
Missouri, St. Louis 107
Mizoram 1, 9

Mohammed 67
Molech 41
Moody Bible Institute 107
Morris, Edmund 82
Moscow . . . . 56, 86, 176 - 177
Moses . . . . .12 - 13, 27
Mother Theresa 107
Mount Nebo 12
Mt. Sinai 14, 37
Mucha, Juan Lopez 85
Muhammed 76, 174
Muhammed, Aishah 76
Munich 86
Music City Christian Fellowship 95
Muslim . . . . .73, 76, 87, 106 - 107, 146, 151, 154 - 155, 162 - 163, 174

N

Nahum 18
Nashville Singers 95
National Coalition Against Pornography, The 147
National Council of Churches 157
National Federation for Decency, The 147
National Right to Life 147
Navigators 58, 137
Nazareth 12, 87, 89, 109
Near East Relief Fund 146
Nebuchadnezzar · 133
Nehru, Prime Minister . . . . 8 - 9
"New Age" movement . . . . .62 - 63
Nero . . . . .43 - 45
New England Primer 142
New Testament, Anglo-American 135
New York 60
New York Bible Sociey 136
New York, Schroon Lake 107
Newton, John 123
Newton, Sir Issac 12, 16, 116, 119
Nicaragua 87
Nichiren 62
Nightingale, Florence 103
Nile 13
Nimrod 18
Nineveh 18, 21
Nipamacha, Pastor 78
Noah 12, 18
Norse 133
Northern Illinois University . . . . , ...7
Norway 91, 128

Nottingham, England 34
Nyerere, Julius 126

O

Ochs, Adolph 115
Ocken, Dr. Harold 157
Oldham, Doug 175
Olivetian 134
Orlov, Dr. Ilia 178
Ovid 46
Oxfam of England 107
Oxford 29

P

Pakistan 11
Palestine 42, 87, 109, 115
Papua New Guinea 85
Parks, Dr. Keith 156
Partnership Mission 7, 165, 169
Pasadena, California 19
Pascal, Blaise 89
Patmos 46
Patrick 43
Patrick, St. 100
Paul . . . . 12, 14 - 16, 27, 31, 45
Pelagius, Bishop (of Rome) 50
Penn, William . . . . .138 - 139
Persia 65, 67, 76
Persian Gulf 11
Peru 38, 99
Peter . . . . .23, 45, 153 - 154
Petronius 46
Pettigrew, William 2
Phelps, WIlliam Lyon 122
Philadelphia 20
Phillipine Evangelical Enterprise 121
Phillipines 39
Phillipines, Cebu 92
Phillips, Tom 93
Pierce, Dr. Bob 11, 106, 107, 130, 175
Pike, Evelyn 38
Pike, Kenneth . . . . 38 - 40
Pilgrims 134, 142
Pilot, Pontius 32
Pishak, Memcha 76

Plato 103
Pliny 46
Plymouth, Massachusetts 35
Poe, Edgar Allen 140
Pollock, John 152
Polycarp, Pastor . . . . .46 - 47
Prague 51
Presbyterian Ministers' Fund 145
Princeton Theological Seminary . . . . .22 - 23
Princeton University 26
Prison Fellowship 94
Promised Land 12, 18
Protestant Public School Society 142
Providence, Rhode Island 35
Prussia 19
Ptolemy 13, 24, 117
Pudaite, Chawnga 78
Pudaite, Chwanga 81
Pudaite, John 113
Pudaite, Mary 113
Pudaite, Mawii . . . . .114, 144, 166 - 167, 171, 173
Pudaite, Paul 113
Pudaite, Rochunga 6, 63, 172
Pueblo, The 58
Pulitzer, Joseph 115
Purcell, Graham 94
Purie, Mr. V.V. 172, 174
Puritans 134, 138

Q

Quakers 110
Quie, Congressman Albert 94

R

Raikes, Robert . . . . 104 - 105
Rama 64
Ramakrishna 63
Ramsay, William 23
Rangoon 36
Raphael 123
Raytheon Company 93
Reformation, Protestant . . . . 51 - 52, 109, 126
Rembrandt 123
Renaissance movement, European 53
Renan 125

Renan, Ernest 54
Resh, Jimmy and Ellen 145
Rickenbacker, Eddie 91
Roberts, Lord 2
Roberts, Watkin .3 - 4, 11, 76, 130, 165 - 166
Robertson, Dr. A.T. 29
Robinson, Dr. Cliff 176
Rogers, Buck 157
Rome . . . . .32 - 33, 36, 44 - 45, 49 - 50, 59, 62, 103, 119
Rosetta Stone 21
Rosetta, Egypt 21
Rossetti, Dante Gabriel 123
Rousseau, Jean Jacques 53
Russia 57, 127, 146, 172, 174, 176
Russian Imperial Library 37
Rust, Eric 25

S

Saint, Rachel . . . . .100 - 101
Salem 133
Salvation Army 105
Samaritan's Purse 107
Samoa 91
Saudi Arabia 8
Scala Sancta . . . . , ... 32
Schaeffer, Dr. Francis 124, 127
Schingothe, Carl 170
Schweitzer, Albert 63
Scotland 11
Scott 122
Scott, Sir Walter 98
Seamands, Dr. John T. 61
Self-Realization Fellowship 62
Seneca 46, 103
Serampore 35
Service-Master Company 92
Shakespeare 122
Sheldon, Charles 141
Shintoism . . . . 66, 72 - 75
Shorrosh, Anis 87, 89
Siberia 55
Sielmat 76
Sikhism 68
Simms Ph.D, P. Marion 132
Simon Peter 15
Simons, Menno 52
Sin, Cardinal 92
Singer, Bashevis 82

Singh, Pishak 76, 78
Singh, Sadhu Sindar 169
Sistine Chapel 123
Slavic Gospel Association 57
Smith, Captain John 134
Smylie, Rev. James 110
Solomon 12, 15
Sophocles 28
South Africa 111
South Carolina, Beaufort 133
South Korea 55
Southern Baptist Foreign Mission Board 156
Southern Baptists 106
Southwestern Baptist Theological Seminary 16
Soviet Armenia 106, 146
Soviet Russia 54
Soviet Union . . . . 1, 8, 55 - 56, 127, 146, 155, 161, 168, 173
Spain 50, 103
Spock, Dr. Benjamin 82
Sri Lanka 61
St. Louis Post Dispatch 115
St. Petersburg 37
Standard Oil 107
Stephanus, Robert 29
Stevenson 122
Stewart, Dr. Walter 26
Stone, Robert 82
Stowe, Harriet Beecher . . . . 110 - 111
Strabo 46
Styron, William 82
Sudan 87
Sudras 70
Suetonius 75
Sutherland, Justice George 132
Sweden . . . . 127 - 128
Syria 11

T

Tacitus 28, 44, 46, 75
Tanzania 8
Taoism . . . . 66, 68 - 69, 72 - 75
Taurat, The 67
Taverner Bible 32
Taylor, Dr. Ken 31, 167
TEAR of Britain 107
Teen Challenge 147
Ten Commandments 12, 21, 140
Tennessee, Nashville 13

Tertullian 16
Thalasius 103
The Navigators 97
Theological Seminary, Dallas 159
Thomas Nelson Company 13
Thomson, Charles 135
Tiberius, Caesar 43
Tischendorf 37
Titus 19
Titus, General 45
Townsend, William Cameron . . . . .37 - 39, 100, 137
Toynbee, Arnold 63
Trajan 46
Transcendential Meditation 62
Trans World Radio 158
Tripura 1
Trotman, Dawson 137
Turkey 146
Turkey, Istanbul 49
Tyndale, William . . . . 31 - 33, 52
Tyre . . . . 17 - 18

U

U.S.A. 10
Ufilas 100
United Bible Societies 40
United Bible Society 161
United Methodists 106
United Nations 88, 98
United States . . 56, 78, 81 - 82, 85, 87 - 88, 96 - 97, 105, 111, 128 - 129, 131, 146
United Way 144
Universal Postal Union 168
University College (Durban, S.Africa) 85
University of California in Berkeley 133
University of Illinois 114
University of Paris 115
University of Virginia 140
University, Auburn 175
University, Brown 143
University, Dartmouth . . . . .143 - 144
University, Harvard . . . . 132 - 133, 143
University, Princeton 132, 143
University, Rutgers 143
University, William and Mary 143
University, Yale 132, 143

V

Vaisyas 70
Van Buren, Abagail 115
Van Buren, Paul 137
Van Dyke, Henry 84, 123
Vaticanus, Codex 36
Vedas, The 65
Victoria, Queen 125
Vietnam, South 91
Vines, Dr. Jerry 15
Vins, Georgi . . . . .55 - 56
Virgil 28
Virgin Mary 75
Vivekananda, Swami 63
Voltaire 54
Volunteers of America 105
Von Braun, Dr. Werhner 90
Vulgate 29, 133

W

Wade, Marion . . . . .92 - 93
Waldensian movement 50
Waldo, Peter 51
Wales 2
Wallace, General Lew 141
Wallis, Widow 34
Ward, Larry 107
Washington, George 135, 139
Watkins, Morris 152
Watkins, Roberts 2
Weaver, Phyllis 177
Webster, Daniel 12, 122, 139
Webster, Noah 142
Wells, H.G. 89
West Soka Gakkai (Value Creation Society) 62
West Virginia, Charleston 59
West, Gilbert 25
West, Morris 82
Westminister Abbey 123
Wheaton College 7, 100, 114, 144
Wheaton, Illinois 31, 35
White Man, Mr. Old 2
White Man, Mr. Other 2
White Man, Mr. Young 2
Whittingham, Pastor William 134
Wilberforce, William 110

Wilkins, Marijohn 95
Wilkinson, Bruce 159
Williams, Roger 138
Wilson, Dr. Robert Dick 22
Wilson, Woodrow 97
Winter, Dr. Ralph 155
Wirt, Dr. Sherwood . . . . . . , ...152
Wisconsin 64
Witherspoon, John 139
Wittenburg 33
Word of Life Bible Camp 107
World Home Bible League 136
World Literature Crusade 159
World Parliament of Religions 63
World Relief Commission 106
World Vision 7, 11, 106, 155, 175
Worms, City of 31, 33
Wycliffe Bible Translators . . . . .37 - 38, 40, 99, 121, 137, 161
Wycliffe, John . . . . 29 - 32, 52, 122, 136, 139, 162
Wyrtzen, Jack 107

Y

YMBA Young Men's Buddist Association 61
YMCA 144
YMCA Young Men's Christian Association 105
Young, Edward J. 16
Youngman, Mr. . . . . 2 - 5, 8, 11, 130
Yugoslavia 8
YWCA Young Women's Christian Association 105

Z

Zabur, The 67
Zhuk, Dr. S.I. 57
Zimbabwe 8
Zoroaster 64, 67, 76
Zoroastrianism . . . . .67 - 70, 72, 73, 74
Zwingli 33

Please send me the following selections:

The Greatest Book Ever Written by Rochunga Pudaite.
A treasure trove of information about the Bible. $9.95

The Truth in Crisis by James C. Hefley, Ph. D. A four volume set
The controversy over the Bible in America's largest evangelical
denomination, the Southern Baptist Convention. $29.95

The Evangelical Dilemma by Herbert J. Milers, Ph.D.
A Southern Baptist educator explains the difference between
conservative, moderate, and liberal theology. Excellent for church
group study. $6.95

Way Back in the Hills by James C. Hefley
Charming story of a boy growing up in the Ozarks. $4.50

What Are They Teaching Our Children? by Mel & Norma Gabler
Study of how morality and America's religious heritage has been
stripped from many textbooks in the nation's public schools. $5.95

Where Is God When a Child Suffers? by Penny Rosell Giesbrecht.
How a Christian family copes with their child's pain. "A classic
book" on suffering, says Dr. Ross Campbell. $8.95

Send books to:

Name_____Address_____

City_____State_____Zip_____
Please add $1.25 postage and handling for first book, .50 each
additional book. (Missouri residents add sales tax)

TOTAL AMOUNT ENCLOSED (Check or money order)$

List books you wish to order on a seperate sheet of paper, enclose
coupon and payment and send to:
Hannibal Books
31 Holiday
Hannibal, MO 63401